The Diagnosis and Treatment of Dissociative Identity Disorder

The Diagnosis and Treatment of Dissociative Identity Disorder

A Case Study and Contemporary Perspective

Ronald A. Moline, MD

JASON ARONSON
Lanham • Boulder • New York • Toronto • Plymouth, UK

Published by Jason Aronson
A wholly owned subsidiary of The Rowman & Littlefield Publishing Group, Inc.
4501 Forbes Boulevard, Suite 200, Lanham, Maryland 20706
www.rowman.com

10 Thornbury Road, Plymouth PL6 7PP, United Kingdom

British Library Cataloguing in Publication Information Available

Library of Congress Cataloging-in-Publication Data

Moline, Ronald A., 1937–
The diagnosis and treatment of dissociative identity disorder : a case study and contemporary perspective / Ronald A. Moline.
p. cm.
Includes bibliographical references and index.
ISBN 978-0-7657-0943-1 (cloth : alk. paper) — ISBN 978-0-7657-0944-8 (electronic)
1. Multiple personality—Patients—Biography. I. Title.
RC569.5.M8M65 2012
616.85'236—dc23
2012029909

♾™ The paper used in this publication meets the minimum requirements of American
National Standard for Information Sciences Permanence of Paper for Printed Library
Materials, ANSI/NISO Z39.48-1992.

Printed in the United States of America

To my wife Barbara, without whose support, patience, and forbearance my efforts as a psychotherapist could not have succeeded.

Contents

Preface

> I do not think anyone really knows what ultimately constitutes an alter personality.
>
> —Putnam (1989, p. 8)

As a psychoanalytic candidate in the 1980s, I was taught that dissociative identity disorder, or as it was then called, multiple personality disorder,[1] was a diagnosis arising from the interaction between a hysterical patient and a fascinated but gullible therapist. This perspective had long roots, essentially going back to the end of the nineteenth century, when Freud, after first agreeing with Janet's thesis (1889/1913) that dissociation was at the heart of psychopathology, abandoned the theory in favor of repression (Freud 1957f). It followed from this thesis that the symptoms of patients with "multiple personalities" were simply unusual manifestations of intrapsychic conflict—that is to say, were defenses against unacceptable impulses.

It is probably the predominant view within psychoanalysis still today; Arlow (1992, p. 70), using this perspective, described dissociated senses of self as the "coalition of fantasy systems," derived from conflictual needs. Ross and Lowenstein (1992, p. 3) state: "Senior psychoanalysts regard dissociation as a symptom, a compromise formation resulting from intra-psychic conflict."[2] Berman (1981, p. 286) describes three cases as "all having issues of oral frustration, and early Oedipal dynamics." In the same article (Ibid., p. 290), he refers to Kernberg's remarks (1973) to the effect that "the therapist should treat patient's insistence on being more than one person as a delusion and attempt for omnipotent control."

Classic psychoanalysis notwithstanding, there is an enormous literature on the diagnosis and treatment of dissociative identity disorder (DID) that includes works by psychoanalysts and psychoanalytically oriented therapists such as: Brenner, 2001; Bromberg, 1996; Davies and Frawley, 1994; Fink, 1986; Gedo, 2000; and Marmer, 1980. Most of these contributions include detailed clinical vignettes. Richard Baer (2007) has recently contributed a book consisting entirely of the detailed description of the treatment of such a patient, which will be discussed in depth in one of the chapters to follow. The division in the world of psychotherapists between those who find the diagnosis plausible and those who don't often seems to correlate, as Chande has observed (in Cohen et al. 1995, p. 36), with those who have been confronted with DID psychopathology in their practice, and those who have not. For most of those who have, the diagnosis seems not only plausible, but compelling.

This book aims to address two questions. First: Can sufficient evidence be adduced, at this point in time, to answer the skeptical critic who challenges the validity of the diagnosis of dissociative identity disorder? Second: Is there sufficient evidence regarding the therapy of this condition to draw conclusions about optimal treatment? The answers to these questions will be sought through a detailed examination of a single case, as well as review of the relevant literature.

NOTES

1. Throughout this book, the terms multiple personality disorder and dissociative identity disorder will be used interchangeably—the former (MPD) when this was the usage of a quoted author or the use during the time period to which I am referring, the latter (DID) at all other times.

2. These authors also note, however, that Freud commented periodically that real trauma, including sexual abuse, did happen to some of his patients, and had psychical effects (Ross and Lowenstein 1992, p. 39).

Acknowledgments

I would like to thank Dr. Rob Marvin for sharing his insights and case material for this book. I would also like to thank Dr. Erika Shavers and Dr. Sean Conrin, both fourth-year psychiatric residents at the University of Illinois at Chicago, at the time this book was completed, for agreeing to the publication of their case material. I am very grateful as well to Mr. Ken Hooker, who did a superb job of editing the manuscript for grammatical errors and stylistic issues. Many thanks to Dr. Robert Bergman and Dr. Jerome Winer for reading an early draft of the manuscript. Not least, I would like to express my deep appreciation to the scholars, mentors, and colleagues who have informed and guided my work in this difficult field, in particular Drs. Merton Gill, Arnold Goldberg, Heinz Kohut, William Offenkrantz, and Otto Will

Section I

Clinical

ONE

"The therapist must be alert to interpersonal problems."

The therapist must be alert to interpersonal problems—they are often a source of trouble.

—Bliss (1986, p. 26)

Well . . . yes.

—Moline (see below)

It is without doubt impossible to present a completely reliable account of what happened in a psychotherapeutic treatment. Schore (2003b) has presented evidence suggesting that psychotherapy, in particular with significant disorders of the self, is a process primarily of right brain interaction between therapist and patient. In other words, it is primarily an affective, rather than a cognitive, process. To the extent that this is true, the task of describing the therapeutic process is made all the more difficult.

Goldberg, however, (2004, p. 191) has warned that there is no affective experience without a cognitive component, nor a psychotherapeutic treatment in which experiencing can stand alone without knowing. Acknowledging the truth of this observation, I would nevertheless suggest that, in presenting psychotherapy to other professionals, we tend to be excessively concerned with what psychoanalysis calls secondary process—left frontal cortex rules of organization, cause and effect, and logic—all of which at times can obscure rather than clarify what happened. In presenting the case that forms the core of this book, I will attempt to describe important *affective* exchanges, in sufficient detail to support my later conclusions, but also to allow the reader to draw alternative explanations.

Sandy first came to me together with her reluctant husband, after she had discovered videotapes of him engaging in various perverse sexual

1

acts with prostitutes, and after he had admitted to having had many casual affairs over the entire course of their marriage. Craig was ten years older than Sandy, and they had met when both worked for the same corporation.

It was my impression that Sandy was suffering from a major depression, and that Craig was a narcissistic man with antisocial traits. After three conjoint sessions, I had come to believe that they both needed intensive individual psychotherapy. Craig was quite open to a referral—a readiness that presaged a failure to stay in therapy. Sandy was ambivalently willing to begin individual therapy with me.

Sandy—not her real name[1]—is an attractive, shy, demure, professional woman. Then in her midforties, she was the mother of two teenage children, a boy and a girl. She had earned an MBA at a prestigious university, and was looking for a new position. Sandy gave me a rather unremarkable family history: she was the oldest of several sisters; her parents were both living and well. Father was a very successful attorney, then moving into retirement. Mother had never worked. Sandy reported that there was nothing either interesting or unusual about her childhood. She had been a good student. She had always been shy.

After several months of first once-a-week, then twice-a-week fifty-minute sessions, I proposed we begin meeting three times a week for ninety-minute sessions. This length of session is extraordinary for me. I had proposed it because of my strong sense that the patient had profound emotional problems—despite my ongoing inability to clearly formulate those problems—and because, for the first forty-five minutes of almost every session, Sandy had virtually nothing to say except that everything was "fine," life was "okay," and "nothing" was on her mind. In the last half of these prolonged sessions, she would give evidence of profound sadness, extraordinarily low self-regard, and implicit signs of torments not yet revealed.

Despite these and other symptoms of major depression—anhedonia, decreased appetite, lack of motivation—Sandy was reluctant to consider medication. (It is my current practice to utilize both psychotherapy and antidepressant therapy in the treatment of this diagnosis.) She revealed, after some months, a lifelong problem with eating—often purging as well as fasting. She tended to think of herself as hideously fat, despite the reality of being on the slim side of normal weight variation. On business trips, she always obtained her meals through room service: she felt too ugly, too repulsive, to go even to the ice machine, much less to a restaurant, bar, or coffee shop by herself. She would leave her room only when it was necessary to go to a scheduled meeting.

The patient's reticence to talk was not a reticence to be in therapy; indeed, she accepted the proposal of frequent and prolonged sessions with little hesitation. She was always on time and did not miss appointments. She had turned to her father to help pay for the considerable therapeutic time to which she had committed herself.

It became clear that a major source of the patient's reticence to talk was that she blamed herself for any and all of her interpersonal or life difficulties. Talking naturally involved talking about her relationships; but to talk about her relationships was to risk revealing encounters with her husband and others in which, she hinted, she had often incurred physical or sexual abuse. This was data she knew I might construe as critical of others—and this was unacceptable to her, since she alone was responsible for her pain. It might also elicit my sympathy toward her— which, I later came to realize, she felt would be unbearable.

It had happened one day, about eight months into the therapy, that Sandy, as usual with considerable prior reluctance, asked me, "How do people think?" I inquired, of course, why she asked.

"Well for me, "she had explained, "there is this . . . conversation. There are these different voices, and they argue different points, and end up making a decision."[2]

I did not realize what I was hearing. I was sure my patient was not schizophrenic, but rather than explore further what was behind the question, I simply normalized what she had told me, answering, in good doctorly fashion, with a description of the psychoanalytic conflict model of the mind:

"Yes, that's how people think. I may want to do one thing, but another voice in me says that's not a good idea, and then maybe there's a compromise."

She said nothing further about the matter. It is obvious, in retrospect, that further exploration might well have informed me of the phenomena that, later, so took me by surprise and shocked me.

Many months after that, Sandy revealed that she had had a recurrent dream, from as far back as she could remember, which disturbed her greatly. She had in fact painted a picture of it, she told me, several years previously. The dream was of a large, unconnected face, staring straight ahead. The face was male; several smaller faces, both male and female, surrounded it. She told me that when she had finished the picture, family members had told her the central face looked like her grandfather. She had felt that was not how she meant the face to look, and altered it. Also in the picture was a large hand, seemingly coming around a corner from a lighted room, about to touch a light switch in this darker space. There was the end-arm of what appeared to be a sofa, in the room.

Sandy had no associations to this dream, other than to comment on how terrifying it was. To my complete surprise, she agreed to bring in the painting, and did so the following session.

The picture was remarkably true to her description of the dream; however, there was one part that she had not mentioned and I completely missed until she pointed it out. In the corner of the darkened room, at the bottom of the picture, was the depiction of a tiny little girl with long hair, sitting with her knees pulled up to her chest. This was the consequence, she explained, of the little girl having first felt grotesquely large, and then swirling into a vortex, shrinking into the figure in the corner. She denied—with a very troubled and anxious look on her face—that the little girl was herself. Looking at the painting and hearing this narrative, I found myself wondering, for the first time, whether my patient had undergone some sort of childhood abuse.

I was enormously excited and intrigued at this new information, and eager to explore it further, after months of the patient's reticence, prolonged silences, and my increasing unease that I was largely in the dark about her obviously serious problems. I looked forward with enthusiasm to our next session. When Sandy arrived for that session, she too, I thought, looked excited and anticipatory. When she sat down, I paused to see if, for what would have been the first time, she wanted to start the session. She said nothing.

"Well," I began. "How are you?"

"Fine!" she responded.

My initial enthusiasm fell precipitously. *Fine.* I had heard that same opening in every session, from the beginning of therapy. Today, I had been expecting something more.

"What was it like bringing in your painting, yesterday?" I asked.

"It was fine!" she replied.

"Fine?" I repeated.

"Yes. It was fine."

"Anything more?" I persisted.

"No, really, it was fine!" she said.

From out of my mouth, unbidden, came: "What the *hell* does 'fine' mean?" The intensity of my reaction took me completely by surprise.

One would have thought I had slapped the patient. She recoiled physically, and appeared suddenly pale and disoriented. She lifted her hand dazedly to her forehead.

"Sandy!" I said. "Are you alright?" I had recovered quickly from my unexpected outburst; she had not. She mumbled something, and slowly shook her head, as though trying to regain a sense of focus.

"My goodness," I continued. "I'm really sorry! I didn't mean to blame you; I guess I was just frustrated that we weren't going to pick up where we left off."

She murmured something more to the effect that that was okay, it was nothing, but she continued to look like someone trying to pull herself together after a horrendous trauma—which, of course, was exactly what was happening. The rest of the session was spent in trying to help the patient recover enough equilibrium to leave the office. Several days after this event, self-mutilation of her arms and abdomen began.

In the ensuing weeks, Sandy revealed an intense attachment to me, which alarmed and concerned her. She had a premonition that she might do something "crazy," that she would humiliate herself or upset me. Oddly, she did not seem to grasp how upset I was by the cutting—which seemed to me more than "crazy" enough—although she herself was upset by it. She admitted to feeling in love with me, but it felt to her both real and unreal. My efforts to relate the patient's ongoing cutting to the trauma of having someone she cared deeply about harshly criticize her led neither to acknowledgment on her part, nor a decrease in the self-mutilation.

As the days turned into weeks, and reports of almost daily self-harm continued, I found myself feeling increasingly helpless. I found myself trying everything in my repertoire of responses.[3] I expressed genuine remorse for my unwarranted attack. I continued trying to explore what my unempathic response had meant to her. I interpreted her self-destructive behavior as a response to guilt, in various configurations. I became authoritatively firm, insisting that this behavior needed to stop and be put into words that we could talk about.

One particular day, Sandy said to me, in a desperate and plaintive voice, "You don't understand. It's not me. Every night there's this battle. I say, 'No, please, not tonight, let me sleep.' And this other voice says, 'No, it has to happen. You've got it coming.'"

To which I replied, "Well, I think I've been talking to the wrong part of you! Say more, what this side of you is saying!"

One could say with some accuracy that I encouraged the phenomenon that I am about to describe, even demanded it.[4] The scientific skeptic would go further, and say that the patient and I coconspired, even if unconsciously, to create it. Without arguing the point at this juncture, let me try to convey what happened.

Sandy replied that she couldn't, and no amount of gentle inquiry, tentative defense interpretation (fear of exposure, shame, etc.), or suggestion, led to further information. Feeling that we were very close to an important understanding, it suddenly occurred to me to say: "I have an idea. Why don't you change chairs? Why don't you sit over here [off the sofa, and in a chair closer to me], close your eyes, and just try to repeat what you hear?"

She replied, "I'd feel foolish."

I answered, "You know what? So would I—but what do we have to lose?"

I had never made such a suggestion to a patient before. Although I had been trained in hypnosis, it is not a part of my ordinary repertoire of therapeutic interventions, and it was not what I consciously had in mind at this point.

Reluctantly, she crossed the room. She sat down, looking anxious and uncomfortable in the new chair. She closed her eyes, but this did not diminish her evident discomfort. "I can't do it," she said.

"Just relax, and try to recall the words that you hear," I replied. "You've already told me some of them. Just say more."

"I can't," she persisted.

"Maybe I can prime the pump," I suggested. "The words that you've already told me are, "It has to happen . . . you've got it coming.'"

There was suddenly a raucous laugh. Sandy opened her eyes, whipped off her glasses, and glared at me with a facial expression— fierce, angry, cold—that I had never seen before. "So what do you want to know?" she said, in a voice I did not recognize.

I was stunned. The patient glowered at me with unblinking eyes, while I found myself inexplicably blinking back tears. "Well . . . what's going on?" I stammered.

"She *deserves* it, the fucking little bitch!" was the hostile reply. "She's a fucking, disgusting, wimpy slut, who deserves everything she gets!" I felt myself, preposterously, in the presence of a hostile, controlling, possibly dangerous male.[5]

She/he continued, "Everything she has is due to *me*—the career, the house. . ." In response to my question, she responded further: "The cutting doesn't matter, and of course it doesn't hurt me. . . . I'm not part of this disgusting body. But she's trying to fuck it up. . . . She wants to kill herself."

I frankly do not remember the few more sentences of exchange that took place, nor did I afterward write them down. I was shaken, and barely felt in control of my own anxiety, much less the situation. Nevertheless, in a matter of minutes, Sandy suddenly put her head in her hands, shook her head, looked up as her usual self and asked anxiously, "What happened?"

What indeed. I had no frame of reference to understand what I had witnessed—or cocreated. Of course I had heard of multiple personality disorder—but it had never been brought up or discussed in my psychiatric or psychoanalytic training, and, as far as I was concerned, it simply did not exist as a real entity. Whether it was listed as a legitimate diagnosis in our diagnostic manual, I could not have told you. Neither did I have a clue how to go about treating the patient following this dramatic development in the therapy. And, yes: Sandy acknowledged that she had thoughts of killing herself, which she had not revealed to me.

NOTES

1. In addition to names, identifying data have been altered wherever doing so does not distort the psychodynamic understanding of the case. The patient reviewed a

draft of this book, and was satisfied both that it sufficiently disguised her identity and was a fair presentation of the therapy.

2. Lyon (1992, p. 74) reports a similar sequence of events in the therapy of a patient with multiple personality disorder: the patient first talked about voices in her head, and in later sessions her "alters" appeared.

3. Hoffman (1992, p. 292) has contrasted an "open-minded positivist approach," in the conduct of a psychoanalysis, to a social-constructivist approach. While my description may sound like a positivist approach—rationally moving from one approach to another, as the efficacy of each was disconfirmed—it in fact consisted neither of pre-planned interventions nor a rational application of various theories. It was rather the saying of whatever I could think of, at any point in time, that I hoped might further understanding or lead to change. Of course, "what I could think of" was informed by previously learned theories, and previous clinical experience.

4. This would certainly be the suspicion of Humphrey and Dennett (1998), particularly astute critics of the existence of this disorder. Their extensive critique will be addressed in a subsequent chapter.

5. Davies and Frawley (1994, p. 68) report an almost identical experience with a patient, "who announced, with burning rancor . . . 'she got what she deserves—it was coming to her.'"

TWO

"It is necessary to meet and interact directly with alter personalities."

In my opinion, it is necessary to meet and interact directly with alter personalities as part of the treatment of Multiple Personality Disorder.

—Putnam (1989, p. 14)

The appearance of the apparitional fierce male presence ushered in a time in the therapy for which nothing in my previous experience had prepared me. Sandy told me that I must have met "Joe"[1]—whom she feared, and whom she regarded as dangerous. She was appalled that any of her "people" had "come out," and alarmed that "others" were telling her that they, too, wanted to come out. She said there were children, including one small child she heard crying inconsolably. There was "Sam," a licentious, promiscuous woman without morals. There was "Vicki," who was crazy and impulsive, prone to temper tantrums and destructive behavior. There were others.

The cutting worsened; "Joe" (no more quotation marks after this) reappeared several times, and informed me that the cutting was part of an agenda, which could not quite be put into words. Joe informed me, after one weekend, that there had been more cuts—wider and deeper. There was a lot of blood. I insisted on hospitalization, which Sandy resisted; for the first time, I met with Sandy's entire family. I explained that the recent disruptions and chaos at home, which had frightened and confused her children, were due to Sandy's psychiatric condition, dissociative identity disorder—a diagnosis I explained as best I could. I told them it could definitely be helped through continued psychotherapy, but at this point it required hospitalization. Craig and the children strongly agreed, and Sandy reluctantly acceded. Craig declined my suggestion that the family be provided some support by another therapist.

A five-day hospitalization was a respite, and it was determined that Sandy's abdominal cuts did not require surgical repair. Joe made one appearance, in which he said that the agenda remained the same: there had to be a purging, a cleansing. It did not necessarily have to be done through cutting—although, he reflected, there was another "part" that loved the violence.

One week after the hospitalization, Sandy came in saying that she had serious cuts on her abdomen again. I insisted she would have to be re-hospitalized, by commitment if necessary, and she begged me to think of an alternative. Despite my insistence, it was not clear to me that yet another short-term hospitalization—essentially the only sort of inpatient psychiatric care available—would make a difference. I decided to have a marathon session, then and there, and cancelled all my remaining afternoon appointments.[2]

A variety of things happened in this prolonged session; Joe made a brief appearance, angrily telling me to back off, that I was getting in the way. Later, I pursued with Sandy a discussion of her feelings about me, which had been in the background since the self-mutilation had become so prominent. She readily admitted that the feelings had not gone away; and by the end of the session we agreed that the self-mutilation was in part a punishment for having allowed herself to get so vulnerable, but also a distraction to keep us from talking about her feelings for me. By the end of the afternoon, I felt cautiously optimistic that the need for further self-violence had diminished—an assessment that seemed subsequently to be borne out.

A few weeks later, I began to talk to the patient about my upcoming vacation, which led to brief, intermittent appearances of other presentations of self. The session prior to my departure, Sandy appeared unusually self-assured. She sat in a chair other than the one to which she had become accustomed, took off her boots in a confident manner, and looked around the room as though seeing it for the first time. I commented that she seemed different today. She smiled, and explained that I was used to talking to Sandy.

"And you are?" I asked. She replied that she was Sandra Ellen. She went on to tell me that Sandy was too emotional, too weak, to show up for this last session. She, Sandra, was not troubled by emotions; she was analytic, efficient, and the one who "got things done." (Yet another one, I silently noted.) Indeed, in the course of the session, Sandra Ellen revealed no feelings about the impending separation; when the time was up, she pleasantly wished me a good vacation, much as one might express to a colleague.

Several weeks after my return, Sandy came to session one day looking quite different than usual: whereas she characteristically wore a conservative suit and low heels, she came in a blouse, loose slacks, and flat shoes. Her hair was held up in the back by a band, rather than falling freely around her ears. She smiled as she came in, giggled as we exchanged initial greetings, sat down, and almost at once suddenly stood up. She went to my bookcase, took out a book, and began to shuffle through it aimlessly. She continued to giggle, a cockeyed grin on her face. I suspected I was in the presence of Vicki.

I urged her to sit down, and to tell me what she was feeling—she ignored me. Her flipping of pages took on a frantic quality, her face took on a crazed aspect, and there was a sense that she was about to explode in some uncontrolled behavior. I demanded that she sit down, at which point she screamed, and fell backward onto the floor. As I tried to regain my bearings, she crawled behind an upholstered chair.

Catching my breath, I said to the patient that she needed to come out from behind the chair and sit down, so we could talk. A childish voice answered, "No." I said that there was nothing to be afraid of; that she could sit in a chair and we could talk. There was no answer for several seconds. Then I heard: "Ouch!"

I could not see the patient behind the chair. I asked what the "Ouch" had been about. Again the childish voice: "Nothing." And then again: "Ouch!"

This repeated a few more times before I moved my chair so that I could partially see the patient behind the chair. I saw that she had a razor, and that there were bright red lines on her arms. "You have to stop that!" I exclaimed.

"Ouch!" Another bright red mark.

Once again, I found myself calling upon all the responses and reactions my years of experience had provided me. I was firm: "You need to put down the razor now, so we can talk." I tried to be empathic: "You must be hurting a lot to want to cut yourself." I was pleading: "I think I must have made you upset. Please put down the razor so we can talk about it." I said whatever else I could think of to try to end this nightmare.

After a couple more cuts, and feeling enormous anxiety, I said, "You need to stop hurting yourself. If you don't put the razor down now, I am going to have to take it from you. I'm sorry about that—I don't want to violate your space. But I cannot sit here and watch you hurt yourself. I will have to take the razor from you."

The patient did not put down the razor. Not sure whether I or the patient would be hurt, deliberately or accidentally, I rose from my chair, slowly moved to the patient, and took the razor from her.[3] She burst into tears, and buried her head on my coffee table.

I said, "I'm sorry to have had to move into your private space. But I could not simply sit here and watch a woman hurt herself."

She replied, amidst sobs, "I'm not a woman!"

"Okay," I said. "I could not sit here and watch a little girl cutting herself."

"I'm not a little girl—I'm a little boy!" the patient said, sobbing.

"Whatever!" I said. "I could not sit here and watch anybody cut themselves up!"[4]

It seemed we were in a phase of the relationship when it was time for me to meet many, if not all, of the characters, whether I wanted to or not. Sam made an appearance one day. The patient came to the session wearing a very sexy outfit, quite unlike her usual dress, sat down, crossed her legs, and began rhythmically rocking the top-crossed leg. She had a sensuous smile and, after a few short exchanges, stood up, stretched languorously, thrusting out her chest, and walked slowly over to my window ledge, providing me a view of her from the rear. She turned, and leaned provocatively on the ledge.

She proceeded to share with me what *her* particular source of scorn toward Sandy was about: Sandy was ridiculously, childishly, inhibited about sex. Sandy didn't know the first thing about men, or what they like. There are all sorts of ways to have sex—"Right?" she asked. Did I have preferences? There are all kinds of ways to take it—and she, Sam, liked them all. Didn't I agree? I was silent throughout this interrogation. There was a fade-out, and Sandy reappeared, unaware of what had just happened.

On a different occasion, Sandy told me about another altered sense of self, who she dreaded my ever meeting. It was, she said, a creature, not a person. It was faceless, hideous, unpredictable, and capable of unspeakable horrors. Much later, as I began to read about the neurobiology of disorders of the self (see section II), I came to imagine that Sandy was describing an "alter" that was almost pure amygdala—with a minimum of differentiated connections and elaborations in the subfrontal cortex. Whether such a concept can be considered anything but metaphorical, or whether it adds anything to the understanding of my patient, remain open questions.

NOTES

1. I will refer, throughout the book, to the altered senses of self by the names that were told to me, and by which Sandy herself referred to them. To my recollection, I never used these names myself in addressing the patient.

2. Cognitive-behavior therapists, as well, perhaps, as some psychoanalytic therapists, might well suggest that such exceptional behavior on my part rewarded the self-destructive behavior and contributed to its continuance, rather than its diminution. I leave it to the reader's judgment.

3. Brenner (2001, p. 58) reports an almost identical incident, describing his anxiety, as he felt impelled to take a razor from a patient.

4. At the time, and up through the writing of the first draft of this book, I had thought this a useful intervention: a declaration that my concern was for the core patient, and that the "overlay" of a particular presentation of self was of much less

concern. Sandy, reading this vignette much later, disagreed, suggesting that there was an attempt here to communicate something to me, which I had not grasped. She was not sure what it would have been, at that belated time.

THREE

"Therapy can be strenuous."

> Therapy can be strenuous. It is often neither a feast of reason nor a tranquil tête à tête.
>
> —Bliss (1986)

My treatment of Sandy was occurring at a time in the history of psychiatry when dissociative identity disorder had become an entry in DSM IV (1994), the official diagnostic manual of American psychiatry, and when volumes had been written about the treatment of this disorder. In the ten or fifteen years prior to the inclusion of this new entity in the diagnostic manual, the frequency of the diagnosis had exploded, and psychiatric units across the country had been set up for the specialized treatment of the problem. The decade had ended in a flurry of lawsuits, which had effectively ended the careers of some "experts" in multiple personality disorder.

This, in turn, had led to a split in the field of psychiatry like few others: much of the field continued to regard the diagnosis as essentially hysteria, with a considerable iatrogenic component, while an embattled minority continued to hold meetings and support their belief that this dramatic psychopathology was real.[1] "False Memory Syndrome" (Yapko 1994) became a new weapon in the fight between professionals; respected scientists (Loftus 1989; Winograd and Neisser 1992) denied that serious childhood abuse could be "forgotten" and come to mind only in adulthood. As for me, I found myself wondering whether I should call the Roman Catholic diocese and ask for an exorcist.

I began to read the literature on dissociative identity disorder, which I found both reassuring and disturbing. It was helpful in the same sense that it had been helpful, early on, to get consultations with a psychoanalytic colleague and a neuro-psychiatrist, both at the university with which I was affiliated—namely, to discover that many therapists had

15

dealt with the very same issues with which I was confronted. It was eye opening to read that the alternative senses of self which I had seen fell into certain common patterns—the angry, controlling male, the promiscuous siren, the administrator, the children (Putnam 1989, ch. 2).

Still, there was something unsatisfying about much of this literature, and with the consultation I received. If the psychoanalytic world from whence I came seemed to hold an unwarranted certitude about the falseness of this condition, the experts in dissociative identity disorder seemed all too accepting, too matter-of-fact in their self-proclaimed understanding of all this bizarreness, and the way to treat it. I found myself recoiling from terms like "multiples," and "alters." In the Braun (1984), Putnam (1989), and Ross (1989) perspective, these words were a shorthand reference to "alter personalities." To me, the word meant: "altered senses of self." I thought there was a difference. I intuitively rejected some of Putnam's statements—for example (Putnam 1989) that, "All individuals with multiple personality disorder have at least one alter *who serves as* [italics mine] the host" (p. 107), and, "The 'personality' of an MPD patient is the sum and synergy of the system of alter personalities" (p. 123). I felt sure who my patient was, and it was not a board of trustees. (These issues will be addressed in greater detail in section II.)

I found myself experiencing a fundamental dilemma, however. How to proceed? Should I in fact be summoning forth, as Putnam and others insisted was necessary, all the various "alters" in order to acquaint myself with them, and them with each other? Was my aim to somehow "integrate" these alternative selves, since they all represented parts of a fragmented whole? Or would such an approach actually lengthen the therapeutic process, by further concretizing what ultimately must be resolved?

In the meantime, I did not know what to expect from session to session. Three months after Sandy's hospitalization, the abdominal cutting resumed intermittently. One day, she said to me, "This has got to stop! Something's got to be done! Yesterday there was blood everywhere. . . . I feel like you and Craig are getting used to it, but I'm getting more and more injured!" I could not have felt more guilty and helpless.

In classic psychoanalytic theory, what was happening in these weeks was a negative therapeutic reaction. We would have what seemed a productive session, but within days, there would be another report of self-mutilation. Psychoanalysis had been troubled by such clinical phenomena from its beginnings, and theorists have struggled to make sense of it. Freud (1957a) was the first to describe the phenomenon: "Every partial solution that ought to result, and in other people does result, in an improvement or a temporary suspension of symptoms produces in them for the time being an exacerbation of their illness; they get worse during the treatment instead of getting better" (p. 49). He goes on to summarize the situation as one in which "there is something in these people that sets itself against their recovery, and its approach is dreaded as though it were a danger" (p. 50). His explanation was that there was a so-called "moral factor"—and unconscious guilt, leading the patient to wish to continue suffering.

Stolorow and Atwood (1992) consider negative therapeutic reactions as "most often produced by prolonged, unrecognized intersubjective disjunctions wherein the patient's emotional needs are consistently misunderstood and thereby relentlessly rejected by the therapist" (p. 105). Whereas Freud's thesis would locate the source of the problem entirely within the patient, these authors would locate it entirely within the therapist, in his/her failure to establish an intersubjective matrix of shared understanding. Hoffman, in his explication of a social-constructivist paradigm (1983, 1992, 1998), suggests that the ineluctable interweaving of transference and countertransference, as experienced and/or interpreted by both patient and therapist, make it impossible to designate either as causal agent.

Sandy, upon much later reflection, had her own understanding. She had come to feel, she said, intensely, helplessly dependent on me; the therapeutic relationship had become the center of her life. It was a familiar feeling to her. Many times in her life she had become intensely dependent on a man, and increasingly "clingy"—to the point that the man had no choice but to reject her. She was terrified that would happen here; but she was equally terrified that she would lose me if she got better. After all, why else would I see her? As a consequence, every correct understanding, she said, was a serious threat. The cutting demonstrated that she was still in need of me. Ironically and paradoxically, it was also a means of punishing her for being so weak.

Obviously, the dependency needs were not only a construction of this relationship, although I certainly allowed, if not fostered, their development. At the same time, I was *not* interpreting the meaning of her self-destructive behaviors in the way just described, because this understanding was not clear to me at that time. One may speculate that if I had interpreted correctly the meaning of the behavior, and simultaneously made clear that our relationship need not end until she felt that terminating was something she wanted to do, it would have made a difference.

In desperation over the continuing intermittent self-destructiveness, I at last presented the patient with Plan A and Plan B. In Plan A, we would devote every session to accessing as many of her alternative senses of self as could be managed. I would attempt to establish relationships with them all (so much for my disagreement with Putnam), and to learn as much as I could about the reasons for the mutilations, in an effort to put their "message" into less destructive form. If this was unsuccessful, Plan B: she would have to be hospitalized for a more extended stay. Sandy reluctantly agreed—reluctant because she found it upsetting and debilitating when she herself was "in the background," and because she desperately did not want the consequences to her external life that a prolonged hospitalization would entail. Privately, I wondered, in any case, what hospital setting could accommodate such a treatment plan, and how extensive a hospitalization her insurance and father's largesse could manage.

It is common in the DID literature to consider such patients readily hypnotizable (Brenner 2001; Bliss 1986; Kluft 1982, 1985a, 1985b; Putnam 1989, 1997).[2] Most of the very long therapy described by Baer (2007) was conducted under hypnosis. Indeed, as Putnam (1997, p. 141) elaborates, "autohypnosis" is a widely accepted theory of the disorder. With this in mind, I proposed to Sandy that we use hypnosis as a way to enhance the emergence of other senses of self.[3] I had some reservations. I was aware of some research strongly suggesting that hypnosis, in patients with DID, induces confabulation (Ellis 2000).

The thought frightened Sandy, but she agreed. In our first effort, she sat in the alternative chair—where I had first encountered Joe—and I attempted to induce relaxation through suggestion. No dice. Sandy closed her eyes—and almost immediately opened them. Her muscles remained tense. She began to glance repeatedly at her purse, seeming more preoccupied with it than with my hypnotic inductions.

After noting this, I asked her if there was something in her purse we should know about. She shook her head, but I was not reassured, and asked permission to go through her purse. She hesitantly consented; I searched her purse, and found nothing untoward. There was a sudden giggling.

Asking what was funny, she answered, "You and Sandy!" The patient then took an eyeglass case out of the purse, and extracted a razor. I told her that I was not surprised; it was perfectly clear to me that, even if I had found that razor, there might well be others. But, I continued, I'm not interested in talking about that—I would like to know more about you (the sense of self in front of me).

This encounter was not so much enlightening as it was chilling. I was told that she had no name, that she was not a person—she was a feeling, an impulse, an action. She liked blood, and she liked cutting—it was exciting, and fun, although in truth it could sometimes get boring. She especially liked all the commotion it caused Craig and me.

I said that I would like to ask her something—not in the way of bargaining, because I felt that I held no chips. (Possibly an incorrect assumption, given Sandy's previous remarks about her dependency, but an accurate statement of my subjective sense of helplessness at the time.) Was there anything I could do or say, or anything that could happen, which would stop the cutting? She thought about this a minute, and said: "I like to paint. I could *paint* blood! In fact, I'm working on a painting of Sandy's abdomen—I could put more blood in it!" I asked if I could see it sometime, and we could talk about it. Her answer was noncommittal. Shortly thereafter, Sandy reemerged, anxious that something had happened.

I asked her about a painting, and she said she'd begun painting a fall scene, with the reds and yellows of autumn leaves. She had thought it would have a blue sky, but it was turning out to be more yellowish. And the foliage now seemed to blend together, in horizontal strokes. I told her what I thought it was actually about, and that I thought the painting needed to continue.

The chaos—without, however, bloodletting—nevertheless continued. One evening I got a phone call from both Sandy and Craig saying that she had overdosed.[4] She tried to argue with me that she hadn't taken that much (of Vistaril, which I had given her for sleep), but I insisted they go to an emergency room. They did, only to leave an hour later without being seen, despite having told intake of the overdose! Sandy went home and slept for twelve hours.

Further efforts at hypnosis, using standard induction techniques, failed. At one point, I suggested that her right index finger would feel very light, as though having a balloon attached to it, and would rise. Her left index finger rose. She noticed, and laughed. I chuckled ruefully.

In that same session, I told Sandy to put her face in her hands, and I asked to talk to the one who did the cutting and the painting. This sense of self (or of mayhem) in fact appeared, but was uncommunicative, and seemed dizzy. Sandy returned; she too, was dizzy—and revealed that she had not taken any nourishment or water at all for about two weeks.

Only later, after consultation with an internist, did I learn that she was in no mortal danger—but not knowing this at the time, I felt panicked, told the patient what I intended to do, and hurried to the lower level mall in my building as fast as I could, bringing back orange juice. She barely sipped it, at my urging.

The patient, over the ensuing weeks, reported that she had resumed taking minimal amounts of nourishment; but other self-destructive behaviors appeared off and on. I began to feel that I truly was not helping her, but perhaps rather contributing to her getting worse, and told her so.

I felt I had to say something more. I told Sandy that she needed to know that I could not withstand further self-destructive behavior—that I could not tolerate what it was doing to me as well as what it was doing to her. I understood that she could not somehow adapt her symptoms to the comfort level of her doctor. I did not think she was untreatable. I simply had to face limits that I had not previously known I had. I could not continue to be her doctor if the cutting or suicidal behavior continued. It was not meant as a threat, or as a manipulation; it was just a fact.

Not so long before, I had said to Sandy that I would never abandon her. Now I was saying that I might have to quit. I both marveled at, and was appalled by, what any analyst could justifiably call my out-of-control countertransference.

In subsequent sessions, Sandy continued to be angry with me, arguing, among other things, that I would make her bear the consequences of actions that she did not initiate. With belated insight, I said: "Sandy, you have already told me that you feel—consciously—that you deserve punishment or injury for caring for me. At night, when your experience is that you do not want such things to happen, but another voice insists that it must happen—is it not a way of disowning what you have already revealed to me as a conscious intention?"

Her response, in essence, was: "Your point?" I said that my point was that if she could hang on to the fact that it was *her wish* that resulted in the self-destructiveness, not some alien "other," maybe she could *feel* it, and it would not be acted upon. I did not, for some time, hear about or detect signs of further self-destructive behavior; unfortunately, this did not mean that it was not occurring, but it apparently had been reduced to more manageable levels.

One day, Sandy brought in two paintings—both, in my opinion, excellent art. One was a landscape, with dead orange trees on one side, and another tree full of fall-colored leaves on the other, but with the leaves flying off in unnatural directions. In the middle of the painting was a "sunset," which I recognized, from the earlier information I had received, as Sandy's stomach. The other painting was of a nude woman's torso, with explicit genitalia and pubic hair, in a somber, misty atmosphere. It was not at all erotic, but rather, in some way, horrific—as though alive, and dead, at the same time.

Sandra Ellen began to appear more often in my office, sometimes without my immediate awareness: smartly dressed, articulate, analytic—pleasant, if unemotional. When Sandy was present as herself, she expressed fear and anxiety, at times bordering on terror, that "something" was going to happen. She often came in seeming fully present, and, by the end of the session, seemed barely to be relating to me, struggling with inner voices. "I'll be fine. . . . I can't let anything happen," she would often say at those times, seemingly oblivious to my presence.

One session, Sandy brought in a list of the things that had happened in the last month, starting from the week before my ultimatum (or surrender). The list started with the last cutting of her abdomen, about which I knew, but also an episode of having cut her breasts—before my declaration, but without my knowledge. There had been two overdoses: one of the Vistaril, which I had known about, but a second of a handful of Prozac, while driving to her parents' home, less than a week previously. There had been two beatings on her legs.

I felt dismayed and confused. Was this, then, a violation of what I had insisted would be a cause for stopping therapy? Had I simply pushed the self-destructive behavior out of my sight, rather than intervened in a way that would either end it or end my involvement? As I thought about it, I realized that my subjective inclination was not to end the therapy. The patient, Sandy, was bringing me a list that she wanted to discuss—analyze, if you will. Consistent or not, I was moved to continue our work together.

She spontaneously associated to her father: she had asked him during their last visit how he had seen her as a child. To her surprise, he said that she had always seemed to him sunny and happy. And to her dismay, he made no follow-up effort over the next few days to continue the conversation, such as asking her how she had seen herself, or why she had asked. In retrospect, it seems to me, she may well have been expressing, through displacement, her disappointment that I had not followed up my ultimatum with questions about self-destructive behavior.

A few days later, Sandy reported that Craig had raped her, after an argument. While appalling, this actually did not surprise me; I had long since learned that Craig's state of mind could vary markedly, from intelligent helper in the therapy to sadistic violator. I suspected that these episodes were cocreated enactments, but that the shifts were also highly alcohol related.

The argument had been in the car while he had been driving; he had pulled over to the side of the road, pushed her into the backseat, and viciously attacked her sexually. She had not dissociated through it. "Rape" was in fact his word—he'd subsequently volunteered that he'd done it because of his frustration and anger.

Despite Sandy's sense of continuity through this painful and humiliating episode, she went on to talk about the fact that she didn't feel there was a core "Sandy" at all—only compartments. There were, she explained, "daily selves"—different than the extreme selves—who carried on the ordinary activities of living. She felt that the Sandy I saw here was not someone who had ever been exposed elsewhere—someone who talked about her thoughts and feelings, thereby making herself vulnerable.

She went on to speak of two Sandys—one, I realized, with whom I had often spoken on the phone at night, who was needy, grasping, and shameless in her efforts to cling; and the other the Sandy in my office, who was vulnerable but not clingy. The needy Sandy had gotten her in trouble all her life, she said; and she realized, at some level, that they were the same Sandy. I framed the issue as one wherein the "other" Sandy—whom I named "Sandy 2," or, as I punned, "Sandy, too"—was akin to a young child, who was desperate for her mother's smile and presence, and who became anxious when mother was out of sight. It made sense to her; she remembered her feelings and behaviors in high school, when her boyfriend would drop her off at her door after a date. He would no sooner have driven away, than she would begin to feel anxious, with an increasingly desperate need to see him. She would begin calling his home as soon as she thought he would have arrived. He would eventually hang up on her, after she had placed several urgent calls.

There followed several sessions that were characterized by some dissociation, but also by good reflective work. Sandy said that she understood my interpretation of some of her parts being expressions of her own, unwanted emotions—sexuality, dependency—but she didn't understand how that applied to "everyone"—for example, Vicki, who was wild and reckless, seemingly to no purposeful end. I acknowledged that I didn't have an explanation.

Sometimes, she said, when she left the session feeling vulnerable, she would begin to feel panicky and needy, just as with her high school boyfriend, and there would be a fusion, or transformation, into Sandy 2. It was she who might well call me later in the evening—a conversation of which Sandy 1 would have no memory.

In another session, she began to wonder whether she was any more real, or more primary, than any of the others. I felt there was not a more crucial question in the therapy, and answered the question with the conviction I felt: she was a truly authentic and unique person, however much she had felt the need to be hidden much of her life, and however much alternative senses of self performed certain functions, both aiding her and weakening her. "Authentic," she repeated, "but *more* authentic?"

Had I the courage of my convictions, the answer would have been an unequivocal "Yes." Apparently, however, a part of me had "bought into" the idea that the alternative senses of self had motivational systems independent of Sandy, because I found myself worried about alienating "the others," with whom I might need to work in the future. I wondered: Would an unequivocally positive answer result in anger and lack of cooperation? I gave a superficial and nominally supportive answer. Had I thought of it, however, I would have liked to have said: "There was a time when there was only Sandy." This important theoretical issue will be discussed in section II.

Toward the end of this session, Sandy said she was feeling again an intense need to get something from me, but she didn't know what it was. At the same time, she felt a build-up of self-criticism, which could lead to self-destructiveness, for foolishly wanting something she couldn't have. Like her sense of continuity during the traumatic rape experience with Craig, this seemed to me, despite the obvious risks, a healthy development: she was *feeling*, not dissociating.

I commented that perhaps it was hard to put into words because it preceded words—something like needing a mother to hold her, and respond to her. She answered, "If that's so, it's hopeless, right? You can't be my mother." I said no, I didn't think it was hopeless—first of all, because her need did not feel so intense all the time, and second, because I hoped she could get *enough* of what she needed, through our relationship and others, to be okay.

She fell into a kind of reverie at that point, reflecting that maybe all the selves have the same need, but their different actions are different ways of trying to get my attention to fill it. I could only marvel at her insight.

By the time of the next session, Sandy had cut herself several times, superficially, on her arm. It hardly seemed reassuring to point out that the self-destructiveness this time around had been relatively minor, but so I felt, inwardly. She was feeling hopeless, helpless. Joe made an appearance: he said that I was foolish not to talk to "them" more—it meant that I missed lots of opportunities. I should tell Sandy to get the fuck out of the way. I answered that I would not do that to him [*sic*], and I would not do it to Sandy, that I respected the person in front of me. Sandy reappeared, feeling depleted.

A pattern began to become apparent: acknowledgments of attachment would be followed by chaos at home including dissociated, provocative interactions with Craig, which in turn led to more physical altercations. Sandy became suicidal—but pointed out herself that she was *talking*, now, about her suicidal feelings, with me and with Craig, which was not the way they were usually "handled." Before, there would only be internal conversations, out of which a decision would be made, and Craig and I would find out after the fact.

Something else had apparently changed in the dynamic of our relationship. I was accustomed to frequent phone calls between sessions, often in the evening, which, rightly or wrongly, had seemed to me necessary as a way of dealing with the suicidal risk. On a particular weekend during this period, however, I found myself getting truly annoyed after two evening calls on Saturday, and two on Sunday evening. They seemed to me unnecessary and elective. During the second Sunday call, Sandy said, provocatively, "Craig says I'm playing games with you with the phone calls."

It is obvious that the appropriate therapeutic response to this comment would be: "What do *you* think?" Or to say that this was an important issue, that we could talk about in our next session. To presume that is what I said next, however, would be to miss the intense affectivity that characterized our relationship at that time. Instead, I responded with irritation: "I don't think you're playing games, but I do think several of the calls this weekend could have been handled in our Monday session. And I think the same about this one. We'll talk about it tomorrow." And I hung up.

In the next session, Sandy expressed hurt and anger that I had first allowed, even *invited*, phone calls, and now was getting angry when she made them. At the same time, her heart didn't seem to be in it. The session after that, she brought in several drawings, which she said she had made over lunch with Craig, of which she had no memory. One was of a female figure bent over a stuffed chair; several were of stick figures, also bent over, seemingly with objects inserted in the anal area. Sandy volunteered that she had not been able to disappear recently when Craig engaged in anal intercourse; it hurt terribly, she screamed, but he kept doing it. After telling me this, she dissociated. Sam appeared, saying that she (Sam) hadn't drawn the pictures, but found them sexuality amusing. She then faded into the cutter, who told me that she had drawn most of the pictures. She showed me a razor hidden in Sandy's purse, which she passively allowed me to take. Sandy reappeared, and agreed to let me search her purse. I found nothing. She looked herself, and discovered another razor, of which she claimed no prior knowledge.

One evening, I got a distraught phone call. Sandy said there were several burns on her body. I felt once again upset, helpless, and angry. Another voice: "Don't you get it? She needs to be punished, until she finally gets the message—she can't trust you, you're just like the others. We're trying to *protect* her, Moline, can't you see that?"

Sandy was stunned that I did not kick her out of therapy. She thought she had violated the bottom line. She had. I didn't. Once again, we had the fruitless discussion about hospitalization.

I proposed that we establish some scheduled phone calls between sessions, in lieu of the irregular calls that had occurred so frequently. This did not entirely stop the unexpected and unwanted phone calls, but significantly lessened them. One evening, however, a laughing voice called to say that she was sticking an electric charcoal-lighter rod up Sandy's anus, and turning it on. Distraught, I expressed my horror; I yelled at her to stop. She hung up. I called back immediately; Sandy answered, bewildered, intact, and unaware of any activity with the charcoal lighter.

In the ensuing days and nights, there were more phone calls, mostly from Sandy 2. I felt they were out of hand; that while phone calls, at an earlier time, might have been arguably necessary, they were increasingly either provocations or simply opportunities for dependency gratification and nothing more. In any case, they could not be explored, because Sandy did not remember them. I told Sandy that the unscheduled phone calls had to stop completely—that I would no longer respond to them. Not surprisingly, she felt humiliated—again, accusing me of having allowed her to depend on my availability, and now taking it away, as though she has done something terrible. I thought, but did not say: But from whom have I taken them away? If you believe that you are not making them, what difference does it make to you? I thought I was bearing witness once again to an inconsistency that pointed more toward the defensive nature of the dissociated selves than to their existence as separate entities.

In the next session, she was no longer angry, but almost resigned. She juxtaposed, without blame, the fact of letting herself feel comfortable enough to rely on me, to open up, and then later having a door slammed in her face. She said it was predictable: it was inevitable that she gets to be too much for the other person.

In response, I talked of many things: my own dismay at replicating that situation; my need to work more on my own self-awareness, so that I don't suddenly and repeatedly discover myself drained, burdened, and angry; and also about how complicated the phone call situation was, because of their multiple sources. I reviewed with her the various psychological origins of the phone calls: 1) my instructions, in regard to scheduled calls, and my acquiescence, in regard to the others; 2) her terror, at times, of being at risk; and 3) the needs and provocations expressed by other senses of self.

I went on to say that it was actually *not* the phone calls by "others" that were most problematic for me, but in fact those in which she, as herself, called, in terror—in other words, paradoxically, the calls that would seem to be the most legitimate. Under those circumstances, I said, I took on the role, and had all the feelings of, a "helpless rescuer": someone desperate to help, but without the means to do so. I said that I thought I needed to get out of that role: it was not good for me, and it was not helpful for her. She said that she pushed me into that role; I answered: yes and no. I thought the two of us created it.

Thus it was that we continued to negotiate, evolve, and experience an intense, complicated, relationship, which I could only hope was more therapeutic than not.

NOTES

1. Hacking reported: "Consider when I subscribed to *Dissociation, The Official Journal of the International Society for the Study of Multiple Personality and Dissociation,* and became an Affiliate of the Society, I received a document designed to look just like a medical school diploma. An accompanying flyer enjoined me as follows: 'Display your professionalism. Be proud of your commitment to the field of multiple personality and dissociative disorders. Display your certificate in a handsome membership plaque ($18.00 including shipping & handling)'" (1995, p. 36).

2. I will discuss hypnosis at greater length in Part II.

3. I have said earlier that hypnosis is not an ordinary part of my therapeutic armamentarium. However, having been trained in the technique during my psychiatric residency by Herbert Spiegel, one of the preeminent authorities on hypnosis at that time, I felt confident in my ability to conduct the procedure.

4. As will be discussed in more detail later, the patient has finally, reluctantly, agreed to take medications.

FOUR

"Nothing happened to me!"

Nothing happened to me! I'm just a perverted piece of shit!

—Sandy

One might think it would have been self-evident by now to both Sandy and me that she had been a victim of childhood sexual abuse. The recurrent dream, drawings, and paintings alone would seem to have attested to this conclusion, together with the somatic response equivalent to being sexually assaulted when she felt that someone she trusted had betrayed her.

In fact, we were both reluctant to come to that conclusion, each for our own separate reasons, but also for one reason that we shared in common: neither of us wanted to be duped. Increasingly, however, it seemed to me that the entire panoply of self-destructiveness, amnesia, and alternative senses of self constituted a highly complex defensive structure—not primarily as defined in the classical instinctual theory of classical psychoanalysis—that is, defenses against unacceptable impulses, but rather defenses against retraumatization. This defensive structure was built on a two-step, paradoxical premise: 1) nothing abusive had ever been done to her, and 2) it was her own fault anyway. More evidence began to accumulate:

- When talking to a man, Sandy would often, unexpectedly, visualize a large penis. In business contexts, this, of course, was anxiety provoking and disruptive; she would get confused and struggle desperately to keep the train of the conversation. At a later time, she was able to tell me that the penis was surrounded by white pubic hair. She felt disgusted and nauseous when it appeared. For most of the therapy, she took these occurrences as further evidence that she was some sort of sick pervert. Her repetitive refrain was, What else

27

could it possibly be? She did not mean this as a legitimate question, but as a conclusion, to which she tenaciously clung.

- Sandy and her parents had many old photos of her as a little girl. She reported a phenomenon that she had never understood in relation to those pictures. She accepted naturally that the photos taken up to age five were of herself as a child. However, she could not identify with the girl in those taken later, who seemed to her to be someone else. She knew rationally that they were pictures of her, but she could not reconcile that knowledge with the "deeper" knowledge that they were not her.
- Sandy had dark, ominous feelings about a certain block on Lincoln Street, the street on which she lived from ages four to six, which was next to her school and two blocks from her home. She was loath to go back there, feeling there was something frightening, even horrific, associated with a certain house on that block. She had walked to and from school, in first grade, and could not have avoided passing it.
- The patient abhorred sexual intercourse—and most often, had no actual memory of it. Indeed, she abhorred sexuality, becoming upset and anxious at any words with sexual meaning, such as "intercourse" itself. To her great dismay, her husband had a lustful sexual appetite, and demanded sex frequently. She realized that "Sam" frequently engaged Craig in sex, particularly anal intercourse, which horrified her.

A fascinating conundrum began to emerge, along with the revelations described above. Sandy was loath to have me assume that "something had happened," and would find reasons to deny the significance of each new piece of evidence. But more upsetting to her—often dangerously so—was any attitude of overly cautious objectivity on my part. For me to say something like, "Of course we can't be sure what this means" was to elicit a reaction of intense shame, humiliation, and anger: "*Of course* we can't! I knew it all along! I'm a perverted piece of shit! Nothing ever happened to me, I'm just a disgusting hypersexed slut who has all these humiliating feelings, visions, and experiences!"

Late in the therapy, Sandy was able to reveal that the only sexual activity that could arouse her was clitoral manipulation. She hated the fact that this aroused her, and more, that she would get out of control when her husband performed this activity. She would resist and dislike the stimulation, until at a certain point, she would find herself intensely aroused, and then helpless in the face of a peremptory bodily demand for climax.

In sessions, Sandra Ellen began again to make more appearances. She warned me not to take the stick drawings too literally—they could be a distraction, she said, from something else. At another point, she began to reflect on the advantages for "the unit," as she described the collective senses of self, in people not realizing that they were talking to different persons. It's the way it always was, she said—until the cat was out of the bag in here.

I asked her how she felt about being in the office with me, at that point in time. How did she experience our relationship? She said she liked it, although she didn't see it as some sort of therapy, working on a problem, because there really wasn't a problem—there was nothing to work on. She went on to insist that they were a well-functioning system, whose combined efforts handled what needed to be handled. I challenged that view: I said it seemed to me often to be a system in conflict, as when Sandy was terrified, whereas she, Sandra Ellen, thought things were fine. She seemed briefly bewildered, but she recovered, saying, "Let's just say it's a glitch in the system."

I commented on the fact that she'd been momentarily unclear. I said that I thought things in general were, in fact, much less clear than she, and the others, would wish them to be. It was my wish or hope that a time would come when there would not be such different senses of being-in-the-world, each with his or her own sense of reality in sharp conflict with another's sense of reality. I said that I had come to believe firmly that these separate senses of reality could exist only by virtue of overlooking significant pieces of information and subjective experience. I deliberately did *not* say "who" was overlooking these various sorts of data. I could have given credence to the idea that Sandy overlooked some things, Sam other things, Joe still others, and so forth. I did not wish to do so; rather, I wished to convey, even if only by inference, my belief that there was an enfeebled core self, whose biological unconscious acted as a central clearinghouse for the particular mechanisms of defense in play at any given point in time.

Sandra Ellen ignored, or didn't catch, the inference. She replied that it would be hard to reconcile such opposites—of temperament, physical appearance, even gender. I said that I understood that.

In the ensuing months, the relationship(s) between myself and the other(s) began to get even more complex, as I became less reactive and more analytic. An important consequence for me was to realize that things were already much more fluid and much less clear-cut than met the eye—or perhaps always had been, as I suggested to Sandra Ellen above. I began to question, or probe, more frequently.

During one session, for example, when we were once again looking at the drawings, and I had asked Sandy to imagine what the girl, bent over the chair, might be feeling or thinking, there was a sudden switch, and a fierce, angry voice said, "Do you know what I'm going to do? I'm going to cut my face, my arms, my body!"

"Why?" I asked.

"Because I feel like it!" was the retort.

"Yes, but *why* do you feel like it?" I persisted. "Why did looking at these drawings make you feel this way?"

"You're trying to trap me!" she yelled. I found this interesting. I had, without intention, revealed a presumption, namely: that the self now in front of me had seen, and was reacting to, the drawings. She had picked up on this presumption, and now was essentially saying, *You're acting like "of course" I saw those drawings, so that I'll reveal to you that I've seen them — when the function of my persona is to deny that they, and what they represent, even exist!*

I answered: "No, I'm not trying to trap you, I'm sorry if I've given you that impression. I am only trying to understand."

The persona faded away. . . .

In the next session, some version of self made a brief appearance and said, "The joke's on us!" I tried to understand the meaning of the comment, without success. The same or another self said, "You are on a mission of discovery but you are being sidetracked. These drawings are naïve, obvious, pornographic—meant to titillate and to distract."

When further exploration produced no further clarity, I said, "That seems obscure, but I believe you are being honest with me."

She (not as Sandy) replied, with evident surprise: "Oh? I'm not always! Or let me put it this way: I am honest, but I may also manipulate, or be covert."

"Yes, I realize that," I said. "But why?"

"So that you don't interfere with my intentions," she answered.

"But how can I do that?" I continued. "I listen, we talk . . . how can I interfere? We are two adults, sitting here, trying to understand each other." Another fade. . .

I had occasion to comment to Sandy, one day, that whenever the fierce part of herself appeared (a more straightforward statement of my unitary premise), my eyes immediately watered. Why was that, I wondered; because I felt helpless? Because I was being put in the same situation she once was?

She was powerfully struck by my having such reactions, "on her behalf." It was terrifying to think, she said, that I cared about her, even though she secretly hung on to it desperately. She ostensibly changed the subject by bringing out an old journal she'd brought with her that her mother had kept on a family vacation in the western states. She was struck, as I was, by how idyllic the journal made the trip sound—like a dream vacation. But, she wondered, how could it have been, with several kids in tow, in a car without air-conditioning, over hundreds of miles? It struck her that this was completely typical of her mother: everything was *always* as it ought to be, everything and everyone were always "wonderful." Feelings to the contrary were distinctly not welcome, and met with silent rage. Sandy wondered if this demand on the part of her mother hadn't contributed significantly to her living in different worlds.

It was a remarkable but increasingly frequent moment: Sandy was allowing herself, tentatively and guardedly, to entertain the possibility that not everything bad in her life was her fault. She was inviting—or rather, cautiously allowing me—to empathize with her, about something that had happened *to* her.

She then brought out more drawings, similar to the earlier ones, and commented on them all: "They're perseverative. . . . They keep emphasizing the ass, never anything else. . . . It's a distraction." I had heard this before, as mentioned above—but never from Sandy as herself.

Almost immediately, Sandy looked frightened, and inwardly focused; she was hearing internal voices, she told me, saying, *Oh-oh! You've said too much, Sandy! We're going to have to take care of this!* Which, of course, left her terrified of more physically self-destructive events.

I said, "Sandy, I can summarize your basic problem in one sentence: 'Don't you dare have hope!'"

By now, we were in the third year of therapy, and some fundamental changes in Sandy's personality structure seemed to be occurring. There were times, in session, when the distinction between Sandra Ellen and Sandy seemed fuzzy, and Sandy would later report that she struggled to stay present even though Sandra was in the forefront. One day she reported that, for two days, she had "receded," and an angry, hostile part took over—*but* she "sort of let it happen," and never disappeared entirely. Most significant of all: she revealed in one session that for almost two weeks she had felt as one—that who she was outside my office was the same person she was *in* the office. She said this had been the first time in her life she could remember feeling whole. She reported that, one day her daughter said to her: "Mom! You just laughed! I never heard you laugh!"

On another occasion, Sandy reported being very upset with both Craig and me. Following her revelation to each of us that she was feeling delighted and proud of her emerging competence and organizational skills at work, she felt that both of us had said that she was "blending" with Sandra Ellen. Craig had said this outright, but she had inferred (correctly) that I had implied much the same thing.

"It's like you're trying to take away *my* achievement, like it's not really *mine*," she said. "I'm discovering that I can master something, and you're acting as if I just 'borrowed' it!"

Apologies given, and accepted.

It did not surprise me that Sandy's family began to react negatively to these changes. There are many ways to understand such phenomena, of course. From a family systems perspective, one could anticipate that the system, seeking homeostasis, would react in a way to pull Sandy back into her usual role. Psychoanalytically, one could expect that, as the patient began to become healthier, others would feel threatened, to the extent that her pathology had served to maintain their own defenses. Craig began to have more outbursts of temper, and was enraged at Sandy's phone calls and emails to me. In reality, these had decreased in frequency, but he nevertheless seemed to feel increasingly jealous of Sandy's involvement with me. He began to enlist the teenagers in a triangulation, scapegoating Sandy. He revealed to them her "sick behavior"—things which they had not themselves witnessed—and he would take their side when Sandy tried to set reasonable parental limits.

Just as striking were the responses of Sandy's family of origin. It had been virtually a tradition that, at holiday family gatherings, Sandy would in some way make a fool of herself, or act out in some dramatic fashion. This was always in the context of heavy drinking, which was also part of the family culture. The morning after, when everyone had sobered up, the previous evening's enactment would seem to be faded history, very much as if some objective had been achieved. Now when Sandy did not conform to these unconscious expectations, family members became irritable, and found other things for which to blame her.

These changes toward "integration," if that indeed is how to conceptualize them, alas, were not accompanied by a smoother, less tumultuous therapy. The core pathological configuration of, first, a cautious expression of trust, second, a reenactment of betrayal, and third, some self-destructive action, continued to play itself out over and over. On one occasion, completely despondent over feeling that she had been a poor mother and let everyone down, she made a serious suicide attempt with sleeping pills and alcohol. She had called me after overdosing, but Craig had taken the phone and denied that it had happened, saying he had grabbed the bottle of pills (which, in any case, he allegedly was keeping, to parcel out the pills one at a time), before she had taken any. He was mistaken, and she ended up in an emergency room, in serious condition.

At another time—after a relatively extended period without self-destructive events—Sandy awoke with more razor cuts. In session, she came to understand the reason for the cutting had been that she had revealed to me—with great trepidation—the existence of a pristine, blonde little girl, who lived deep inside her, and whom she had never, ever wanted to reveal to anyone. She resisted the idea that this was herself, and that she must have looked very similar to this image when she was a little girl. Instead, she contrasted the little girl's perfection with her own grotesque, filthy self. As she told me this, she began to have body dysmorphia, feeling that she was transforming into something huge, and hideous.

She was able, however, with great difficulty, to reveal that she had harbored the secret hope that, if only she someday got everything perfect, she could *become*, in fact, the little girl. That was the whole point of her "dieting" (starving herself), and of much of the self-mutilation: if she could exhibit perfect control in some way, it could happen.

Next session, she asked, cautiously, whether an unwanted touch could nevertheless be pleasurable. I answered promptly, "Of course! Nerve endings have no conscience! But why do you ask?"

She did not answer, but went on to ask if a child could be made to have an orgasm even if she didn't want to. It felt like one of those remarkable moments when Sandy both knew and didn't know. If I had confronted her with the obvious fact that she was referring to something that had happened to her, I knew that she would be severely threatened, and shut down. We continued to talk about what might happen to "one."

She repeatedly returned to the premise that, "Nothing like that could have happened to me—if it did, it would only be because I wanted it to happen, otherwise I would have stopped it."

I asked her, "How do you suppose you could have done that? A child, amidst several adults?" She of course had no answer, but neither did the question seem compelling to her. Several times she came close to dissociating, but did not. I made a joke of it: "Here comes Greyhound—leave the driving to us!'" We laughed together.

A month later, she reported, terrified, that "a decision has been made"—that is, that there would be a suicide. She thought it was in response to having had a sudden insight, working in the garden a few days previously, that she *mattered,* profoundly, to her children, and that it was both incredible and horrifying that she had ever tried, to kill herself. In the telling, she switched to another sense of self, who said, without affect and matter-of-factly, "Of course I'm important to the kids. I'm their mother."

This was followed by lots of apparent self-confidence, denial of problems, and so forth. I did not ask "who" I was talking to. I did ask her what she thought had been going on, leading to this "decision," and she answered that it related to Sandy having distanced herself from "the resources." I said, "You *do* matter, you know!" Once again, my intention was to address the core self, without challenging the presentation of self before me. She blushed, and faded.

FIVE

"Nice life."

Nice life.

—Sandy

I have in my records a note written by Sandy without a date. It could have been written any time in the midst of the therapy, but it is striking in its contrast with the bland history she had given me at the beginning of therapy. The note read:

Some hard and fast truths:

- I was overly preoccupied with things sexual when I was young (seven or eight through thirteen or so).
- I did sexual things with friends and family members that embarrass me and humiliate and frighten me now.
- I did things to myself in that area [*that were*] embarrassing and humiliating and painful.
- During my teens and 20s, 30s, and I guess even 40s, I *have found myself* [italics, ed. See discussion below] in situations where I am pushing for some strange sexual something to occur, yet not really. It's just something that I can't seem to help and I've always hated it and always wondered what kind of pervert I was. Everyone else just thought I was some kind of nympho.
- I "flirted'" with anorexia when I was 17 or 18. I would like and intend to have a serious relationship with it right now.
- Destructive things that I have done to myself:
- Preteen: standing in the snow barefoot, sticking my hand in a frozen stream and holding it there . . . being in the wrong place and the wrong time, more??
- Teens: Third degree burns on my legs, hand through a plate glass window, provoking a fist fight with a group of black women (I

35

knew what they were going to do to me and I wanted them to);
refusing to eat; more????

- Late teens and twenties: serious drugs, alcohol, repeated suicide attempts, standing outside in a nightgown in 30 wind-chill weather, walking late at night on campus hoping that someone would attack me, more?????
- Thirties and now: beating myself, repeated suicide attempts, walking late at night, trying to freeze myself, self-mutilation, alcohol, bulimia, "flirting" with anorexia, provoking beating by others, more?????
- Nice life.

One of the most interesting aspects of this autobiographical note, I believe, is the *ownership* of the pathology. It is indistinguishable from the history a borderline patient might give, and only in the italicized phrase is there a suggestion of dissociation. What does this say about dissociation in Sandy's pretherapy life?

Sandy's own explanation of this phenomenon is that she does not distinguish in the note—as indeed she did not in her life—between what she consciously brought about and what she "found herself" in the midst of. Her life had been a blur; and virtually none of it was very clear. Her family often thought she was crazy; *she,* on the other hand, thought that, since she had obviously brought the tumult about, however much of it she remembered, she was some sort of debased and worthless troublemaker. It happened on her watch, so to speak, leaving her feeling both responsible and not responsible.

It seemed to me that most of the behaviors and events that she had written down were those I associated with the "Sandy 2" sense of self, in the course of our therapy. It reinforced for me the idea that Sandy 2 was a barely dissociated manifestation of a deep-seated dynamic in Sandy's psychology. Fairbairn (1944, pp. 114–17) referred to this dynamic as split-off senses of self that are dependency-driven to seek relationship with the only sort of object they know: a rejecting, unavailable object and/or an exciting, frustrating object. Kohut did not provide an accounting for this compulsive seeking after bad objects, but Bergman (2008, pp. 79–80), from a self-psychology perspective, has proposed that we refer to such behavior as seeking out "false selfobjects."

In Sandy's note, there was no description of violent behavior toward others, destruction of property, athletic prowess, or, for that matter, calm and collected proficiency at intellectual or practical tasks—all behaviors that I had either witnessed firsthand, or were reported to me by her husband. I suspect the explanation lies in the fact that all those behaviors associated with other senses of self were completely foreign to Sandy, and thus not reported in her list. Her only allusion to these dissociated aspects of her life occurs in her description, "I have found myself in situations where I am pushing for some strange sexual something to occur, yet not really."

In rereading what I have been describing in the past two chapters, it seems to me a case can be made that the therapy was proceeding satisfactorily. At the time, it felt anything but satisfactory. The repeated appearances of alternative senses of self felt like anything *but* progress, Putnam et al. notwithstanding. Outside of therapy, Sandy's life continued to be as chaotic as the earlier life she had described. In the process, more and more memories—or "pictures"—came into focus. Most frightening, and disgusting, to Sandy, was one of herself as a child caressing the genitals of an older woman, and of the woman doing the same to her. She refused to let herself think about this image, or associate to it. By this point in the therapy, it seemed to me to be a snapshot of the most traumatic event of her childhood, but we reached an impasse in trying to access it further. Meanwhile, there were further self-destructive acts.

Whether or not therapy was progressing, I was becoming increasingly desperate, and exhausted. In my ongoing efforts to understand and cope with a seemingly endless array of bewildering, frightening, and destructive behaviors, I came upon the idea that, in classic Freudian terms, Sandy was acting, rather than remembering—and that our task was to continue to mobilize her memories. However, I proposed we attempt to access more memories in a very unanalytic fashion. I suggested to Sandy that we devote several sessions entirely to memory reconstruction, using the technique of EMDR (see below). If there were further self-destructive events during this time, we would immediately hospitalize her, but continue the work of regaining memory with this technique. She agreed.

Eye movement desensitization and reprocessing, or EMDR (Shapiro 2001), was a technique gaining some degree of recognition, in the years of my treatment of Sandy, with many reports of success, particularly in the treatment of posttraumatic stress disorder (Boudewyns et al. 1993; Carlson et al. 1998; Marcus et al. 1997; Wilson et al. 1997). Zulueta (2004) reported the ongoing utilization of the technique in the treatment of dissociative identity disorder patients at The Traumatic Stress Service, Maudley Hospital, London—a sufficiently august recommendation, I thought, to warrant my consideration of the technique.

There were several theories about why EMDR was effective (Shapiro 1995)—presuming that *it*, and not other therapeutic factors, was mutative. Most of them involved the idea that unprocessed memories, feelings, and thoughts could be reprocessed and "metabolized" during the eye movements, by reorganizing the neural connections between the two hemispheres—perhaps similar to what happened during the rapid-eye-movement (REM) cycle of dreaming sleep.[1]

The therapeutic protocol for doing EMDR has been well elaborated and manualized (Parnell 1999) and will be discussed in greater detail in chapter 14. The expectation in treatment was that, as the patient followed

the therapist's metronome-like finger movement, while instructed to visualize some aspect of the trauma, she would, after stopping to thorough-
ly describe her feelings, bodily sensations, cognitions, and so forth, be
able, on repetition, to become desensitized to the event. In describing my
experience with the procedure, I will state the caveat that I followed the
protocol only loosely—without expectation, in fact, that the patient
would become "desensitized."

My own hunch about the method was that it was a variant of
hypnosis—a variant with a minimum of "surrender" on the part of the
patient to the therapist's authority—and it was in that sense that I resolved to try it with Sandy. My aims, in fact, were more like the aims of a
hypnotic session than those described as an EMDR session.

While I did not expect desensitization, I had several reasons for using
this particular form of intervention. First, because of the relentless self-
destructive threats and actions, I was losing faith in one of my core
psychoanalytic beliefs, namely that the therapeutic relationship itself, together with interpretation of the transference, would prove transforma-
tive, over time. Second, through a combination of previous training, clinical literature, and wishful thinking, I hoped that a cathartic experience
would provide a significant alleviation of her symptoms. Third—and
perhaps most rational—was my sense that the patient's sexually imbued
experiences—be they bodily sensations, hallucinations, interpersonal encounters, or bits and pieces of historical memory—seemed to her so disparate and ego-alien, that her *only* conclusion could be that there was
something perverse and "sick" about her. I hoped that reexperiencing the
origin of these symptoms would provide Sandy a more coherent narrative—one that would finally help her to make sense of her life history and
experiences, in a way that interpretation of the transference alone could
not provide.

Over the course of the next several weeks, I conducted EMDR sessions
irregularly—depending on whether there were more pressing real-time
issues that it seemed to me urgent to address. The experience, for her,
seemed to me very like what is reported in hypnotic sessions with DID
patients, with the exception that she could remember, and talk about, the
images that had emerged. They included the following:

- She saw the image of a woman fondling her sexually, and recognized her as a neighbor lady. An image appeared of the woman
  sweetly inviting her into a room. She then saw herself on a table;
  candles were being put into her vagina and anus.
- An adult (a man?) appeared, holding her hand, walking her from
  one room to another, forcing her to lie down on a hard surface.
  There was a light overhead. Candles were put in her again. It was
  not clear to her that it felt bad; it was confusing.

- On another day, she saw similar images: she was led into the house, and a man was saying, "Just for a little while." There was talk of playing "the special game." She was put on a table, and someone kissed her "down there."
- Another: she was being fondled, which went from gentle, feeling-good touching, to more urgent, sexual stimulation. She felt herself transforming into something swollen, grotesque. She felt she was getting huge.
- She visualized the recurrent dream that she had painted and brought to therapy, and it became real. She could feel *herself* physically shrinking, in a desperate effort to get away from something going on with her "down there." There was a sense that the woman with her hand on the switch was doing something wrong, something that would hurt.

At a time of calmer reflection, Sandy said that there were two meanings to the hand on the switch. One was the literal reading: someone was turning on or off a light switch. The other, she said, was of a hand manipulating her clitoris (my translation of her considerably more veiled description).

These EMDR sessions were terrifying and intensely difficult for the patient. The "seeing" was in fact a reliving, but, unlike her previous experiences of somatic sensations which could, with some justification, be considered "body memories," or flashes of sexual visual imagery, this reliving consisted of visualized vignettes. As the patient struggled with the experience, I could see on her face alternative senses of self, as I had experienced them and come to know them, drawn into the experience — for example Joe, looking stunned, angry, upset.

Meanwhile, the time between sessions was not improving. Sandy reported, however, a new phenomenon: the recurrence of feelings she remembered vividly from her childhood. She would awake most mornings terrified, absolutely convinced that something catastrophic was going to happen. She would lie in bed trembling, trying not to move, as though she could somehow avoid what she felt was inevitable. She was consumed, during the day, with thoughts of killing herself. I suggested that these were feelings that I could well imagine a child having, if she knew that she was powerless to prevent being abused by adults, later in the day. She agreed; she could remember those feelings.

There were various debacles at home, usually involving heavy drinking, which included physical altercations with Craig, suicide attempts, drug overdoses, and also running away from her home, later "finding herself" in strange locations. She reported one day that she had taken a mild overdose the previous night — not as an attempt to kill herself, but as an attempt to just obliterate consciousness. She asked me, in desperation:

What was going to cure her? How was this therapy going to ever make a difference?

Obviously, I was, during this period, in full-bore medical-model mode. I was the physician, who not only prescribed medications, but had prescribed a treatment (EMDR) in which I actively intervened, and she passively received. Thus it was that I answered her question, authoritatively. I said that, one, the ongoing discovery that her previously unaccountable feelings, thoughts, and images were connected with remembered (reexperienced) events of her childhood, would provide her an alternative explanation to her assumption that she was simply perverted and a horrible person. Two, I believed that, over time, she would be able to incorporate into herself my own positive regard for her.

I sensed, by her look of questioning and skepticism, her unspoken query: *Did* I have such regard for her? My psychoanalytic self reemerged: I gave voice to her unvoiced question. She acknowledged it. I responded: "How could you doubt it? I have been with you through terribly difficult times. I have had to acknowledge to you things about myself that I have not even done with many friends: self-centeredness, unjustified anger, and insensitivity. What other explanation could you have?"

She felt enormously better. For weeks afterward, she made reference to the huge difference my remarks had made for her. Whether because of the EMDR technique or because of her increased acceptance and trust of my caring for her, exploration of Sandy's childhood became a recurrent, and less threatening, part of our conversation. More snippets of apparent memories appeared, as well as more coherent sequences of events.

She recalled that they had moved to a new home when she was just five years old. In this location, she would walk back and forth to school, which was just a block away. She pictured a brick house that abutted the school grounds, separated by a row of shrubs. She remembered being terrified of going past that house, "for some reason." They had moved to their new home in the beginning of winter. In February of the new year, she had a very severe genito-urinary (GU) infection. Her mother has had occasion to refer to this medical problem from time to time, in Sandy's adulthood, and their physician's puzzlement about this sort of infection in a young girl.

Mother seems to have been a self-preoccupied woman with little interest in her daughter's emotional life and development. I think it quite possible that she was chronically depressed. Father, for whom Sandy has always felt more affection and who she has tended to idealize, was nevertheless largely absent, uninvolved in her upbringing, and predominantly interested in her academic—and later, work—success and performance. It is striking to imagine the impact in the life of this depleted, needy, child of the horrific and at the same time intensely stimulating events which may well have happened at a particular time, in a particular house, around age five or six. She was the center of attention; she was also rendered helpless. She was caressed, complimented—and she was also humiliated, sexually overstimulated, and physically hurt. She was seduced; she was also coerced. She was made to feel special; she was made to feel dirty. Did she want it? Did she hate it? Variations of these events, and of these questions, had dominated Sandy's life ever since.

Despite the vivid experiences and imagery that emerged during EMDR, and despite the evident grappling with the material by alternative senses of self, Sandy would often, after the fact, deny the meaning of it. "I don't know what that was about," she would say, "but nothing happened." She finally asked me one day: "Why can't I believe it?"

I countered: "What would be lost, if you believed it? What is the payoff for *not* believing it?"

She was thoughtful, and then replied, with apparent sorrow, "That would mean that the ugliness was outside of myself . . . that I was just raped, that's all, it didn't mean anything. I would lose the belief that they liked me. . . . It would mean that I was just a stupid gullible little kid."[2] It was a poignant manifestation of Goldberg's conclusion (1999): "No one gives up a split-off sector without a penalty or a price" (p. 134).

NOTES

1. Goldberg (1999, p. 37) reports that Basch (1988) likened the occurrence of disavowal, entailing a disconnection between perception and affect, to neurological disconnection between the hemispheres of the brain.

2. The perceptive reader will note that there is a hint of paradox in this comment by Sandy. The issue will be further discussed in chapter 16.

SIX

"What is wrong with my mother?"

What is wrong with my mother?

—Alice, Sandy's daughter

All psychiatric treatments, psychoanalytic or otherwise, influence the significant others in a patient's life, and are influenced by them. While only
family therapy specifically aims to alter the dynamics between a so-called
"identified patient" and significant others, it is surely always a hope on
the part of therapists and psychiatrists that treatment will change the
patient's relationships for the better. In Sandy's case, involvement with
family members was inevitable—first, because her father was paying for
much of her treatment, and second, because her pathology so profoundly
involved behavior as well as subjective feelings, her spouse and children
were inevitably impacted.

It is my custom to provide information about a patient's treatment to
any family member who is paying the bill. To me, this has always seemed
an ethical issue, about which I have no ambivalence. First, of course, I get
permission from the patient; I then write a summary of the reasons for
therapy, at the time of the initial treatment contract, or later of treatment
progress. I then have the patient read this draft, and together we finalize
the letter that will be forwarded to the appropriate person. In Sandy's
case, as I have said, this was her father.

Sandy's father can be characterized as a hard-headed, business-orient-
ed professional, and a very intelligent individual. He was a quintessential
American success story, having begun life with few advantages, but having become an extremely successful and wealthy man through his own
talents. He was also a man of exacting standards, expecting of himself
and his three children full-throttle effort at all times, in whatever endeav-
or was at hand. He believed there were few obstacles in life that could not
be overcome through sheer determination. The scorn and disgust that

several of Sandy's altered senses of self displayed toward her "weakness" sounded very much like the internalization of a child's reading of her father's demanding superego. Her father was skeptical of the diagnosis of dissociative identity disorder, but to his credit, was willing to suspend disbelief in the service of therapy that he fully agreed his daughter desperately needed.

Sandy's mother was herself a strong-willed woman, although, as I have earlier suggested, given to denial. For her, family happiness was not a matter of working through issues, ups and downs, or muddling through. It was achieved by *willing* it to occur. On the other hand, it was evident that she felt considerable guilt over her daughter's problems. Neither Sandy, in her conversations with her mother, nor I, in my communications to her, ever explicitly confronted her with her apparent complicity in the childhood antecedents to Sandy's problems, but the implications were unavoidable.

In the course of Sandy's treatment, I saw her parents on one occasion, together with Sandy, and wrote to them several times. I include three of these letters below, for two reasons. The first is to demonstrate what I have described above—that is, the way in which I involve family members who are paying the bill. The second, and more important, is to provide a unique overview of the stages of therapy with Sandy, written in present tense, rather than in retrospect. Obviously, I cannot help but put my best foot forward in these letters, in terms of explaining and justifying the treatment (although this is less true of the second letter, which was never sent), but the letters nevertheless provide some insight into how I viewed what was going on at the time from a more reflective, considered perspective, stepping back from the scene of the action.

The first letter was written early in the therapy, when I learned that Sandy's father would be paying for the increased amount of time per week that I had recommended to Sandy.

Dear Mr. and Mrs. F:

I am writing this letter on two counts. One is that it is my personal belief that you are entitled to some information about the process and progress of Sandy's psychotherapy, in that you are contributing truly significant amounts of money to help her pay for it. The second is that I believe Sandy herself has a difficult time making clear either the nature of her problems or their status—and that it is difficult for anyone other than myself to maintain a real sense of how serious these problems are.

Let me say at once that it is my opinion that Sandy's problems are very serious indeed. It is for this reason and this reason alone that she continues to be engaged in this intensive, long-term psychotherapy. Indeed, her condition is one of the few for which this kind of therapy is the only real alternative, unlike so many other conditions for which modern psychiatry has found biological corre-

lates and medical treatments, or which are responsive to shorter-term psychological interventions.

I will review for you some of the reasons I believe her condition to be serious, and I am sure as I do so you will find yourself in agreement. On the other hand, I think I understand as well why at other moments you may well find yourself feeling that this whole thing has been exaggerated, blown out of proportion. A major reason for the latter viewpoint is that Sandy herself feels that way much of the time, and conveys to you and to the world that things really are basically "fine" — that she simply needs to buckle down and work harder at her goals. For that matter, she not only feels that way much of the time, but acts accordingly. Thus she continues to be a very good mother, and an ambitious and competent businesswoman. When her difficulties do surface, coming into public view, they are very likely to look primarily like marital difficulties. Those difficulties indeed are there and are in themselves not insignificant; but they are not her core difficulty.

You have already been apprised of some of the symptomatology for which Sandy is being treated, but let me go over this again. Sandy has true periods of quite profound amnesia, during which time she acts in a purposeful manner, makes decisions, and interacts with other people. At those times, she looks and seems truly like a different person to those who may witness her behaviors. I have experienced this many times in my own office, and Craig can and probably has attested to the same phenomenon to you. I presume this phenomena must be familiar in some fashion to you as well. At times, Sandy in a certain state of self-presentation can be "super-Sandy" — more efficient, more competent, more focused and energetic, than she ordinarily thinks of herself as being. But at other times — again, as you have heard before — her presentation of self can be self-destructive in the extreme. Thus she has at times made deep, serious, multiple cuts across her upper torso, for which she has no subsequent memory.

I regard the symptomatology I have described above, however — as dramatic and at times alarming as it may be — as secondary. It reflects a way of coping with what she must experience as overwhelming stress, which increasingly appears to have developed when she was an adolescent, or younger. We do not yet know what sorts of intolerable stress might have led to these extreme coping mechanisms; it is possible that we will never know. We do now know of some very disturbing events having happened that, while insufficient in themselves to account for any long-term destructive sequelae, may serve as examples of what in more severe form could have had such an outcome.

[I refer at this point to Sandy's adolescent diary, in which she had recorded incidents with the family's minister that sounded as though he had engaged in some quasi-sadistic behavior with the patient in the guise of "horse-play," for example at a pool. I thought at that point in the therapy these events might have been instrumental in causing her dissociative symptoms. They later seemed of secondary importance, as we explored experiences and events of her earlier childhood.]

What is important about [these episodes] is, first, that they happened at all—truly unacceptable behavior in an adult on whom Sandy had an intense (and normal) teenage crush—and second, how Sandy reacted to them. She blamed herself. She must have done something, she wrote in her diary and said to me, to provoke the man. She was too tomboyish, or teasing, or flirtatious, or whatever. Wrong. She was the child, he was the adult. And finally, her reaction includes: amnesia. She has absolutely no memory of the events about which she has written.

Did Reverend Pete do other things, perhaps much worse, of a violent, sadistic, or sexual nature, of which Sandy has no recollection? I have no idea, and neither does she. But I can say with confidence that it is this kind of experience—including the sense of betrayal and humiliation—that very likely in some form occurred with someone, during those formative years, which has resulted in lifelong problems.

I have now alluded to what I believe to be Sandy's core problem, as opposed to the secondary coping mechanisms which are problematic in their own right. That is: her lack of any sense of self which is worth anything at all. She feels herself to be a nothing—or, at moments, worse: a something which is destructive to those around her, utterly lacking in any redeeming values. And as a result: bleak, terrible depression, mostly defended against.

At this point, you may be finding yourself less sure that I am accurate in my assessment. You may be feeling, "Well, yes, Sandy has always had trouble with self-esteem, but aren't you overstating things a bit in that description?" All I can tell you is: I think not. I believe Sandy has opened up to me to a degree she has never done with another person, and this is what I hear, and experience.

The aim of this treatment is, obviously, to change this state of affairs. How? Primarily, by providing Sandy with a safe relationship in which, gradually, she can come to see reflected by me a view of herself as OK, solid, and a person with whom it is truly worthwhile to be in relationship. This is beginning to happen, but slowly, and in glimpses. She is capable at moments of saying, now, "I don't deserve this"—whether it is a behavior by Craig, or an unempathic remark by me—without immediately turning it into a self-excoriation. Much of the time, she still cannot. But I do see signs of change, and I am hopeful.

I am also hopeful that you find this rather lengthy letter useful in terms both of understanding what is going on with Sandy, and of reinforcing your support for this elusive, difficult-to-describe, therapy, a version of which one of Freud's patients, a hundred years ago, called: "the talking cure."

Sincerely,
Dr. Ron Moline

The contrast between this letter—self-assured, professional, insightful—and the letter below could hardly be more dramatic. The following letter, written about two years after the one above, was never sent—a decision I am sure the reader will agree was a wise choice. In retrospect, writing it was motivated less by a wish to apprise Sandy's parents of the current state of things than by a need on my part to gain some sort of distance and objectivity about what was going on in a therapy that felt disorganized and chaotic. As will be evident, it followed upon my having finally realized that Sandy had rather desperately needed me to act on her behalf in the face of her profound ambivalence about being hospitalized.

Dear Mr. & Mrs. F,

I want to give you a summary of Sandy's brief hospitalization: before, during, and after. As I told you on the phone, this hospitalization did not take place because Sandy was more depressed or more suicidal than she had been over the past several weeks, although neither was she less so. Rather, I hoped, first, that it would convince Sandy at a deeper emotional level that I, as her therapist, really did hear her plea that it was not safe to depend on her impulse control alone to get her through this period; second, that in taking this step Sandy would feel that she herself was able to say: "I need help — and I am deserving of help"; and third, that it would get both of us over the uneasiness of the unknown, i.e., that we would both learn about the specific procedures involved in hospitalization and what we could expect from hospitalization.[1] Fourth, that we would consider whether the inpatient setting might be a good place — because of its safety — to do more exploratory EMDR work.

You may know that the initial attempt to get Sandy hospitalized was a fiasco, because of the incompetence of hospital personnel. I began at 9:00 a.m. to try to arrange for the hospitalization, and they finally set up an "assessment interview" with her at 6:30 p.m. — after the clinical intake person with whom I'd been talking all day was off shift.

Then, Sandy appeared at the appointed hour, only to be told by a valet at the front door that patients weren't allowed to enter there (the hospital was having an "Open House"), and that she should go to a building in the back. She did so: the waiting room was somewhat shabby, and the only person in attendance seemed to be a security guard who, when Sandy explained why she was there, set about trying to find an assessment clinician. After almost a half-hour, Sandy, agitated, told the security guard that she was going to leave, to which he replied, "Okay!" Then she called me, completely distraught.

After hearing the story, I was almost as upset as Sandy was. She ended up saying that she would do whatever I said she should do. Thinking that this mess could still go on for God-knows-how-long, if I tried myself to reach the hospital intake person and then get back to Sandy, I suggested she go back home and we would try to get this done properly the next day. Apparently she and Craig then left and went to a nearby restaurant. As she calmed down, she apparently also felt that all the reasons why the hospitalization made sense in the first place were still in place — including her distrust of her impulse control — and she told Craig she wanted to go back. Craig proceeded to get angry and upset, saying it was a terrible idea. He followed her downstairs to the ladies room, and when she emerged began, in her words, to "shove her around," leading a waitress to call the police. The police came, and she told them she wanted to go to the hospital.

Craig impressed the police as being perfectly in control and capable of taking her to the hospital himself, and he did so—where he literally dumped her off on the doorstep. Somehow, she was admitted.

From the hospitalization itself, Sandy and I learned that it served one function very well, but one function only: it was a place to feel safe. It most decidedly was not a place to do more intensive therapy. I discovered that private psychiatric hospitals today are no more set up for therapy than public or university hospitals: the interview rooms were tiny, were right off the corridor, and were barely soundproof. On one occasion when we were meeting, someone mistakenly entered. Another time, a phone in the room began to ring. The entire unit was not a calm, soothing environment. The nurses seeming burdened by too much to do, there were often many patients milling around the nurses station, and most of the patients seemed much less highly-functioning than Sandy—many of them psychotic, some of them indigent (private psychiatric hospitals make much of their income, I learned, off Medicaid patients). Several of them came up to me begging to see their doctor, whom they apparently had not seen in days.

Not surprisingly, Sandy was eager to be discharged the morning after admission. I told her I really did not want to do that, and she agreed to stay. We both realized, though, that the holiday weekend was approaching, that I would be out of town from Friday through Monday, and that the hospital program, such as it was, would undoubtedly be curtailed. Sandy called me late Wednesday afternoon from the hospital, and asked what I thought of discharging her on Thursday morning, allowing her to keep our previously arranged downtown appointment later the same day. She sounded in good shape, and I had felt good about how she had seemed during our session in the hospital. It made sense to me that we could have a more fruitful therapy session in my office, before the long weekend, than we possibly could in the hospital, and thus, I agreed. When we in fact did meet in my office, I continued to feel very pleased and impressed with what this whole experience had accomplished: Sandy felt good about herself, she did not feel suicidal, and she felt good about our working together as a team.

However, there was a mix-up. Sandy had thought we were going to be meeting for 90 minutes and had told Craig so; in fact, I had only scheduled 60 minutes, and consequently, after the session, they missed each other. When they finally did meet and go to lunch, the atmosphere apparently turned tense. As I understand it, Craig was angry and critical of Sandy for having gone to the hospital at all and then for having stayed such a short time. He conveyed to her that she was selfish, self-indulgent, neglectful of her family, etc. He ended up grabbing her suitcases and, according to Sandy, literally running to the car and taking off, leaving her stranded downtown. In short, Craig was, in my view, emotionally assaultive, and quite effectively undid much of the good that had come from the hospital experience.

Sandy now was in the position in regard to her kids of having Craig return home alone and tell them some story about their crazy mother. In addition she was left to figure out what to do. She did not know that Craig had dropped her suitcases off at Janet's apartment [Sandy's sister, who lived in the city]. She of course thought that that was where she would have to go, but she felt humiliated and defeated to appear on Janet's doorstep, under such circumstances, without so much as a toothbrush. She called me, and sounded very, very precarious. I had visions of her dissociating, and of me getting a call later from a policeman, bus driver, or whoever saying that I had a patient who seemed disoriented, or worse. I spent some time with her on the phone, trying to calm her down, and encouraging her to in fact go to Janet's for the evening. This was not easy; by now Sandy was feeling—as she inevitably does when someone is critical or hostile toward her—that this was all her fault, that of course she's the problem because she's such a piece of shit, that nothing matters anyway, that she might as well do . . . whatever. She did eventually get to Janet's, but later that night went to a hotel. I think it would have been better had she stayed at Janet's, actually; going to a hotel did not make things better.

At this point in time, Sandy is exhausted, disgusted with herself, dispirited, and can not imagine how things can ever get better. She is, thankfully, not suicidal. I have reminded her that the hospitalization did open up to her some new feelings which were positive and which can, over time, be recovered. I have said that her feeling defeated, flawed, and vulnerable after the hospitalization was not her fault or a reflection on her, only revealing the fact that she is still profoundly susceptible to emotional attack and insensitivity.

Sincerely,
Dr. Ron Moline

Below is the last letter I had occasion to write to Mr. and Mrs. F. Late in therapy, things were very much improved—but we also seemed to have reached something of an impasse. Sandy and her father had reached an agreement some time previously about how jointly to pay for her therapy, which was in any case less costly because of our having reduced sessions to once a week. But, feeling we were at an impasse, I thought the only way through it was to resume more frequent sessions, which Sandy by herself could not afford.

Dear Mr. & Mrs. F:

This observation, it occurred to me, is as good a measure as any other of how long I have been seeing Sandy: the first two times I provided you an update, I sent it via first class mail, with no thought of any other alternative. This report, obviously, is coming via email; and the idea of sending it via the post office got very short consideration indeed.

The good news I have to tell you is old news, and that in itself, in considerable measure, is good news. The gains that Sandy has made have been sustained. The fears that we harbored—Sandy and myself, but no doubt the two of you as well— that there would be regressions, possible episodic crises with old, dangerous behaviors—have not occurred. Sandy is Sandy—all the time, in the face of whatever stresses she encounters. The internal voices that plagued her entire youth and early middle age have simply ceased, as have those voices' more physical representations.

The downside of good news being old news is that the remaining psychological problems have changed very little over the past couple of years; and it is for that reason, that I feel obliged to ask you to consider, yet again, sustaining the cost for Sandy of increased therapy.

Sandy herself is extremely reluctant to ask you even to continue funding her current therapy, much less resume a greater financial burden. She will often argue with me that her problems at this point are not psychiatric, but personal, and have more to do with her failure to make difficult life decisions than with psychopathology. I disagree.

There remains in Sandy a very serious and very core problem which can be summarized like this: she has a deep need to view any misfortune which is visited upon her, or any mistreatment she receives at the hands of others, to be a consequence of her own deficiencies and even "badness."

To be sure, this trait has lessened dramatically over the past many years. There was a time when, if Sandy realized in a therapy session that she was taking pride in something, or daring to think she was successful or competent, there would be a sudden and dangerous change in her psychological state — as though she'd been caught in a terrible lie, and now needed to be punished for it. There were often serious physical consequences.

No longer, thank God. But what continues to happen is that, when Sandy approaches the idea that there are things she could do to be happier, to lead a more satisfying life, she almost automatically slips back into a psychological state in which she tells herself NO — that cannot be. Nothing can change, nothing can get better, until I prove myself worthy. To the absolute mystification of anyone outside Sandy herself, her subsequent determination to change often takes a completely maladaptive route — as, for example, by putting herself on a near-starvation diet.

In Sandy's previous employment, the number and length of therapy sessions per week were dictated almost entirely by when she was in town, and could free up the time. While I was not satisfied with this — I, of course, always prefer that decisions about therapy be made purely on the basis of psychiatric assessment, not external exigencies — I will say that I hoped lesser intensity of treatment at that point in time would prove sufficient to get Sandy where she needed to go. I regret to say that that has not proven to be the case. What has happened with once-a-week therapy — or less — has been that Sandy gathers her defenses, spends the first three-fourths of the session trying to convince herself and me that everything is basically "fine" — and only in the final minutes acknowledges that things are not fine at all, and that she is at times barely functioning.

Because of this, I am recommending that, as her employment permits, Sandy resume twice-a-week sessions, of at least an hour and fifteen minutes each. I hope you can agree to this.

If you would like to discuss the matter further with me, please feel free to contact me, although, as always, with the understanding that Sandy needs to

know of any such contacts, and that I am limited in what I can tell you without
Sandy's permission. (She of course has given her permission for this letter.)
  I hope you are both well.
  Sincerely,
  Dr. Ron Moline

As important as Sandy's parents were in her life, the more compelling,
complex, and important relationship in her current life, of course, was
that with her husband, Craig. In the presenting marital crisis, after Sandy
had found the videos of Craig engaged in sexual activity with prostitutes,
Craig was clearly disturbed and agitated, but seemingly less out of shame
and guilt than out of the possible repercussions on his marriage. The lack
of shame and guilt over his behavior led me initially to think of him as a
sociopathic personality, but I came to see him as a much more complex
individual. The sexual behavior itself—driven, repetitive, clouding his
judgment—was more characteristic of a sexual addict than of a pattern of
antisocial behavior. Indeed, it appeared that he had married the patient
in considerable part because "Sam" was a partner as interested in sexual
activities other than vaginal intercourse as he was.
    Some of the material above points toward Craig's further problems.
At the same time, he was a devoted father to his children and, indeed,
could at times be a devoted husband. I learned over time, however, that
the marital relationship was a never-ending tumultuous series of crises,
often involving violence on both their parts. Sandy felt almost persecuted
by Craig's endless demands for sex, not all of which apparently could be
"handled" by dissociation; he in turn could be enraged by Sandy's frequent, at times inexplicable, provocative behavior. At the same time, they
were constantly together, as much as business and family responsibilities
allowed, and when apart, in continuous cell phone contact with each
other. (This changed significantly in the last years of the marriage, when
Sandy began an affair.) There were few boundaries between them, and
the idea of personal privacy seemed virtually foreign to both.
    I have referred to the role alcohol played in Sandy and Craig's rela-
tionship. Both of them were, at the least, alcohol dependent, if not outright alcoholics, and both could exhibit markedly different behaviors
when under the influence. Midway in the therapy, Sandy one day announced that Craig had once again beaten and raped her, over the weekend. Something startling had happened the following day, however: she
had tried to talk to him in a neutral, problem-solving way, about his rage
and his violence. This led to their mutual realization that Craig had absolutely no recollection of his behavior at all! Presumably, Sandy's psychological growth allowed her to create a context in which a discussion of
such emotion-fraught behavior could be broached, but neither, apparently, could have predicted how the discussion would unfold. The impact of
this revelation was even greater on Craig than on Sandy. He was

stunned, confused, and—for one of the first times—remorseful. This event led him to attend some Alcoholics Anonymous meetings, and to markedly curb, if not stop, his drinking.

I met with Craig and Sandy together on many occasions, almost always in regard to some serious, safety-threatening crisis. I had no illusions about Craig—his psychopathology, his contribution to the maintenance of the problems, his ambivalence toward Sandy—but I had, perforce, at times to interact with him as though we formed a treatment team.[2] I could not keep Sandy safe at home—Craig, potentially, could. Somewhat to Sandy's and my chagrin, Craig began to regard himself as, indeed, a cotherapist—for example, referring to me by my first name, as opposed to Sandy's continuous use of "Dr. Moline." He became an expert on dissociative identity disorder, reading virtually as much on the condition as I had. I have mentioned elsewhere that he claimed this literature to have been a revelation: it made explicable, to him the heretofore inexplicable behavioral changes he had witnessed in Sandy.

I met a couple of times with Sandy's children as well. Given their chaotic parents, I found it astonishing that both of them seemed to be reasonably psychologically healthy teenagers. Both were doing well in school, neither engaged in serious acting out behaviors, and neither struggled with severe depression. It must be said that both Sandy and Craig functioned best in life as parents. To a remarkable degree, they managed to shield the children from the acting out and bizarre behavior that characterized so much of their relationship. Sandy, in fact, had what I considered to be exceptional relationships of trust and openness with both her son and daughter. Each had, on occasion, confided in her and turned to her for advice in ways that I as a father could only envy.

I met with the children the first time relatively early in the therapy, at Sandy's request. She was sure they often were confused, if not mystified, by her behavior and the turmoil between her and Craig, and hoped that I could clarify her problems for them in a way that didn't sound like she was simply crazy. The session with the kids seemed to go well, and I was subsequently given feedback that they had found it helpful.

Sometime during the middle years of therapy, Sandy engaged in some unusual out-of-control behavior. On a Saturday night, she ran out of the house after a fight with Craig, got in the car, and began to drive. At some point she blanked out. Four hours later, she became aware that she was in a hotel with a man, without recollection of how she had gotten there, and even unaware of what town she was in. Terrified, she got the man to leave, and, ascertaining the name of the hotel and the town (about thirty miles from the suburb in which they lived), she began to search for her car, without success. At that point, she again blanked out. Apparently, at some point shortly afterward, she called her daughter on her cell phone, told her where she was, and said she needed help.

The result was that in the early morning hours, Craig, together with the children, came to get her and to find the car. Sandy called me the next day, distraught that she had involved her children in her problems, and distraught that they were refusing to talk to her. Craig had been enraged with her for involving them, and she could only agree. She had implored the kids to have a meeting with me, but they refused. I proposed I write them a letter, to which she eagerly agreed. It was the only letter I ever wrote in regard to her that she did not read and edit first. The letter said:

Dear Ted and Alice,

I have several things I would like to say to you. One: I have told your mother that you have every right to be really angry about what happened last night. She says—correctly—that she, Sandy, your mother, did not choose to do what happened last night. As I told her, however, it impacted big time on your life, and that doesn't change just because she didn't choose it or doesn't remember it.

Two: Why did it happen? I believe because of several extreme stresses taking place all at one time in your mother's life: the incredible pressure of starting her new job, the blow of seeing a For Sale sign in front of the house you all love, and feeling totally cut off from me, because of my vacations and my illness [I had had a retinal detachment], this summer.

Okay, you say, so she was under pressure. Why did she do what she did? There are a million ways to deal with pressure, some good, some not good, but why this way?

I will tell you what I told her.

When your mother feels extremely overwhelmed—feels she can not really depend on anyone to be able to help her carry her load—she is vulnerable to turning to an old way of coping—a very poor way, but one which was imprinted in her brain at a very early age. I believe that when she was around five years of age, and was feeling like it was her duty in life to be a very good little girl and not bother her mother or father about anything, especially feelings, it was her very bad luck to run into some adults who said, "Hey! We'll care about you a lot! We'll tell you how nice you are, and how pretty, and how terrific—while we do some other things to you, which you might not like, but which will be your fault anyway because you asked for it."

In other words, as you already know, I believe your mother "learned"—only it really was more like something getting lasered into her brain—that when you are feeling extremely needy, there is only one way to go about getting your needs met. And that's what happened last night. Except that, there was still a healthy part of her available to call you, to let you know something was happening that needed to stop, and in fact finally to come home, without anything really bad happening. I don't know why she called you instead of your father, unless it was because they had had a fight earlier in the evening.

I hope this helps.

Sincerely,

Dr. Moline

NOTES

1. Sandy's first hospitalization, a couple years prior to this occasion, had been an admission to the university hospital with which I was affiliated. It proved unsatisfactory in several respects, including the fact that the system was not accustomed to attending physicians admitting their private patients, and the fact that a psychiatric resident, not I, was the accountable attending physician. The hospitalization described here as to a private psychiatric hospital to which I had gotten admitting privileges specifically for the purpose of hospitalizing Sandy.

2. A significant exception to this characterization is that I never talked with Craig about Sandy without her being present except under extreme circumstances, and on those occasions would later provide her a full accounting of our exchange.

SEVEN

"The intense symbiotic dyads are very difficult for the therapist to penetrate."

The intense symbiotic dyads [of the borderline patient] are very difficult for the therapist to penetrate, as the quality of the therapist-client
relationship does not have the power of the symbiotic one in which the
client is engaged.

—Celani (1993, p. 46)

Toward the end of the fifth year of therapy, the appearance of altered
senses of self in my office had ceased. Sandy reported that her "voices"
had become weaker and less intrusive; episodes of an altered sense of self
fully taking over her life were rare and brief. In the sixth year, both the
voices and the appearances ceased altogether. Our relationship seemed to
be moving toward what Celani (1993), summarizing several theorists'
views, refers to as "resolution of symbiosis" (p. 77). The intensity of our
relationship had attenuated, and we both felt as though we were emerging from a deeply important but fading experience. I began to imagine a
healthy, growth-enhancing termination. And is it ever thus?

To my dismay, an old figure in Sandy's life reappeared, through no
initiation (to my knowledge) by Sandy. Bill had been a hugely important
love object for Sandy, beginning in high school and continuing through
the next decade of her life, reemerging off and on ever since. In high
school, the relationship had become tumultuous, largely because of
Sandy's dependency (or selfobject) needs. She would return from a date
deliriously happy, only to begin, almost immediately, to fall into a panicky sense of loss and abandonment.

The first ending of this relationship occurred in high school one day
when Bill had driven her home from a date, and Sandy had refused to get
out of the car. He eventually pushed her forcibly out and drove off, as she
tried to hang on to the car. She went inside her house, cut and bleeding,

and her parents—appalled—insisted she break off the relationship. The relationship resumed when Sandy moved away from home, to attend a nearby college.

Certainly the information I have just provided is consistent with the diagnosis of borderline personality disorder. Does it correlate with, or explicate in any way, the diagnosis of dissociative identity disorder? Sandy had, in fact, given me additional information about the relationship that was not typical of borderline personality disorder. For example, she had no memory of ever having had sexual intercourse with Bill. She was sure that it had occurred: she has memories of driving to secluded areas, kissing, and embracing, followed by—blankness. She would regain awareness as they returned home, suspecting that intercourse had taken place.

Bill had occasionally alluded to Sandy's passionate nature; it seems likely that the sexual aspect of their relationship played a prominent role in his continued interest in her, despite the tumult. He seems to have had his own problems, however. Even in high school, there were times when he would suddenly disappear from Sandy's life, seemingly independent of her behavioral contribution to their difficulties.[1] He would then suddenly reappear, professing his love, often when Sandy had despairingly given up hope.

Eventually, Bill married and had children. Sandy also married, but she and Bill continued to have an occasional secret rendezvous, despite their marital status. Each time, however, after one or two meetings and various phone calls, Bill would abruptly disappear again, ceasing all contact. Sandy had not seen or heard from Bill for many years, until the day toward the end of our fifth year of therapy when he called, "to say hi." I was concerned, though Sandy insisted that she was aware of the pitfalls of seeing Bill once again. Despite my expressed reservations, she arranged to see him in what she felt would be "safe" surroundings, with the single intention of bringing each other up to date about their lives.

Of course it did not stop there. Within weeks, the changes in Sandy's attachments were startling. I all but ceased to exist as a libidinal object—my words in therapy could as well have been written on paper and handed to a stranger. Craig became little more than an obstacle, around which Sandy had to maneuver in order to see Bill. Interpretations—of avoiding the pain of termination of our relationship, of a resurgence of masochistic self-inflicted pain due to guilt, and of the siren call of an ancient imago of Fairbairn's "frustrating-exciting" object—were useless. In short, it was as if I were beginning therapy with a classic borderline personality disorder.

Frequently, Sandy and Bill would make elaborate, secret plans to meet at a bar in a town midway between their respective abodes. They would confirm the rendezvous hours before the agreed time—and Bill would not show up. Sandy would be crushed and distraught. She would email him: there would be no response. She would call him at his office: he was either unavailable, or would respond curtly, "I can't talk now," and then hang up. Eventually, she would get an email from him that was like bad haiku: brief, impenetrable, paradoxical. All Sandy's pain and rage at abandonment would suddenly become emotionally unavailable to her. She would start making excuses for Bill's conduct, and would find reasons to blame herself for having somehow disappointed or misunderstood him, as an explanation for his conduct. Contact would be reestablished. Another rendezvous would be planned. Bill might or might not show up. The cycle would repeat itself.

I had not imagined that I would be revisiting my reservoir of helpless, impotent feelings this late in the therapy, given how things had improved over the previous months. There were many sessions in which I wondered why in the world Sandy bothered to come, or what point, if any, there was in our meeting together. It was as if we were engaged in what Searles (1961), in his therapy with schizophrenics, and Celani (1993), in his work with borderlines, describe as the first, "out-of-contact" phase. I found myself reminded of Celani's statement that, "There are on occasion patients who never get beyond this point and therapy turns out to be a fruitless and frustrating experience for both parties" (Ibid., p. 75). It felt as if our six years of therapy together had never happened. Fortunately I was able intellectually, at least, to tell myself this could not be the case.

These countertransferential feelings prevented me, for a long time, from recognizing that something different was happening in Sandy's revisiting this old, pathological relationship. In addition to the repetitive thoughts and feelings associated with each stage of these reenactments, she also began, from time to time, to be able to reflect on the relationship—something that had never happened before. She volunteered one day that she didn't know what would happen if Bill and she were not each married; she was not at all sure he would be someone she would want to spend the rest of her life with. For one, she said, even if there were usually good reasons for his failures to show up (I bit my tongue), she recognized that he had a striking inability to communicate his feelings. Second, there were major sociocultural differences between them: Bill had never gone to college, never left his hometown, and had little or no knowledge of cultural, social, or even political events.

Of far greater interest and importance, however, were the changes that took place in the relationship between Bill and Sandy at the level of intimacy. There came an occasion when, for the first time in her life, Sandy did not become amnesic during intercourse, but experienced it instead as a loving, caring, intimate act. Bill had said, "I love you, and I always have." Whether or not he had ever said those words previously, and whatever they may have meant to him, she had never heard them before.

Like any therapist, I have had many experiences with patients in which I have learned things about myself, human nature, or the human condition, that I hadn't known before. Few experiences, however, have left me feeling as awed by the complexity of human motivations, psychological growth, regression, morality, and paradox, as this one. I had initially regarded Bill as little more than a "bad object" (or again quoting Bergman, a "false selfobject") for my patient, and her attachment to him as solely pathological. After Sandy shared her experience of intimacy, however, and continued to speak of Bill as a man who had serious flaws, but whom she loved, I found that there was no single thing I could say about this relationship that would capture the truth of it—that, in fact, there was no overarching "truth." I learned what I suppose I should have learned decades ago: that there are probably very few relationships that do not contain the potential both for growth and for destructiveness.

The encounters with Bill began to attenuate, both in frequency and in emotional intensity. Both parties seemed to begin to realize the futility of their lifelong fantasies about each other, and the unreality of their imagined future together. It was as if the termination between Sandy and myself was taking place vicariously. It seemed to be one more paradox: an acting-out of the transference seemed to be leading to a *resolution* of the transference. Within sessions, Sandy and I resumed relating to each other in a way that reflected our years of working together.

At a point in time when, for a period of months, Sandy had had no episodes of amnesia, suicidal thoughts, overtly self-destructive behaviors, or dramatic fights with either her husband or anyone else, she was offered a work opportunity in another city. For some time, she had been wrestling with whether or not to leave her husband. One child was in college; another soon would be. She was unsure. A part of her, she said, still loved Craig and felt grateful to him for having stuck with her through years of turmoil; but she also felt resentment at his emotional, physical, and sexual abuse, even while recognizing that she had cocreated some of it. Most troublesome to her was the feeling that she could never experience sexuality as loving and satisfying with Craig, whereas she now knew that she was capable of it with someone else.

She decided to accept the work position and to make the move without her husband. In terms of therapy, while we had begun to talk about termination, neither of us felt that this external event should determine our ending. We reached an agreement that felt right to both of us. Since she expected that the new job would bring her back to Chicago frequently, she would continue sessions as she was able.

In fact, her return visits happened much less often than she had anticipated, and we were able to meet only once every six or eight weeks. These sessions did not seem to go well. Sandy was reluctant to let herself become vulnerable without follow-up sessions, and I could not find a balance between "cutting to the chase," or being excessively tentative in my explorations. We agreed that we would stop formal therapy. We also agreed that we would not terminate our relationship, but would meet, perhaps once or twice a year, when she was in town, in an informal (office) session.

This sort of encounter happened only once. We both felt it went well, but, despite occasional emails updating me on her life, Sandy did not request another meeting. Her employment was going extremely well; it was a job she liked, and one that provided a substantial income. She had divorced Craig, and begun to date. In her emails, she sometimes made reference to feelings of depression, usually in response to conflicted feelings about various men with whom she had gotten involved. She had thought about finding a therapist in her new community to deal with these issues, but she said she was reluctant to risk the sort of dependency she experienced during our long therapy. I emailed her that I doubted that that would happen again. She was not so sure. She had had no dissociative symptoms for over seven years when I ceased hearing from her altogether.

As the final draft of this book was being written, however, Sandy sent me a brief email. It had been two years since I'd last heard from her. She said she hoped that I was well, and that she had exciting news to share — which was not included. I emailed back, briefly acknowledging that I was indeed doing well, and asked about her news. Below is part of her response:

> My news is that I am getting married! I met a wonderful man last May and he proposed this March. We had been talking about an eventual permanent relationship, but the proposal itself was a complete surprise. We plan to get married in August of this year. He is sweet, kind, generous, loving and has the most spectacular sense of humor, and, I think, is very handsome as well (see attached picture!).

She went on to describe how they had met, and something about her fiancé's work accomplishments. She continued:

> I would very much like to have you meet him and was wondering if we all might have coffee together when I am next back in Chicago? We are planning a trip in June — probably around 7th/8th. Let me know if that might work for you.

I answered back that I would be happy to meet her and her fiancé, but that I wanted her to think through how this might go. For example, how would she characterize our work together? What did she anticipate he might say, or ask? How would she want me to respond?

I was taken completely by surprise when Sandy replied that she had told her fiancé virtually everything about her life and her therapy. She had even explained honestly how she had gotten the scars that remained on her abdomen. She said that her revelations had taken place gradually, over time, with lots of dialogue, but she felt that she couldn't commit herself to a relationship if she was keeping secrets from her partner. She had of course been frightened at the risk to the relationship in doing so, but was subsequently enormously gratified that this man was understanding and sympathetic.

At the time of this writing, the proposed meeting over coffee has not taken place. I expect to feel—indeed I do feel—considerable pride in having helped Sandy arrive at this point in her life.

NOTE

1. This, of course, is impossible to know, particularly given Sandy's markedly unreliable memory. However it proved characteristic of him in the time of their renewed relationship during therapy.

EIGHT

"God, I'm going to miss little Claire."

God, I'm going to miss little Claire.

—Baer (2007, p. 208)

As the reference list to this book makes clear, the patient and the treatment I have been discussing are hardly unique in the literature; indeed everything I have described can be found in many previously written articles and books, albeit almost always with shorter clinical vignettes. *Switching Time* (Baer, 2007) is a notable exception—a book-length description of an eighteen-year therapy by the author. As a therapy conducted according to the methodology of the leaders in the field, it provides a valuable foil to the therapy I have described, and bears in-depth consideration. There are both similarities and dissimilarities between the two patients and their treatments, some quite striking. Certain aspects of Baer's narrative would seem to add plausibility to inferences I have drawn from my treatment of Sandy; others are more troubling.

It must be noted that *Switching Time* was written for a different audience than this book. It is not a scholarly work, and in fact takes the authenticity of dissociative identity disorder as a given. It presumes a lay readership, to whom Baer often "explains" the work of a therapist—the reasons for certain lines of inquiry, the use of pauses and silences, open-ended questions, and so forth. There are many brief descriptions of the therapist's intense emotional reactions to what is happening in the therapy, but they are peripheral to his main intent: to describe the physical and sexual abuse incurred by the patient, his therapeutic attention to the altered senses of self, and what he calls the "integration" of the disparate selves.

There is early evidence in Baer's therapy that his emotions will be engaged in a way that is unusual when doing psychotherapy, particularly with a patient suffering from depression. After only a few sessions, he

61

reports a growing sense of irritation with the patient, as she speaks in a reluctant monotone and seems indifferent to his interpretations. He reports feeling, "As if she's walking all over me" (Ibid., p. 11). A bit later he adds that, of all the many depressed patients he had worked with over the years, none got to him as Karen had.

Whether or not such unanticipated and unwelcome feelings led Dr. Baer to verbally accost the patient in some way is not recorded. Let us hope that Karen escaped less scathed than Sandy.

Baer learns that his patient is chronically suicidal, in addition to chronically depressed. He begins what becomes an endless, unsuccessful attempt to find the right antidepressant medication, and the right dose, to address her depressive symptoms. Soon he is scheduling evening phone calls, and fielding many unscheduled calls, in an effort to forestall self-destructive behavior. Soon too, the patient confesses feeling utterly dependent on him, and says that he has become the most important person in her life.

The therapist interprets the bind the patient feels she is in (p. 31): "It sounds like you can't live with me or without me." He does *not* comment upon the binds that *he* is being put in, as in a letter he receives one day (p. 30):

Dear Dr. Baer,

I need to let you know that I lied to you about the last time I hurt myself. I told you it was three months ago, but it's been less than a week. . . . I'm really scared there's something terribly wrong with me. I need your help. . . . I hurt myself like this during high school but stopped when I was 19 years old. It started again last October and has increased during the time we've talked about the sexual abuse. I don't know how to stop it.

Needless to say, neither does Dr. Baer. He believes that talking about childhood sexual abuse is crucial to Karen's improvement, but is being told that to do so may be dangerous, even lethal. Karen confesses to a wish to cut her genitals. She in fact injures herself by inserting a coat hanger into her vagina. Sandy "displaced upwards" her wish to injure her genitals, by seriously cutting her abdomen (something Karen also does at one point). *Help me!* these patients cry out. And proceed to increasingly and secretly mutilate themselves.

The similarities between my patient and Baer's, and between our experiences within the therapy, are obvious and striking. My patient, Sandy, however, is unusual in the literature in her prolonged adamant denial that she ever endured sexual abuse as a child. I have briefly referred to some material that emerged in the early middle phase of therapy—much of it described in a diary—involving things that happened to her during early adolescence. Some involved interactions with a young minister; others involved descriptions of being in a woods, held to the ground with her legs spread apart, her clothes torn; boys laughing, and looking at her. Exploring this material was painful, even excruciating to Sandy, but she did not resist it with the adamancy that she did interpretations about earlier life events.

Such descriptions are jarring to read; one resists believing them, preferring to conclude that such memories are—just as Sandy wanted to believe!—the sado-masochistic fantasies of a perverse adult mind. The critical inquirer cries out for some sort of corroboration, and there is none. I would like to think that my efforts to lay out the evidence in Sandy's case have been both plausible and persuasive; but now comes Karen, whose bizarre reports of childhood trauma may reawaken the critical reader's skepticism about the relationship of adult dissociative identity disorder to actual childhood events.

Karen describes horrendous, sadistic, terrifying experiences as a child at the hands of adults. Remarkably, there is some corroborative evidence of the perverse and destructive impulses her parents harbored. At one point, she hands her cell phone to the therapist to listen to a series of voice messages left by her mother. They include (p. 71):

> Call me! I need something. After all I've done for you, you owe me! Call me! Don't be so fucking rude, bitch! (beep)

> This is your mother! Call me! What the fuck! The least you can do is call me. You owe me the money I spent on you your whole life! Call me or you're dead to me! (beep)

> You're nothing but a fat-assed slob! Don't ever ask me for a fucking dime. If you can't help me, you can kiss my bloody ass! (beep)

> I'm calling your precious Dr. Baer and telling him you're a no-good piece of shit! I wish you would've died at birth! Screw yourself and rotate! (beep)

At one point during Baer's therapy with Karen, her father is arrested and charged with the sexual abuse of her niece, filed by her sister-in-law. Both her parents become relentless and adamant that the patient must testify on his behalf, describing him as a good and decent father. She refuses; she has, in fact, many memories of sexual abuse at his hands. He is eventually found guilty of sexually abusing the niece, but dies from cancer before serving much of his sentence.

The patient initially finds it almost impossible to talk about this material. Like Sandy, she says that it proves that *she* is "no good," and she is afraid that the therapist will want nothing to do with her after he hears it. Unlike Sandy, she says there is more—much more—from her childhood that she remembers, but is afraid to share. The therapist proposes that she put it on a tape recorder, at home, and bring in the cassette. She reluctantly agrees. What follows in the book are vivid descriptions of what is often called, in the literature, satanic ritual abuse.

There are three main clusters of memories involving groups of adults engaging in torture and sexual abuse, with religious connotations. The first is recorded on the cassette referred to above. In it, the patient describes being awakened at 2 a.m. and taken by her father and grandfather to the basement of the factory where her father worked. There are ten or so other people, men and women, some unclothed, including an employee who worked under her father. The room is lit by candles. The patient is undressed, and her grandfather begins to bellow exhortations about "evil children," "God's word," "necessary punishment," "Mother Mary," and so forth. She is made to clutch the blade of a knife, and an adult squeezes her fingers around it, until her fingers are cut and bleeding. She is raped. Other visits to this factory are described, and a ritual called "The Midnight Host" is described, in which a piece of the girl's nipple, ear, or vagina is cut off.

The second cluster of memories occurs at a funeral home, which in reality existed not far from her family's house. The patient is taken to the funeral home, and tied to one of the stainless-steel tables. She is penetrated with objects, and later put in one of the coffins, and the lid closed. When she is allowed out, a woman tells her that she is alive and reborn. The third cluster involves being called to the office of a priest at the Catholic school she attended. Her father and a police officer are there. Karen's nephew has also been summoned, and they all proceed to the church basement, where a makeshift film studio has been set up. The children are forced to engage in sexual acts, while the priest directs the action. When the boy demurs, he is screamed at, told that he is a sinner and that the devil will do terrible things to him, and locked in a closet.

There are also memories associated with Halloween. She remembers at age thirteen being pinned to the bed in her home and having her mouth taped, while her father, a police officer, and other men don Halloween masks, tell her that her body now belongs to Satan, force her to swear her allegiance to Satan, and rape her, while intermittently giving candy to trick-or-treaters at the door. Another later Halloween memory is of the police officer—apparently named Bert—apologizing to her (location unstated), saying that he can't live with what he's done, and committing suicide by shooting himself in the head in front of her. She remembers that his hand made a mark in blood on the mirror.

What in the world is the reader to make of these stories? Reading this material in the twenty-first century, one cannot help but be reminded of the era initiated by the infamous McMartin preschool trial, begun in 1983, in which several teachers and administrators of a preschool in California were formally charged with sexually abusing scores of preschool children, on the basis of children's testimony as elicited by counselors using an interview technique involving "anatomically correct" dolls. The testimony of many of these children included stories of what came to be called satanic rites—candles, robed figures, dead babies, cannibalism, and so forth.

This ushered in what some have called a "moral panic" (Benschoteen, 1990; Cohen, 2002; Conte, 2002), a time in which, especially in the English-speaking world, there were widespread "revelations" of childhood sexual abuse, including satanic sexual abuse. At times, these included accusations of conspiracies in high places to promulgate such atrocities. In 1986, the largest-ever symposium on child abuse was held in Australia, with several leading exponents of the theory of satanic cults as featured speakers. Coincident with the "uncovering" of such childhood abuse, was the emergence of a previously rarely diagnosed condition, multiple personality disorder (MPD), as a common outcome of such abuse. MPD began to be diagnosed so frequently that several treatment centers were created in the United States to address it. Also during this time, certain psychiatric professionals became known as experts in diagnosing and treating MPD. They produced a plethora of books and articles on the disorder—many cited in this book—including virtually manualized methods of treatment.

In 1990, the last of the accused McMartin preschool defendants was found not guilty, all others previously having either been found not guilty or had the charges against them dismissed. Across the country, family members who had been accused by their adult offspring of abusing them as children, began suing their offspring's psychotherapists for actions (induction of false memories) that led to defamation of their character. They began to win—with enormous economic and professional consequences to the therapist-defendants. The frequency of the diagnosis of MPD began to wane; treatment centers were closed. In 1997, the publishing division of the American Psychiatric Association published a book titled *The Dilemma of Ritual Abuse: Cautions and Guides for Therapists* (Fraser 1997)—basically sounding the death knell for this alleged form of childhood abuse.

And now we read of Karen—treated when belief in these events and their sequelae were at their height, but told to us, in printed form, almost twenty years later, when there has been almost universal dismissal of such narratives by both the psychiatric and legal professions. I know of no external corroboration of satanic cults that ever emerged. No "plea bargains," no remorseful confessions, no discovery of secret altars or religious paraphernalia hidden in forests—nothing ever led to the uncovering of groups of people abusing children in the name of Satan, or otherwise incorporating religious elements into their abuse of children.

Baer acknowledges that the question of how much of this is "true" always comes up when he reflects on or talks about his patient's horrific stories. He is apparently satisfied, however, by the convincing way in which she tells these stories: with obvious pain, depression, and torment. She seemed reluctant, in fact, to tell him these "memories."

And there's the rub. We are up against what a therapist must think, must do, in a dire clinical situation, as opposed to what an objective observer might conclude. Baer goes on to say that after giving him the tape, Karen becomes continually suicidal, requiring telephone calls every other day to assess her risk.

Is the patient's increased suicidality, after revealing these stories, further evidence of their veracity? Possibly. It is what a therapist is most likely to feel, under these circumstances. Is it not also possible, however, that some part of the patient, conscious or unconscious, feels intense guilt and shame at the enormity of her accusations, to which she cannot honestly attest with absolute certainty? Or, even more troubling, could she have come upon a way of redoubling her therapist's attention and concern? Baer himself raises the question, and answers it by saying that he cannot imagine what purpose such a deception would serve. He had, after all, already seen her for over four years, and he cannot conceive what "secondary gain" (my phrase) would be achieved so deep into the therapy that other behaviors would not already have achieved. Further, he wonders if indeed she did not have reason to worry that such revelations might jeopardize the treatment, rather than further his already intense involvement.

In the end-phase of therapy, Baer's patient, who is in the process of "integrating" separate senses of self, writes him an extraordinary letter describing detailed experiences of satanic abuse. After warning him that what she is about to describe will be very upsetting, she describes the different levels of satanic belief to which she was introduced, which culminated in praying to Satan and giving him control over her soul. She remembers, she says, white sheets with blood on them, as well as animal sacrifices. There were "important people" from her neighborhood, who wore robes and masks during sadistic rituals. One of her altered senses of self was tortured in "unbelievable ways." She was warned that if she told anyone, she would be killed. One concludes that the patient has no doubt—even after years of therapy and significant improvement, when there can be no question of her therapist's dedication and steadfastness—that she endured and remembers satanic sexual abuse.

It is impossible to prove a negative. Lack of evidence does not prove that something could not have existed, and in the field of psychosocial phenomena, we have no scientifically demonstrated theorems or laws to confidently predict that apples will always fall, and never rise. What I have cited, thus far, are fashions, or currents, of thought. In the twenty-first century, we are, on the whole, convinced that satanic sexual abuse is a myth; in the late twentieth century, we were, on the whole, open to the possibility. Neither is provable.[1]

We are speaking, then, of plausibility and implausibility. Here are my reasons for thinking it highly unlikely that Karen's convictions correspond to actual historical events.

First: Karen, like many other reports in the literature (particularly in the 1980s and 1990s), implicates "important people." In one early cluster of memories, both a policeman and priest are present—important people in the eyes of a child. It is difficult enough to give credence to groups of adults engaging in satanic sexual abuse rituals—but leaders of the community as well? This is the stuff of conspiracy theories, which comprise a long history of confabulation and deep resentment against those who hold power.

Second: what we understand about the origins of pedophilia, including sadistic pedophilia, is that it is rooted in individual histories of childhood abuse in the perpetrators. Classical psychoanalysis theorizes the defense mechanism of "identification with the aggressor." Trauma theorists speak of attempts to undo, or master, childhood trauma. Outside of the literature on dissociative identity disorder, one does not encounter pedophiles who interweave religious, or "antireligious" ideation with their abusive conduct, and we are not surprised by this. It would be beside the point, in meeting their pathological needs.

Third: we live in an age when powerfully felt belief in Satan is not a part of the general milieu—and certainly not in a cross-section of people serving in positions of power in communities. People who do evil things are not generally inclined to attribute their behavior to a malevolent spirit—and if they do, we find it strong grounds to consider a psychotic illness. Centuries ago, the Western European mind regarded the world as completely inhabited by spirits, malevolent and benign, the apotheosis of the former being Satan and the latter God.[2] The sense of "agency" was not confined to oneself and other human beings. Rather, behavior, like events in general, was the consequence of an indissoluble and indefinable amalgam of human desire and spiritual forces. One could attempt to further one's aims, seek support for one's intentions, or avoid negative consequences, through acts of worship and sacrifice meant to alter the balance of power in one's favor. In that context, one might pledge one's allegiance to whatever forces one considered consonant with one's aims and capable of powerful intervention on one's behalf. For a very few, this was the devil.

We do not live in such a world. People naturally claim agency for their own behavior, albeit wishing, at times, for God's blessing, or attributing good fortune to His grace. Even in very conventional religious groups, however, such claims may be more conventions of speech than deeply felt experiences. The devil is given his due in hortatory sermons still today, in some churches in various denominations, but more perhaps in the service of inducing moral behavior in young children, or for political ends, than as a Being we must resist in fear and trembling. It strains the imagination to think of a nonpsychotic individual past the Middle Ages who feels a deep affiliation with, or need to placate, a sentient, external, evil spirit, who intervenes in human affairs. It is even harder to think of such people finding each other and organizing sadistic, ritual-laden, quasi organizations that focus on the abuse of children. Today, like-minded pedophiles can communicate with each other and form groups via the Internet, and law enforcement agencies have found large numbers of these. Such groups, however, are not bound together by satanic or other quasi-religious trappings, and their actual pedophilic behavior tends to occur solitarily, or at most serially, rather than jointly.

Let us turn to the issue of alternative presentations of self. I have raised the question, in my treatment of Sandy, of whether I might at some point have induced, even unconsciously demanded, the patient to assume a false sense of self. I believe it is indeed possible; the next question then is whether what happened in response to my demand was the creation of something *de novo*, or the unveiling of something that already existed. My astonishment—even horror—at the subsequent display of disparate self-presentations seems to me at least partial evidence that I was not aiding and abetting such presentations. Like Baer, I had a hard time conceptualizing what was "in it" for the patient. Sandy, like Karen, could not know whether such bizarre and dramatic events in the therapy would further involve me in her therapy, or incline me to judge her "too sick to treat." Still, Baer's description of his "discovery" of alternative presentations of self seems problematic.

Karen did not present alternative self-presentations for over four years of psychotherapy, although she described from the beginning periods of amnesia. Nevertheless, Baer, for reasons he does not elaborate, considered the diagnosis of multiple personality disorder quite early on.[3] During that extensive period of therapy, there was no talk of "voices," or reports of other people accusing the patient of out-of-character behavior. Baer reports one behavioral peculiarity, however, about which he does not comment but which perhaps contributed to his suspicion; namely that the patient, who persistently presents as a helpless victim of both historical and current abuse, nevertheless also reports having on occasion inflicted actual bodily harm on her husband, in physical altercations. To the reader, such aggressiveness seems markedly inconsistent with the debilitated, depressed, woman otherwise described in Baer's sessions. He also reports that, quite early on, in the course of a hospitalization, the patient presented him several pages of written material about her childhood, which included a list of questions, centering on hopes and fears of therapy, written in a printed handwriting much different from the cursive writing of the rest. The patient does not invite his attention to this oddity, nor does he appear to have reacted to it at the time.

Then, in the fourth year of therapy, one day not long after having given Baer the tape describing the ritualistic torture and abuse, Karen begins a session by saying that she has "spells," which she calls "switching." She goes on to say that there are periods of time—even months in duration—for which she has no memory. Interestingly, she includes the information—identical to my patient's admission—that she has no memory of sexual intercourse with her husband. Baer reports that he is "excited" that she's brought this up "at last." He reveals to the reader that he has been reading up on multiple personality disorder, and he is clearly eager to have this diagnosis confirmed in his own patient. Nevertheless, he is initially cautious, and his first interpretation of dissociated senses of self is circumspect.

A month after the above quoted remark, Karen brings in a dream in which her mother and several different people come to therapy session with her, and begin to engage in a variety of behaviors toward the therapist. Baer tells her that he thinks the people in the room represent different sides of herself. The next day, he receives a letter in the mail (obviously written before the session above), hand-printed in pencil, in childish script. The writer identifies herself as "Claire," claims to be two years old, and expresses the wish to be able to talk to Baer—and to get help tying her shoes.

The letter demonstrates one of the many incongruities and inconsistencies of altered presentations of self: a two-year-old who writes and spells like a six-year-old—a necessary glitch, one may assume, if the patient—however conceived—felt the need to broach multiplicity with this particular presentation, and with the safety of a written communication, rather than face-to-face. In the next session, the therapist brings up the letter with Karen. Gently, but firmly, he tells her that he has been thinking for some time that she is suffering from multiple personality disorder—that he thinks it is the only explanation.

She responds (p. 93), "'I wasn't prepared for this.'" She goes on to say something quite intriguing, and, one suspects, important: "Sometimes I think I'm not very important to me."

Baer says he's not sure what she means by that, but ignores it and now proceeds to ask if she has ever heard of this disorder before, or seen the movie about MPD, *Sybil*. She says she's heard the term, but always stayed away from "those movies."

I find two interpretations of Karen's cryptic remark plausible. The first is, I suspect, along the lines of what Baer himself thought. The core self of a patient with this disorder often feels herself diminished by the very existence of alternative senses of self, as well as by being the recipient of "their" scorn and rage. However, it seems to me that there is another plausible interpretation. It is possible she meant: *Sometimes I think I'm not very important to me—or to you.* Could it be that, exquisitely attuned to Dr. Baer's moods, attentiveness, nonverbal communications, and so forth, Karen senses Baer's increasing interest in the external manifestations of her pathology, and the drama of her story, at the expense of her core self?[4] Is there an enactment about to unfold, in which a neglected and abused child feels she can only get the positive attention of a disinterested parent by some type of performance?[5]

Baer proceeds to explain to the patient how MPD works: we all have different sides to our personality, but for her, there are separations to the different parts, and they're not fully aware of each other. When she leaves, he asks her to call him that evening—he's even more concerned than usual that she might hurt herself. This added interest and concern on Baer's part could hardly have been lost on the patient. He reports that in the following sessions, she seems to have much more awareness of the other parts inside her—"especially in the evening and during the night." He asks her one day how many voices she hears. She answers (p. 95), "I think about six."

Baer is full of emotion. He asks her, "trying to hide my exasperation," why she hadn't told him about this before. But he's also aware of how excited he is to have a patient like this. The paragraph quoted above ends with Baer reflecting, "What do the voices say? Six of them! Only six?"

Not to worry. There are many more, which, over time, will be revealed to Baer in ever-increasing numbers. He is given a series of lists, with ages, descriptions, and functions, even diagrams, showing the relationship of one to another. Baer used the metaphor of a roller coaster, early in his book. Now, he steps onto a roller coaster, we may say, of a particular design. Despite the terrifying rises and falls to come in this prolonged treatment, the narrow tracks define the path he will perforce follow: the solicitation, with the help of hypnosis, of all the "personalities," as he calls them; the gathering of careful histories from each of them; extensive involvement with many of them, at the expense of time spent with Karen as herself; and, ultimately a long process of ritually integrating them into one personality. A very different therapeutic approach than the one I have described. A not-so-different therapeutic course.

Baer eventually is introduced to seventeen different personalities. Unlike the presentations of self that I encountered in my treatment of Sandy, these selves quite openly identify themselves as serving specific functions in defense against the experience of traumatic pain. Even the children alters readily acknowledge that they came into existence at particular moments in time when the patient could not tolerate what was happening to her. This did not make some of them any less prone to self-destructiveness. "Pain relieves pain," was the mantra of some; suicide was the aim of others. Some were biblical in their harsh morality: *If your right hand offends you, cut it off.*

Baer's efforts to elicit the cooperation and support of the various self-presentations, to call now upon this one, now upon that one, and to solicit information known to some but not to others, seems to have done nothing to avoid the rocky, quasi-traumatic sort of course (for the therapist as well as the patient) that I have described in detail in my treatment of Sandy. Unlike myself, Baer has a fairly clear plan of action, and he sticks to it doggedly, through quiet times and chaotic times. What is revealed, however, in this detailed narrative, is an extraordinarily intense therapeutic relationship that is certainly unique in *both* their lives, and may even have significantly impacted Baer's personal life. The reflective reader begins to feel that something is missing in the portrayal of this therapy, as if a three-dimensional edifice were being painted in two dimensions. The *trompe l'oeil* is extraordinary, and the therapist brings all his skills and analytic abilities to bear on the utterly dramatic, bizarre presentations of selves and their vicissitudes which comprise this complex picture. Meanwhile, the reader realizes that immense currents of emotion are flowing between the therapist and the patient, seemingly unexamined. At times, the author simply fails to tell us what reactions he had in circumstances that could not have failed to elicit strong feelings. At other times, he is frank about his intense reactions, as when he gives, as an aside, that in response to an alternative self saying that he wanted to cut off Karen's breasts, he "felt like running screaming out of the room" (p. 166).

Most of Baer's references to his own emotions, however, tend to be given as asides, basically acknowledging "countertransferences" (although he does not use the psychoanalytic term), in the sense of feelings toward the patient that are obstacles to the work at hand. He seems to have very little sense that the intense emotional relationship he formed with the patient may at times have made her worse, at other times better, and ultimately been crucial to the outcome of the case.

Baer is courageous and honest in describing the evolution of the therapeutic relationship, and the evolution of his personal life as well. It is all the more striking, then, that he does not reflect on, or analyze, what he has told us. In one prominent example, he reports spending hours on the phone with Karen each week, which he tries to do after his children have gone to bed, but which he acknowledges is upsetting to his wife. He tells us that difficulties have arisen in his marriage, of which the phone calls with Karen are only a part—but a part, nevertheless. He reports, following one long phone conversation (p. 178):

> After I hang up, my wife turns over and beats her pillow with her fist a few times, as if it's her pillow that's keeping her awake. I lie awake, looking at the ceiling, feeling the unrelenting burden of Karen and all her parts. My marriage has lately been full of complicated issues, of which Karen is merely one. It would help matters at home if I tried to set more limits with Karen, but I fear what the effect on her would be—and after everyone in her life has let her down, I can't be just one more.

Does the author worry at all that perhaps he has a choice to make, between his spouse and his patient (or his way of treating his patient), and

that he is in the process of choosing the latter? Is he not at all angry—
enraged, even—at his patient, who is at the very least confounding his
problems with his wife? If so, he does not tell us.

There comes a time when Baer decides to take an administrative position that will necessitate markedly cutting back his private practice. This
is not a problem in regard to Karen, who he has been seeing only once a
week, the other many hours of "unbilled" time each week occurring on
the telephone. Some time afterward, however, his employer apparently
demands that he work full-time, and thus, Baer will no longer be able to
maintain an office practice. This occurs at a time when he has separated
from his wife. Terminating therapy with Karen, however, is out of the
question—and so he arranges to see her in his apartment. Of this fact he
says only (p. 184): "After some initial turmoil, Karen adapts to this
change of treatment setting, and we resume our work together."

In writing this chapter, I debated, as a grammatical or stylistic issue,
whether or not to end my last sentence above with an exclamation mark.
In fact, it requires, from an emotional perspective, at least two exclamation marks. What was this woman coming to mean to the author in his
life, and what was the patient's experience and interpretation of his involvement? Most important: Were the meanings of these changes in ar-
rangements, or the evolution of their relationship, talked about? Did the
patient know of her therapist's separation and subsequent divorce? Did
she know she had become his only patient?

To raise these questions is not to say that Baer's choices were necessarily inappropriate or inadvisable. It is to say that his choices were without
question having significant impacts on the emotional life of both parties
involved in this treatment, and to continue to conduct the therapy according to the Putnam, Kluft, et al. paradigm, without exploring these
feelings in depth, would seem a serious oversight, regardless of one's
theoretical orientation. It is quite possible Baer did just that, however,
and has chosen not to tell us about it. If so, he has misunderstood what is
important for a reader of his book to know about the conduct of this
therapy.

In the seventh year of treatment, the therapist can no longer avoid
acknowledging a serious dilemma: the patient has accrued a debt of
$5,000 through failure to pay her bill. No experienced therapist will be
shocked or moralistic about this state of affairs; it happens, and it is
embarrassing to admit to one's colleagues. Baer has provided us some
previous material pointing to reasons for his having neglected this problem: an earlier reminder to the patient about an overdue bill had led to
self-destructive behavior, as it apparently evoked in the patient memories
of father demanding she hand over money acquired when he basically
pimped her out. Now, however, the problem is very serious indeed, and
the therapist feels he can no longer avoid addressing it. What Baer does
next, however, is extremely unusual: concluding that the patient will

never be able to make up this debt, particularly as it continues to accumulate for the foreseeable future, he volunteers to see her without charge.

Again: exclamation point omitted. The reader has now been presented, however, with a therapist treating only one patient, who may have played some indeterminate role in his divorce from his wife, and who he is seeing in his personal living space, without charge, in an open-ended therapy. Again: it is courageous of the author to have honestly presented all this information in his work. It seems extraordinary that none of these powerful interpersonal events are reported as having been explored in the therapeutic process, nor are they explored in terms of the author's understanding of how the therapy progressed. After the decision not to charge for therapy is reached, eleven more years of therapy ensue. Was the issue ever raised again? Did the patient ever pay her therapist for any of those endless hours of his devoted efforts? We are not told.

Baer wants us to be as fascinated by the strikingly presented and disparate self-presentations as he was—and indeed we are. There are only so many ways the human mind can attempt to escape from overwhelming trauma, and the possible defenses are arrayed before us in their usual DID format: the efficient, asexual manager; the siren who takes charge of sex; the "never again," aggressive male; the "wild" one; the sequestered, suffering children; and the unnamed, always lurking, always dangerous, Angry One. Baer tells us that his conduct of therapy changes after he is introduced to the cast of characters: from then on, following the standard recommendations, he spends only a brief initial time with Karen, and the rest of the session talking with the others, under hypnosis. In my therapy with Sandy, I was always cognizant that prolonged time spent with other self-presentations was debilitating and demoralizing to Sandy. Karen also reacts to this therapeutic approach, but seemingly with less distress.

In the eighth year of therapy, one of the self-presentations suggests to the therapist that it is time to "integrate," and proposes a method (utilizing hypnosis in a procedure that could be described as "guided imagery"). The author is grateful, because he claims to be uncertain how to proceed in this phase, finding the fusion rituals described in Putnam (1989) vague. "Holden," the self-presentation giving the advice, says Baer must guide Karen, under hypnosis, to a safe place, explain to her what he will be helping her to do, introduce an "alter" and review with Karen his/her function, and then ask the alter to step into Karen's body. (Interestingly, very much in accordance with Putnam's suggestions.) Over the next two years, Baer does just that. There are more diagrams, drawings, and letters. Meanwhile, during that time, the chaos, mayhem, and self-destructiveness waxes and wanes.

Baer tells us that, after the final fusion—a point at which Karen seems to have many of the mannerisms of the altered self-presentations, and most of their memories—therapy is hardly at an end. He reports that she was "fully integrated" in April 1998, but they continued to work together for another eight years—strengthening her resilience and her tendency to despair in the face of the ordinary exigencies of life. He is gratified to see her gradual growth and increasing resilience.

Therapy is terminated in June 2006. Their last session, as one might expect, is touching and poignant. The patient expresses regret that the relationship has always been so one-sided, and then, interestingly, says: "I've never exceeded our boundaries; I was always attuned to you; I could sense what you'd allow" (p. 341).

At first reading, this comment seems almost outlandish—just as in my treatment of Sandy, the boundaries of this treatment have been stretched beyond anything that could be described as a generally accepted therapeutic framework. But I think she has pegged it right: she has never exceeded the boundaries *that the therapist has set*, which were, in fact far outside ordinary parameters. And indeed, she surely was very attuned to him and could sense what he could allow.

In a postscript, the patient, Karen, comments on her experience of the therapy. It is a moving commentary, and concludes with this remark (p. 343):

> Actually, *Switching Time* is a kind of love story. After being hurt so badly all my life, I didn't have the ability to love myself or anyone else. . . . Whether real or fantasized, Dr. Baer's patience, understanding, and unconditional care made me feel accepted and, yes, loved.

I am persuaded that Karen has captured far more accurately the curative factors of this therapy than all the techniques so meticulously described by Dr. Baer.

I have wondered how I would have responded to Karen's, and the other self-presentations', vivid description of satanic abuse. Surprisingly, Baer seems not to have availed himself of Freud's seminal concept of *psychic* reality being the reality that matters in treating a patient; rather, because of Karen's sincerity and distress in revealing her memories, he apparently accepts them as veridical. But how else might a therapist address these issues when a patient—wanting to know if she can trust her therapist, wanting someone, finally, to understand her—asks him if he believes what she is telling him? The interpretation of "psychic reality" can sound to the patient like a dodge—which, in a certain sense, it is.

I think I would have had to tell Karen that I believed her—and did not believe her. That I was utterly convinced some terrible things had happened to her, but that I did not think we could trust her memory to provide us a reliable history of what those terrible things were. And there would be hell to pay, in the subsequent days and weeks of the therapy.

NOTES

1. I was astonished to find that Hacking—clearly a cautious, analytic, and thorough investigator of the phenomenon of multiple personality disorder—in a footnote of his 1995 book (p. 284) offers the opinion that it is quite possible there were and will continue to be satanic abuse cults, and claims to know that goats are sacrificed to Satan on the rooftops of warehouses just a few blocks from his home. I take his word for it, but would almost surely bet that these are rituals of an African or Caribbean subculture within his neighborhood, and are completely unrelated to the sorts of satanic groups of white Americans described in the MPD literature. Hacking's opinion seems to be based on his unhappy view of the capacities of the human soul for depravity, rather than on an analytic perspective of historical and sociocultural contributions to human behavior, which he otherwise so keenly exhibits.

2. This observation as well as the generalizations made in the remainder of the paragraph are to be found in Taylor (2007).

3. Dr. Baer's precise opinions are somewhat confusing, in that he diagnoses dissociative identity disorder very early in the treatment, but states that he "suspected" she further had multiple personality disorder. This is in fact the same diagnosis in different iterations of our diagnostic manual. In the context, it appears that the author means to say that he was certain the patient had a dissociative *disorder*, which was characterized by prolonged periods of amnesia, but suspected the further sub-category of multiple personality disorder.

4. Later, Baer questions whether his patient, whom he comes to identify as "Karen 3," actually *does* represent the "core self," following upon the theories of Putnam et al.

5. Such enactments, as many theorists attest, are inevitable in intensive psychotherapy, and are not an indictment of the therapist. Neither does the term imply that the therapist has fully entered into a repeat of a patient's childhood traumatic experience—only that some aspect of his behavior has been a trigger for the patient—*and been triggered by the patient*—with the result that she experiences it as a repetition.

NINE

"It would be premature to cast the syndrome of multiple personality into a rigid form."

It would be premature to cast the syndrome of multiple personality into a rigid form by proposing a restrictive definition, although many have been offered.

—Bliss (1986, p. 119)

OUTLIERS

I have made clear that, in one important respect, Sandy is an outlier in the firmament of dissociative identity disorder, in that she did not present with a history of childhood sexual abuse, nor did she even accept that such things might have happened to her until well into the therapy. A recent multicountry naturalistic study of the diagnosis and treatment of dissociative identity disorder (Brand et al. 2009), involving almost three hundred patients, exemplifies the demographic and biographical data reported in the literature of such patients: 95 percent were female; 89 percent were Caucasian; 78 percent had some education beyond high school; 86 percent had been sexually abused as children. Once past her initial demurrals, Sandy classically fit the profile. I have had exposure, however, to several cases of dissociative identity disorder that did not correspond to the typical description. They provide interesting comparisons and contrasts.

Dolores is a lower-income, forty-five-year-old African American divorcee who has been in twice-a-week psychotherapy treatment with a psychiat-

77

ric resident (psychiatrist-in-training) for almost two years. She is the mother of three adult children, and currently lives alone. She has been a psychiatric patient in the university system for almost a decade, treated in various therapy programs, utilizing various therapeutic modalities, but never previously in intensive psychotherapy until assigned to her current therapist, who I consider a gifted psychotherapist. For the first time, in all those years, the patient is making significant progress.

Dolores' primary diagnosis has always been major depressive disorder, recurrent, characterized by chronic anhedonia, insomnia, crying spells, and hopelessness, as well as social phobia. It is not clear from the old records whether anyone previously ever took very seriously other debilitating symptomatology, which is best characterized as posttraumatic stress disorder: flashbacks, traumatic dreams, anxiety attacks, and intrusive memories. The source of these symptoms lies in a childhood of neglect and sexual abuse. Her mother relentlessly belittled her, describing her as ugly, mean, and stupid. The patient states that, because of her dark skin and big nose, she was bullied and teased by other children at school. She has memories, beginning around age five, of her father taking her to their Baptist church, when it was empty, and sexually accosting her, including intercourse. She became aware, over time, that father did the same with her two sisters. She is certain her mother knew what was going on, but chose to ignore it.

At age sixteen, she became pregnant, eventually marrying the father of her child. He proved an abusive man, who at various times held a gun to her head, beat her with a telephone, and raped her. He was the father of all her children. Dolores' subsequent relationships with men were little better. Much of her social phobia proved to be a fear of and rage at men, which, among other things, sharply limited her ability to take public transportation.

In her initial work with her current therapist, the patient excoriated herself for being ugly, stupid, and an unworthy patient. Her mood varied from moderately to severely depressed. The therapist helped the patient realize that, as an adult, she criticized herself in almost the identical words her mother had used when she was a child. Over time, the patient began to speak of other feelings, for example, as though she had a "river inside," that wanted to burst out. At other times, she described this as a "scratching," or "clawing." The therapist helped her to identify this feeling as anger. The patient feared its expression—she didn't know "what might happen."

Together with the emergence of angry feelings, Dolores began to recall more events from her childhood and youth. Among the first to emerge was a memory of having been beaten up by a group of girls at school. The next day, she recalls, she went to school prepared for battle: she had sharpened her nails, wore a shirt without buttons, and was prepared to accost the ringleader. What happened? The patient doesn't remember. There was a fight, she is sure, but she has complete amnesia for the event. She hinted that there had been other episodes of suspected violence, for which she had no memory.

In the second year of psychotherapy, the patient revealed that, when she enters the church she now attends, a strange thing happens: she experiences herself as a little girl, in a frilly dress. "Is that you, or someone else?" the therapist inquired.

"No, it's me," was the reply—"but that's just how I see myself."

Over the ensuing months, the therapist cautiously explored the possibility that the patient suffered from dissociative identity disorder. She learned that the patient identified several "girls" inside her—who were both her and not her. One was a girl in a dark hole; another a girl in a cage. When the patient "saw," or experienced, these images, it was terrifying to her, and in fact the experiences proved impossible to distinguish from flashbacks to actual traumatic events. On one occasion, the patient likened her experience of sitting in the comfort and safety of the therapist's office to that of another girl, an adolescent, sitting on a blanket in the sun. Again, whether the adolescent girl was the patient herself, an "other," or a fantasy, remained ambiguous.

The patient denied hearing voices. She also denied prolonged periods of amnesia, and had never been told that she had been acting "not herself," or strangely, without memory of such behavior. In recent months, her depression has lifted considerably, as she has been able to take in her therapist's positive regard. She was recently stunned that her therapist could name, and inquire about, all of her children—no one had ever acknowledged her role as a mother, before, or shown the slightest interest in how her kids might be doing. There has been no recent talk of fearing an outburst of uncontrollable rage, and fewer reports of flashbacks. She has begun taking off her sunglasses in sessions, for the first time. There has been nothing further to suggest dissociative identity disorder, except for this intriguing, recent remark to her therapist: "I feel like my girls are starting to come together."

Another current psychiatric resident at the university had occasion to tell me about Bill, an African American man in his midfifties, for whom the resident was the inpatient psychiatrist last year at the Veterans Administration Hospital connected with the university. The patient had previously been in prison for several years, for robbing convenience stores. He had gained a certain amount of notoriety for his *modus operandi,* which included entering the stores he robbed cross-dressed as a female. At the time the resident was his psychiatrist, the patient was on parole from prison, but rehospitalized because of having been forcibly restrained from throwing himself in front of a subway train.

The patient is described as a large, imposing man, muscle-bound from years of weightlifting in prison. Prior to his suicide attempt, he was on the verge of being declared in violation of his parole because of his persistent approaches toward his ex-wife, who had an order of protection against him because of previous abusive behavior. Throughout most of the hospitalization, according to the resident, the patient spoke and behaved like a nine-year-old child. The therapist worried that the patient was putting himself in harm's way by this behavior, which could easily have been taken as provocative by other, equally tough, hospitalized veterans. The patient seemed confused about why he was in a hospital at all, and incredulous that he had ever been accused of being abusive to someone. Despite being "only a child," he knew that he was married to his wife. He had no recollection of ever having robbed convenience stores.

During the course of the hospitalization, the patient's wife withdrew her order of protection, and the patient reemerged as his adult self. There was something of a reconciliation, and he was discharged as improved. At no point in the patient's history, including this hospitalization, was the patient diagnosed as having dissociative identity disorder.

In the course of supervising this resident on his outpatient cases, he presented to me another case, an African American woman named Tracy. The patient was a thirty-eight-year-old mother of two, recently hospitalized for depression, who was trying to get on disability, being otherwise unable to pay her bills. She had a long psychiatric history, with diagnoses including major depressive disorder with psychotic features, anxiety disorder not otherwise specified (NOS), and personality disorder NOS, with borderline features. She also suffered from sickle-cell anemia. Prior to her referral to the resident, she had been treated predominantly with medication and monthly follow-up visits.

The patient's husband—who she described as a drug dealer—had died a few months previously, and early on, much of the weekly therapy consisted of the patient working through her very ambivalent feelings toward this man. She also made puzzling references to the family's "walking on eggshells" around her—implying, but never quite saying, that she was prone to violence. Sometime later, she referred to herself as the "enforcer" in the family—but again, without clear explication of what behavior that designation entailed.

Some months into the therapy, after Halloween, the patient came in describing her rage at one of her sisters, with whom she had a long history of not getting along. The more she talked, the angrier and more agitated she got, somewhat to the therapist's alarm. Part of her anger had to do with the sister's failure to adequately control, in the patient's opinion, her three-year-old child. Suddenly, in the session, the patient's voice became menacing and malevolent, and with what the therapist described as "an evil smile," she described feeding the child Halloween candy, piece after piece, until eventually the child became sick. She claimed great amusement that she had "gotten away" with this, without the mother ever having realized what made her daughter sick. The therapist was completely nonplussed, and found himself smiling weakly back, uncertain what to say or how to respond. The patient missed the next two sessions. Upon returning, she had no recollection of the story, but said that she needed help with the "urge to hurt people," because "that's not right."

The resident began to get more history: the patient's parents had separated at her birth, and she was predominantly raised by her mother, who was demanding, overprotective, and jealous of her outside relationships. She would beat the patient when she had her periods, as though she were doing something wrong. Tracy spent some time each year with her father and stepmother, in the South, who were supportive and encouraged her to be a strong woman. However, her stepsister once sexually molested her, and her stepbrother began having sex with her when she was four years old, which continued until she was ten. An uncle also forced her to have intercourse, which she remembers as intensely painful.

The therapist began to discern that the patient presented herself in markedly different ways, from session to session. He became familiar with a very organized, pleasant presentation who was usually in good spirits, and who described herself as a member of a "sisterhood" of professional African American women—despite not having employment herself. At other times, she appeared disheveled and disorganized. On one occasion, the therapist found himself in the presence once again of the angry, intimidating presentation, who was preoccupied with a cousin who had slapped her rear end obscenely at a family party. Glaring at the therapist—almost daring him to disagree—she described in detail how she was going to entice the cousin to her home, implying to him they could have sex—and then kill him.

The resident's intervention was brilliant. He said that he could only admire how the patient [in her current presentation] had kept Tracy safe, throughout the years, preventing men from abusing her, just as she was wanting to do now. He wondered, though, if there might be other ways, at this point in time, to go about accomplishing the same goal, without putting "themselves" at so much risk. The cousin seemed to be a "lowlife," true enough. But could he not be confronted, forcefully, and warned to keep his distance? The therapist role-played some possible responses—and the patient's rage seemed to dissipate.

The patient later acknowledged that she heard many voices, and often felt she had to mediate between them. One was a male voice; another was named Shantee. "I don't think the others have names—should I name them?" she asked her therapist.

"I don't see the point of it," he responded.

Although the therapeutic "contract" had been for weekly sessions, the patient had in fact never kept to this schedule, coming mostly every two or three weeks. The arrangement was eventually formalized into monthly sessions, which, despite their infrequency, seemed surprisingly productive. The resident continued to focus on helping the patient develop a greater repertoire of assertive, limit-setting behaviors, with an apparent corresponding decrease in dissociative events.

Dr. Rob Marvin, an associate professor of clinical psychiatry at the University of Illinois at Chicago, has kindly provided me information on the following two cases.

Sam was a gay, African American man in his midforties, who was admitted in the late 1990s as an inpatient because of suicidal ideation, substance abuse, "hearing voices," and periods of "blacking out." He had no previous history of psychiatric treatment. He had finished college, and had spent three years in the army. He was an accomplished pianist and oboist. During the hospitalization, he was discovered to be HIV positive, and began antiviral treatment. His psychiatric condition improved, and he began outpatient therapy with a psychiatric resident, during which time he was diagnosed as suffering from dissociative identity disorder. Nine months later, he was transferred to the care of Dr. Marvin.

The therapist was soon introduced to several alternative presentations of self, including Hobbé, dangerous and aggressive; Marie, a holder of traumatic memories; Sherman, a child needing protection; Matriarch, his internalized mother; Bobbé, a trickster; and Little Sydney, possibly his core personality as a child. Dr. Marvin saw the patient for approximately a year, during which time he never learned details of the early traumas that Marie allegedly held as a closely guarded secret, although they were frequently alluded to. The patient would state that, "there's something big back there." Sam was able to talk with the therapist about other painful matters, however, including the unavailability of his mother during his childhood, her death (not long before he began therapy), and a conflictual relationship with his brother.

Dr. Marvin reports that it was not always clear which "part," as Sam referred to them, was active during a session, although it was clear through grammar, intonation, body language, and varying memory content that changes were occurring. The therapist was not certain, in fact, that distinctions were always definitive, and he felt it neither wise nor necessary to seek clarifications. Marie, however, was distinctive, but also reticent to engage in therapy. Her entire *raison d'être*, after all, was *not* to reveal traumatic events. Over time, "she" and the therapist developed a metaphor that seemed to capture her evolving role in the system: she was like the little Dutch boy who put a finger in a hole in the dike, to prevent the dam from bursting. Or rather: she was like the dam itself, with a floodgate, which allowed her to siphon off just enough water to prevent a catastrophe. In her words:

A little bit at a time because I don't want to overwhelm myself. I don't have the capacity to deal with it all at once. So just a little bit at a time, as much as I can handle. To keep things going that water has to go somewhere. We have to figure out where best that water can go, and not cause a flooding some place else. . . . Just shifting the problem from here to here, is not what I want to do. Make sure that the water that goes here is absorbed somewhere. The process of getting totally to that point there will take some time. I'm realistic to know that. I don't expect things to happen overnight.

Later, the patient began a session addressing a question the therapist had raised: what was the fear in letting emotional memories come through? The answer:

With the integration of the parts, with the parts being able to get feelings or emotions out there, being able to talk about them in here, I'm wondering, and that's why I go back to the top one, am I going to be overwhelmed by all of that? [pause] Am I going to be overwhelmed? I really don't know what to expect. Again, it's the fear of the unknown. You ask me what the fear is. That's what the fear is. You ask me what is the worst thing that can happen. [pause] Insanity, being totally overwhelmed by these feelings that are all coming at once. I guess if there is any one real fear, it would be as if the Boulder Dam was to break and I would be right down there. That's how I feel about this whole thing. I wouldn't be able to deal with the pressure and force of it all.

The problem is, as I foresee it, is this. It all sounds wonderful on paper. For right here and right now, it sounds wonderful. My real fear is that when that process starts to happen. Sure, in a controlled setting, I am fine. In here, I am able to deal with it. What happens over the weekend when I'm home alone and these thoughts come? Now in the past the way I have dealt with things was to set up a support group. But sometimes when the going gets rough, I am unable to call them. . . . Other times, there's a part of me, a part of me acts out. I don't to have deal with this.

In the ensuing month, the patient dealt with some difficult experiences that had occurred during his military service, the first time he had allowed painful memories to be processed in therapy. His reaction was to become disorganized for several weeks. Attendance became sporadic. Ultimately, though, he realized that he had not, indeed, become overwhelmed, and had been able to master the experience. He subsequently expressed concern, though, about where this would ultimately lead.

"We'll survive, but will that part [Marie] survive? That's the question."

The therapist asked, "What are they [*sic*] going to do?"

He answered:

> That's a perfectly legitimate question. That part is really afraid of com-
> ing out there, letting people look in there and see what's there. That
> part is really afraid of that. The fear, you ask, realistically, there is
> probably nothing to be afraid of, but that part does not know that. . . .
> To undo this mechanism, this machinery, is to undo that part.

The patient continued to make progress in the remaining months of his
work with Dr. Marvin.

Ann is a Caucasian woman, now in her early fifties, divorced, the mother
of three children and college-educated, who self-published a book titled
Ann's Multiple World of Personality (Garvey 2010). She was apparently
sexually abused by her grandfather, from infancy up to adolescence;
mother, seemingly oblivious, was also at times physically abusive. The
patient was a depressed, overweight, lonely adolescent, who fixed upon
a plan to kill herself on her eighteenth birthday. As the day approached,
however, other "parts" increasingly pushed forward, taking over her life.
Some of these altered selves proved remarkably adaptive.

Ann's place in a chapter on "outliers" will be considered below, but it
may be noted first that there is much in this case that is prototypic. Ann
(or "Corey," the altered sense of self who does most of the writing) reports, in her book, that there are twenty selves, each with names, and
running the full gamut of ages. Once listed, early in the book, the reader
does not hear about most of these alternative presentations thereafter.
The book is predominantly a journal about the day-to-day life of the
patient, and much of it is focused on work-related issues and relationships. There is very little about the childhood abuse that presumably
played an etiological role in the patient's condition.

For those unfamiliar with the dissociative identity disorder literature,
it may be surprising to learn that autobiographical accounts of the disorder are not uncommon. Indeed, Ann reports finding forty-seven such
accounts, from articles to full-length books. Of these, I have only read *A
Fractured Mind* (2005), by Robert Oxnam, a self-declared "multiple," and
former president of The Asia Society. An earlier book, *Multiple Personality
Disorder from the Inside Out* (Cohen et al. 1991), provides autobiographical
vignettes from 146 individuals.

In her book, the patient early on makes quite clear that "we don't
believe in integration." Her therapeutic goal, she states, is communication, between parts, and smoother, more functional transitions and accomplishments of tasks. It is fascinating, however, to read, in bits and
pieces, how the patient struggles with these issues, and with how to use
therapy. At one point, she joins an online support group of DID patients,
referring to themselves as the "multiple community," and is eager to
understand how other such individuals view themselves and their problems. She states/asks: "We are working on our own belief that we have a

core and she holds our one soul, we realize every system is coming from a different place with this, and sometimes (to us) this seems a little threatening because the parts have handled so much of life, and we don't want to give it up (hate the thought of integration), but are there those of you who've been able to adapt to having a core with some good potential to the system?"

That is: the patient is raising the question of whether there is a "role" for the core personality in the multiple system! I now face a dilemma: I would wish to be able to define such a patient—a patient whose life is so prevailingly characterized by alternative presentations of self that she/ they are virtually putting belief in the core personality up for a vote—as an outlier, but in fact I do not have grounds to do so. The problem I face is that Ann's perspective may well not be uncommon in patients with this syndrome, as revealed in the online world of the "multiple community," and thus not deserving of outlier status at all, however much I may find its implications troubling. Behind the bravado of the alternative presentations of self, in their writings, and their communications with one another (intra- and interpersonally), there lies a reality: not infrequently, it seems, the core personality has all but disappeared in the plethora of task-oriented, anxiety-deflecting, elaborated defenses. You will recall that Sandy herself once told me that the self that I saw did not exist outside of my office, only the presentations whose wardrobes filled her closet— which, rightly or wrongly, I took to be hyperbole.

Remarkably, Dr. Marvin has stated in regard to Ann that only in the past few months has the core person, Annemarie—also known to the alternative presentations as Dear Heart—actually identified herself in his office. In retrospect, he states, he realizes that she had previously made brief appearances, from time to time, judging by mannerisms, cognitive characteristics, and so forth, but overwhelmingly his entire many years of therapy with the patient had, until that point, been with alternative presentations of self! Annemarie has very few skills, either interpersonal or practical. Her growth and development were essentially arrested in her late teenage years, when alternative presentations took over life functions, and she is foggy about many life events that have occurred since that era. She is depressed, passive, prefers most to watch TV, and lacks knowledge about the world around her.

In discussing the case with Dr. Marvin, I asked, in the role of devil's advocate, why, in fact, he would call Annemarie "core"? What's the evidence? Why, when she is so debilitated and lacking in even basic tools for living, give her such a privileged position? I found his answer remarkably astute: she is the only "person," among the many presentations, who *hears voices.* They in fact nearly overwhelm her. All the other presentations *are* a voice, or its acted-out manifestations. One could of course augment his answer with the observation that the personality system itself has declared Annemarie "the one true soul" (or is at least thinking about it!), but it seems a profound insight that the *I* in, "I hear voices," is the core patient.

However, I am troubled by a particular approach to the treatment of dissociative identity disorder that this case would seem to exemplify. It is captured in the following quote:

> Last night we met with Dr. M. When we were getting up to leave, we couldn't help but notice his always cheerful face was shining even brighter than normal. Confused, we asked if he was laughing at us, but he said, "No." Then, he volunteered some very kind words about his pride [in all] of us! Although we hadn't sought this praise, nonetheless, it was not only satisfying, but as well, as encouraging as the older people's applause! It's a job worthy of being done, and we can do it! (Ibid., p. 49)

My reaction is similar to that to which I alluded in the previous chapter, in quoting Dr. Richard Baer's fondness for "little Claire." The alternative presentations of self would wish to be seen as separate personalities, fully capable of engaging in interpersonal relationships, like anyone else. It is clear that many therapists, or some therapists in some cases, fall into such an understanding of the nature of their therapeutic relationship. It is not my understanding, and, further, raises for me the question of whether such an alternative understanding does not help fix into place a way for the patient to be in the world that is fundamentally inauthentic.

It strikes me as quite possible that, behind many of the memoirs describing relatively adaptive lives of multiplicity, behind the "We're multiple and we're proud," blogs and declarations, lies just this particular kind of therapeutic relationship. Dissociation is fundamentally not conducive to living a regulated, productive life, fully engaged in human relationships; to live a life that gives such an appearance may require a therapist who provides the "glue" that holds the dissociative lives together, smoothes the rough edges of transition, and helps the patient avoid the abyss of traumatic memories.[1] I will readily admit that this may be all a given patient will allow the therapist to do. I think this may well be true in the case of Ann, as Dr. Marvin seemed fully devoted in his therapy with Sam to working through the patient's childhood traumatic experiences. And there can be no question that it is fruitless for a therapist to attempt to define for a patient what her goals for therapy should be. I worry, however, that such therapy is doing a disservice to the weakened, beleaguered self who is "hearing voices," and who once was whole before experiencing cataclysmic events.

NOTE

1. Against this idea is the fact that, in the online blogs of the multiple community, it is not uncommon to find intense anger at the therapeutic community for being excessively focused on "integration," the implication of such entries being that those people are not in any therapy at all. However, it is perhaps the "multiple community" itself that provides the supportive function I am postulating may be necessary to function in a quasi-adaptive manner as a "multiple."

Section II

Theoretical

TEN
Psychiatric Diagnosis

> The tendency has always been strong to believe that whatever received
> a name must be an entity or being, having an independent existence of
> its own. And if no real entity answering to the name could be found,
> men did not for that reason suppose that none existed, but imagined
> that it was something particularly abstruse and mysterious.
>   —John Stuart Mill (1863)

Let us return to Sandy. I have raised the question in previous chapters of
what she could, and needed to, believe. What should *we*, as psychotherapists and psychoanalysts, believe? DID remains one of the diagnoses
most subject to skepticism (Aldridge-Morris 1989; Chodoff 1987; Fahey
1988; Hacking 1986, 1995, 1998; Simpson 1995; see also subsequent chapters). A study of the opinions of North American psychiatrists a decade
ago demonstrated the extent of this skepticism. There is no reason to
think opinions have changed in the ensuing years. Pope et al. (1999) sent
questionnaires to 367 American psychiatrists, asking their opinions regarding the diagnostic status and scientific validity of dissociative amnesia and dissociative identity disorder. Only about a third of the 82 percent
that responded felt these diagnoses should be included without reservations in DSM IV. The majority, in fact, believed they should only be
included as proposed diagnoses (pp. 321–23).

This same group of investigators (Lalonde et al. 2001) surveyed five
hundred Canadian psychiatrists, with virtually identical findings. Of the
80 percent who responded, only about one-third thought that dissociative amnesia and dissociative identity disorder should be included in the
diagnostic manual. The Canadian psychiatrists were possibly even more
skeptical than the Americans, with only one in seven feeling that the
diagnoses were supported by strong scientific evidence.

What is the nature of the "scientific evidence" that apparently satisfies most psychiatrists about the DSM classification system on the whole, but not about dissociative identity disorder? What scientific criteria does DID fail to meet, that other diagnoses have attained? It may be useful to consider the scientific status of the entire enterprise.

In 1980, the classification of psychiatric problems underwent a major philosophical revamping, which resulted in the *Diagnostic and Statistical Manual of Mental Disorders III* (DSM III). In addition to bringing the American classificatory system into closer correlation with the International Statistical Classification of Diseases and Related Health Problems, there was a conscious effort to rid the system of theoretical assumptions about causation (primarily based on psychoanalytic theory, in the previous system), and to present a "theory-neutral" classification based on purely operational and objective symptomatology. The result was akin to the classificatory system of the botanical world created by the eighteenth-century botanist, Linnaeus, with a time frame added: x number of stamens plus y number of petals, together with z number of variegated leaves—for more than two weeks—equaled a separate entity. The Linnaeus system, like the DSM system, made no effort to account for *why* the entity emerged in its own unique fashion, or how it related—other than phenomenologically— to similar but different entities.

Integral to the *medical* classificatory system of disease is etiopathogenesis; but given that there are few psychiatric conditions for which an etiology has been demonstrated scientifically, the conditions described by DSM III were labeled "disorders," not illnesses.[1] Still, the fundamental question of a medical taxonomy remains: how to distinguish a "disorder" from a "nondisorder"?

With very few exceptions,[2] both the medical profession and the lay public have never had difficulty accepting the reality of mental disorders, for centuries quarantining the most socially offensive of such individuals in public institutions different from prisons. (Sadly, this may be less true in the United States today than it was fifty years ago.) A major problem has always been, and remains, where a disorder begins. The current edition of the DSM (IV-TR, 2000) takes over wholesale the definition of mental illness given in the DSM IV version (1994): "a clinically significant behavioral or psychological syndrome or pattern that occurs in an individual [which] is associated with present distress . . . or disability . . . or with a significant increased risk of suffering" (xxi–xxii).

It further states that "no definition adequately specifies precise boundaries for the concept of 'mental disorder' . . . different situations call for different definitions," and that "there is no assumption that each category of mental disorder is a completely discrete entity with absolute boundaries dividing it from other mental disorders or from no mental disorder" (xxii).

Obviously, these terms of definition are rife with ambiguity. There can be no question, however, that DSM III, and more specifically its later iterations, DSM IV and DSM IV-TR, have been of enormous value for research into, and treatment of, the major psychoses. The field, on the whole, is far beyond the time when sane individuals could feign symptoms that resulted in their commitment to institutions, from which they were then unable to obtain discharge solely on the basis of their demonstrations of sanity.[3] With the objective distinction between bipolar disorders and schizophrenia, based on separate clusters of symptoms, and the advent of mood-stabilizing medications, we are now able to treat these disorders in a much more targeted and effective fashion than previously. But how scientific is this classificatory system, on which the entire psychiatric and clinical psychology professions rest?

A philosopher of science, Dominic Murphy (2006), has pointed out several serious problems with both the scientific legitimacy of the system, and its usefulness as a tool toward further scientific understanding. He states that its claim to scientific legitimacy is based on construct validity, which is defined as "some postulated attribute of people assumed to be reflected in a test performance" (p. 217). An example would be anxiety, which can be rated on a scale using standardized testing measures. But, he argues, the concept of anxiety is not defined in the DSM beyond the folk psychological, as modified by clinical training. Something is being measured, but what is the "something"? Further, few of the over three hundred diagnostic entities in DSM IV-TR have even construct validity, much less any underpinning to an underlying reality.

Murphy (p. 310) likens the system to diagnosing a malfunction of television sets according to the final state of the malfunction, for example: blank screen disorder. Subtype: blank screen disorder with wavy lines (my diagnostic contribution). Or, making the criticism a bit less fanciful, Murphy suggests that if medicine were to formulate diagnoses in the same manner as DSM, it would have such entities as "cough disorder" — with the number of coughs per hour, whether productive or unproductive of sputum, and so forth, as the defining characteristics. Such a system, he points out, might prove quite reliable, with objective measurements that could be agreed upon by objective observers. It would also have nothing to do with an underlying causation, or reality.

Murphy's second major objection to the system is that, on the one hand, it is defining disorders that involve derangements of capacities that are studied by the sciences of the mind—the cognitive sciences, affective neurosciences, life sciences, and social sciences—while on the other completely cutting itself off from these sciences. By definition, a disorder is a deviance from what is normal—but the DSM has no definitions or concepts of normality, and is cut off from the sciences that are furthering our understanding of normal memory, reasoning, planning, affect regulation, and so forth. He regards this approach as "absurd" (p. 333). As a deceased friend of mine, a Piagetian scholar named Dr. Terrance Brown, once put it: "Any psychiatrist can tell you what a thought disorder is— but he is clueless when asked to define normal thought!"

It is common knowledge that the creators of the DSM III and its revisions were/are biological psychiatrists (Guze, Frances, Spitzer, et al.) and, as such, espouse the "medical model" as the foundation of modern psychiatry. As Murphy repeatedly points out in his critique, however, the medical model that the authors seek to emulate classifies illnesses according to their underlying etiology and pathogenesis, while these authors make a point of ruling out such intentions. Murphy argues that, even if we cannot yet postulate etiologies for most psychiatric disorders, the classificatory system ought to lend itself to, or incline toward, etiological explanation, rather than to eschew it.

It seems to me likely, however, that the authors of DSM III and IV, despite their disclaimers, actually think that they are doing just that, by articulating separate classificatory constructs which can be reliably diagnosed, and then looking for underlying genetic, anatomical, and physiological abnormalities that correlate with them—thus at least pointing to causal biological relationships. Further, the constructs they have formulated—in particular the psychoses, which are foundational to the very identity of psychiatry as a profession—frequently lend themselves to investigation through pharmacological research, an approach that has proven fruitful.

What they do not do, however, is provide any avenue of exploring pathogenesis at a *psychological*, or *psychobiological* level. Even if the approach to understanding a disorder in terms of a neurobiological lesion were successful—say, the improbable discovery that a particular sequence of gene irregularities is correlated with a particular subform of schizophrenia—it would not explain the jump from the base biological irregularity to the symptom manifestations. How would the genetic abnormality affect normal thought processes to produce paranoid delusions? What definition of "delusion"—other than the folk psychological—would characterize it as an aberration of normal thought? What cognitive dysfunction differentiates the symptom from normal cognitive function? The DSM is so designed as to effectively eliminate the possibility of multilevel explanatory constructs—which for most disorders almost certainly will be required for a satisfactory and comprehensive understanding of pathogenesis.

Schore (2005), in an article focusing on the recent advances in affective neuroscience, has put it this way: "Although the role of early expressed genetic factors is an essential focus of current study, it has become clear that genes do not specify behavior absolutely; prenatal and postnatal environmental factors play critical roles in these developmental origins. The social environment, particularly the one created together by the mother and infant, directly affects gene-environment interactions and, thereby, has long-enduring effects" (p. 204).

Let me return to dissociative identity disorder. It is my thesis that psychiatric researchers and clinicians generally have a bias toward diagnoses that: a) have—or more often, *seem* to have—construct validity, b) lend themselves, or seem to lend themselves, to a predominantly biological etiology, and c) respond to specific pharmacological interventions. None of the diagnoses in the section on dissociative disorders, in DSM IV-TR, can be so described.

In subsequent chapters, I will explore in depth some of the critiques in the literature of dissociative identity disorder, and take as a given the DSM diagnostic category and its definition. Here, however, let us consider the first criterion for making the diagnosis, according to DSM IV-TR: "The presence of two or more distinct identities or personality states. . ."

There is no construct validity here, and no time constraint on how long this condition must have existed. "Personality disorder" is elsewhere defined, but several of the alternative senses of self I encountered in the treatment of Sandy—not unlike some of those described in the literature—do not, in any case, meet the diagnostic criteria of any of the personality disorders. But even more confounding: "the presence of two or more distinct identities or personality states," according to whom? The patient? The perplexed parent or spouse? The empathic—or open, or nonjudgmental, or gullible—clinician? How to answer, with any scientifically objective evidence, the critique of such an astute observer as Otto Kernberg when, as quoted in the preface of this book, he states that the condition is simply a patient's delusion, and must be confronted as such? (I have often pictured the redoubtable Kernberg in these circumstances as a righteous prophet of old, pointing his finger at an alternative presentation of self and declaring: *Get thee behind me, Satan!*)

The problem, it seems to me, is that dissociative identity disorder is best described as the diagnosis of a particular way of engaging in interpersonal *relationships*, not a brain disorder—or rather, not a brain disorder in the way the authors of the DSM consider brain disorders. Murphy points out that the brain is best described as a social and cognitive organ (op. cit., p. 114), and that, as such, can never be fully understood separate from the environment in which the brain/mind of the person being investigated is situated. The brain responds to, and is shaped by, culture, and culture is built by the ideas in people's brains. DID shoves that inconvenient (from the perspective of phenomenological classification) fact in our faces.

Another source of some of the most intense critiques of DID—as will be addressed more fully in the following chapter—is the claim that the disorder is a consequence of childhood sexual abuse. Here, it seems to me, there are both legitimate and illegitimate grounds for raising serious questions about the disorder. I have already discussed, to some degree, the legitimate concerns in chapter 8, namely that the claims made by some patients and some clinicians to childhood histories of satanic cults involving conspiracies of prominent community figures is simply implausible, and has never been corroborated by objective evidence. Less legitimate, it seems to me, is the suspicion accrued among some simply by the act of elevating a psychosocial phenomenon to an etiological role.

At one conference, I heard a critic scoff that, if DID is always a consequence of childhood abuse, it would be the first psychiatric diagnosis to have a known etiology since neurosyphilis. This, of course, is not literally true: the substance abuse disorders have a clear etiology, as do some of the dementias.[4] However, one senses in the critical literature an objection to the very *idea* of a psychosocial etiology to a mental disorder. Whether such an etiology for DID has been established will be considered in detail later; but what seems at issue is how difficult it is, even at a conceptual level, to imagine childhood events producing such truly bizarre adult behavior. It is even harder to conceptualize how such radical and complex behavioral changes as "switching" could reflect a brain disorder of the sort believed to be at the basis of other serious mental symptoms such as paranoid delusions, racing thoughts, panic, compulsions, and so forth.

One novel explanation for the diagnosis of dissociative identity disorder is offered by Hacking (1986, 1995, 1998), whose skepticism I have referenced earlier. Hacking has a nuanced and complex vision of dissociative identity disorder, but fundamentally considers it a "transient" mental disorder—evident only now and then, in the history of the Western world over the past two and a half centuries, and not a "natural kind" of the sort he would consider schizophrenia. He makes clear, however, that he does not mean to say that the disorder is, in some way, fictitious, iatrogenic, or "not real." The fact that a certain type of mental illness appears only in specific historical or geographic contexts, he says, does not mean that it is manufactured (Hacking 1995, p. 8). On the other hand, he also describes multiple personality disorder as providing "a new way to be an unhappy person."

This author (1998) likens the disorder to a peculiar illness diagnosed in nineteenth-century France, called *fugueur*—the mad traveler disease. The disorder was characterized by individuals being overtaken by an irresistible urge to travel to far-off places, which travel would take place without the patient's ordinary conscious awareness—that is, the patient would "awaken" or "find himself" in some distant location, with no memory of how he got there. The first case was diagnosed in April 1886, and before long became literally an epidemic, at least in Bordeaux. The diagnosis virtually disappeared in France (it apparently persisted some years longer in Germany) at a conference of alienists and neurologists in Nantes, in August of 1909. At this conference, the behavioral phenomenology of *fugueur* was declared attributable to a variety of other conditions, of which it was only one manifestation: epilepsy, melancholia, and dementia praecox, as examples. Some few cases were considered close to the original diagnosis, and were categorized as "dissociative fugue," which is still found in DSM IV-TR—although Hacking suggests it has been "grandfathered" in, and that few, if any, cases of the disorder can be found today.

Hacking believes DID, like *fugueur*, is a constellation of symptoms that has come mistakenly to be regarded as a "natural kind," because a confluence of sociocultural processes allows it to fill a kind of ecological "niche." For a niche to exist, Hacking postulates, four principal vectors are required: medical taxonomy, cultural polarity, observability, and release. Fugue, in the nineteenth century, fit comfortably as either a kind of hysteria, or epilepsy. When hysteria disappeared as part of the taxonomy, toward the end of the century, and epilepsy became more specifically defined, fugue lost its status as a widely diagnosed condition, and became relegated to one kind of dissociative state. Cultural polarity, in Hacking's thinking, requires a kind of tension between two prominent and opposing strands of social thought and emotion. For *fugueur*, these consisted of the new phenomenon of romantic tourism, together with increasingly common and feared criminal vagrancy. *Fugueur* became widely discussed and a source of fascination for the nineteenth-century European middle class, thus satisfying his criterion of observability.

Hacking (1995) tells us that the existence of dissociative phenomenology, in which an individual acts in ways that are totally out of character, and has no memory of such behavior, goes back as far as the twelfth and thirteenth centuries (p. 147). He refers to a French historian, Bourreau, who has described a syndrome whose sufferers were referred to as "sleepers," in France during those centuries. These individuals went into a kind of trance and acted in violent or otherwise forbidden ways, after which they would "awaken" with no recollection of what they had done. The syndrome emerges again in writings of the eighteenth century, in France, referred to as "somnabulism,"[5] and in England as "double-consciousness." By the early nineteenth century, lengthy and detailed descriptions of the bizarre behavior of individuals so afflicted can be found in England, America, Germany, and France. Interestingly, such individuals were not regarded as having "two personalities." The presumption was that there was one person, the described patient, who would enter into altered states of consciousness. By the late nineteenth century, cases of "double-consciousness" were not uncommon, but almost always in patients who exhibited other symptoms that fit with the diagnosis of hysteria: anaesthesias, hyperaesthesias, partial paralyses, unexplained bleeding from various orifices, *globus hystericus* (a sensation of something obstructing the throat), and so forth. The famous case of Anna O., by Freud and Breuer (Freud 1957e), would seem to fit this description very well—an hysterical patient, whose symptoms included double-consciousness.[6]

The very first case report of a "multiple" — that is, a patient with more than two different states of conscious behavior — was reported in the 1880s, in France, and was a man (Hacking 1995, p. 175). Much of what was written about this individual by his doctors, according to Hacking, was quackery, but one facet of fateful historical importance, in this author's opinion, was the introduction of memory as significant in the syndrome: each of the patient's presentations of self were associated with different memories. Not long afterward, Freud would famously claim that hysterics suffered from reminiscences.

Back to the present day. Hacking believes that DID has filled a modern niche, just as *fugeuer* did in another time and place. For his principle of cultural polarity, he juxtaposes a modern sense of the fluidity and changeability of identity (even including the medicalization of the concept of changing one's sexual identity), together with the widespread belief in the evil and life-changing nature of child abuse. As for observability, he contends that newspapers, afternoon television shows, and confident clinicians — who also provided the medical taxonomy — made MPD a virtually universally known and accepted entity. Finally: release. The condition, like *fugueur*, allows for a way out of what is experienced as a constraining, untenable, painful state of being.

Within such a context, Hacking identifies a mechanism by which these conditions are perpetuated and elaborated upon, which he calls "the looping effect." Popular dissemination of the lore associated with a diagnosis causes people who fall under it to behave as is popularly expected, but also, at times, to evolve in their presentation. Clinicians note the changing behavior and respond by changing their conception of the disorder. Thus what may appear as a new discovery about a diagnosis does not reflect an accumulation of knowledge about a stable condition. It reflects a change in the self-understanding of its members.[7] He regards schizophrenia, on the other hand, as a "natural kind" — a genuine mental disorder. I have not found a succinct statement in his writings that clarifies his reasoning in this regard, but I surmise that, first, he believes that the discovery of underlying biological causes is within reach; second, that the prevalence rate is fairly constant in the Western world; and third, that the symptoms seem less related to psychosocial factors.

In commenting upon Hacking's consideration of DID, let me make my points using another diagnosis that is less controversial. Bulimia, a reasonably clear-cut diagnosis, is a disorder in which, clearly, psychosocial factors play an etiological role.[8] Because of these factors, however, Hacking — in a very brief discussion — raises questions about it being a "real mental disorder" (1998, p. 8). Would it not be more aptly described, he asks, as a consequence of stereotypes of female beauty, combined with a way of rebelling against parents? It seems that, if culture seems to play a meaningful role in the expression of a disorder, Hacking finds it something less than a genuine medical illness.

There are reasons to consider bulimia more than simply a cultural disorder. For example, Steigler et al. (2001) found that platelet-binding of the antidepressant, paroxetine, is significantly lower in bulimic women than nonbulimic women, suggesting a reduced uptake of serotonin at central synaptic sites. The same study found lower levels in bulimic women of the protein, prolactin, produced by the anterior pituitary gland and pointing to down-regulation of postsynaptic serotonin receptors. The authors could not decide whether to consider their findings to be a product of the bulimia (if so, it is by no means clear how this would come about), or a biochemical abnormality that leaves some women susceptible to the sociocultural factors that are intrinsic to the disorder. The biological abnormalities that have been found in research to correlate with DID will be discussed in a later chapter; but I would suggest that the presence of such abnormalities, presuming they are replicable and not aberrant findings, taken together with clear alterations in normal thought and affect expression, ought to weigh more heavily in considering whether one disorder (bulimia, DID) is of a similar kind to another, such as schizophrenia, than Hacking seems inclined.

A few more words about schizophrenia, Hacking's prototypic natural kind of mental illness: clearly, this disorder has a more stable set of symptoms, seen across generations, than a condition like bulimia or DID, and for this reason, one may plausibly conclude that sociocultural factors play less of a role in its expression. There are, however, cross-cultural differences in the presentation of schizophrenia, as well, and we in fact know very little about how this illness may have manifested itself prior to the Industrial Revolution. In my own lifetime, I believe I have seen significant changes in how paranoid schizophrenia manifests itself, and is perceived.[9]

As a resident and young psychiatrist working with psychotic patients, I found it was not difficult to discern the association of paranoid suspicions and delusions in men with the presence of homosexual conflicts, as Freud famously postulated in the Schreber case (Freud 1957b). A chronic paranoid schizophrenic man, attending the day hospital through which I rotated as a first-year psychiatric resident, was sitting in a group consisting of the ward personnel, including social workers and psychiatrists, and all the patients. It was my first day on the unit; the group was to say goodbye to the previous resident, Dr. Michael Lipkin. This was the heyday of the "therapeutic community," in hospital psychiatry, and people, both staff and patients alike, were expected to attend groups and honestly express their feelings.

The head nurse asked people how they were feeling about Dr. Lipkin's departure. There were a few desultory comments, when the schizophrenic man—a short, swarthy individual, probably in his late thirties, chewing fiercely on an unlit pipe—spoke up.

"I want to know why Dr. Lipkin fucked me in the ass!" he said loudly and strangely impassively. The group froze. Nobody spoke.

The head nurse was the first to recover, and made what almost certainly was the correct interpretation: "Joe, I think you're referring to the fact that, when Dr. Lipkin first came to the unit, he did a complete physical examination on everybody, including a rectal examination. He did that because he wanted to make sure that neither you nor anyone else had some medical problem that wasn't being attended to."

Dr. Lipkin picked up on this understanding, saying, "That's right, Joe. I was doing a medical procedure, and I did it on everyone. But I can imagine it felt to you like it was invasive, and humiliating. I'm really sorry if that's how it seemed to you."

Another nurse said something similar. Joe listened, still impassive, and when there was a pause in the comments, he spoke again:

"No, you people are talking about metaphors, or poetry, or something. But that's not what happened. *He fucked me in the ass!*"

When I tell this story to modern day psychiatric residents, they are stunned and perplexed. They have never heard of this early psychoanalytic interpretation of paranoia. And they have never seen homosexual issues in their paranoid patients.

Perhaps Sandy's diagnosis of the nature of her problems was as astute, and accurate, as anything psychiatry has yet come up with. At a point in the therapy when I was seriously discouraged, and raised with her the question of whether this treatment was actually helping, and whether we should consider transferring her to another therapist, she answered with a challenge: Did I really think that she'd gotten nothing out of this relationship, that the destructive aspects defined the whole thing for her?

"Let's agree," she said, "that I handle difficult situations—often incredibly difficult—differently than most people, okay? Even what you call the destructive things serve a purpose. They're necessary."

NOTES

1. According to Murphy (2006, p. 112, footnote) it was also the case that the American Psychological Association threatened to sue the American Psychiatric Association if the term "mental disease" was used.

2. One highly controversial but popular professional exception was Thomas Szasz, MD, who wrote a book titled *The Myth of Mental Illness* (1974).

3. D. L. Rosenhan (1973), "On Being Sane in Insane Places," *Science* 179, no. 4070: 250–58.
"What did you do, Mike," I asked, "tell them you're hearing voices?"
"Of course!" was the reply.

4. Why some dementias that result from known neurological disorders, like Huntington's Disease, are even in the psychiatric nomenclature, is not entirely clear, but that is another question.

5. Neither the French diagnosis of "sleepers" nor of "somnambulism" referred to sleeping states, during which patients would behave differently. Their transformations would take place when they were fully awake.

6. Borch-Jacobsen (1996), however, has done a critical and in-depth analysis of what is known about the case of Anna O., which concludes that little can be trusted about what Freud and Breuer reported in their case study.

7. This is essentially what I was getting at in my consideration of those people who claim quite adequate life adaptations as "multiples."

8. I am paraphrasing a discussion by Murphy (2006, ch. 7) to my own ends, as a point of comparison with dissociative identity disorder.

9. Hacking acknowledges that the presenting symptoms of schizophrenia have varied, over time.

ELEVEN

The Syndrome I

> Each of the mental disorders is conceptualized as a clinically significant behavioral or psychological syndrome or pattern that occurs in an individual and that is associated with present distress (e.g., a painful symptom) or disability (i.e., impairment in one or more important areas of functioning) or with a significantly increased risk of suffering death, pain, disability, or an important loss of freedom.
>
> —DSM IV-TR (p. xxxi)

In a certain sense, one might consider the existence of dissociative identity disorder as a diagnostic entity a settled issue, since it appears not only in the diagnostic manual used in the United States, DSM IV-TR, but in the International Classification of Diseases as well. Here is the DSM IV definition of the disorder:

- The presence of two or more distinct identities or personality states, each with its own relatively enduring pattern of perceiving, relating to, and thinking about the environment and self.
- At least two of these identities or personality states recurrently take control of the person's behavior.
- Inability to recall important personal information that is too extensive to be explained by ordinary forgetfulness.

The criteria go on to include conditions that must be ruled out to make this diagnosis.

It appears that DSM V will continue to list DID as a diagnostic entity, little changed from the above definition. Nevertheless, it remains one of the diagnoses most subject to skepticism and challenge. For more than a decade, some of the most persistent and indefatigable critics of the validity of the DID diagnosis have been H. Merskey and A. Piper (Merskey 1992, 1995a, 1995b, 1998; Piper and Merskey 2004a, 2004b). The title of their last two jointly authored papers, "The Persistence of Folly: A Critical Examination of Dissociative Identity Disorder, Parts I and II" (2004a, 2004b), perhaps suggests that subjectivity and strong feelings are not limited to one side of the debate. Indeed, in their opening remarks, Piper and Merskey flatly claim that the diagnosis has wrought "significant harm" in North America (p. 592). I will consider these articles in some detail, since they represent one of the more extensive critiques to be published in the last decade.

The first critique that Piper and Merskey raise relates to the alleged association of the diagnosis with an etiology of childhood abuse, and makes three claims: 1) an association between a diagnosis and childhood trauma does not prove causation, 2) no study has ever demonstrated that DID patients as a group have experienced repeated and overwhelming childhood maltreatment, and 3) there have been no studies to determine what percentage of people with histories of trauma *fail* to develop DID (p. 592).

The first critique invites the question: Who is making this claim? Most clinicians who have worked with patients suffering from this syndrome find histories of sexual abuse. Few among them, however, would claim a simple cause and effect, but more often postulate that patients who develop profound dissociative symptoms in response to trauma likely had *a priori* vulnerabilities. The literature on posttraumatic stress disorder would seem relevant here. Steele (1986, p. 35) has stated: "We are convinced . . . that the more significant element [in the reaction to trauma], at least from the standpoint of producing psychological damage, is not the strength of the stimuli themselves, but the failure of the protective shield which would engage the psychic apparatus to assimilate or counter the stimuli."

Psychoanalytic perspectives on DID will be considered in depth later, but in this context, Goldberg's observations (1999) about a different but related psychological concept, disavowal, are relevant, introducing the developmental milieu in which someone might develop such mechanisms:

> The fundamental feature [of early manifestations of disavowed behavior] resides less in the manifested behavior and more in the parent's inability to form and maintain an integrated image of the child. (p. 34)

and:

> Whatever the origin [of the specific disavowed behaviors], the parent is unable to see the fear of the child both because of her own limitations *and because of the fact that the unhappy child is no longer around. The child who has disappeared has found a solution.* (p. 36)

Piper and Merskey's second point, regarding the absence of studies demonstrating a history of serious abuse in DID patients, seems counter to the literature, until it becomes clear that by "demonstrated," these authors mean *proven*—through objective documentation other than the patients' reports. The authors properly point out that patients' uncorroborated accounts of past mistreatment must be viewed with scientific skepticism. They then proceed to review the various published accounts of documented childhood abuse in DID patients (Coons 1986, 1994; Hornstein 1992; Kluft 1997; Chu 1999), and, with varying degrees of persuasiveness, find methodological flaws in all of them. They do not cite Bliss (1986), who refers to thirteen cases in which collateral evidence was obtained to confirm early childhood trauma.[1]

Their third claim would appear to be true but pointless: only a prospective study, following a group of children known to have been subject to physical and sexual abuse into adulthood, and comparing them to a control group, could demonstrate whether there was a correlation between the abuse and subsequent dissociative disorders. But what sort of representative sample would it be feasible to obtain, when the traumas being referred to occur in early childhood, inflicted by adults who have every reason to keep their abusive conduct secret? Such a cohort would have to be culled either from families that had encountered the criminal justice system or clients of social service agencies willing to participate in such a study—and in either case, the difficulties of gathering a representative sample, and adequate follow-up, would be almost insurmountable.

The authors go on to ask: If childhood trauma leads to DID, why have there been so few reports of the condition in psychiatric history? Have not childhood trauma and abuse been a part of the human condition throughout history? Their question would seem to reveal an insufficient reading of history; as I have documented earlier, there have been several waves of dissociative disorders, reported under different names—and with various manifestations—for centuries. Why there has not been a relatively stable prevalence rate throughout history is another question, which however touches as much upon fashions of diagnosis among medical taxonomists as it does on patients' syndromes.

Piper and Merskey ask further, where are the cases of childhood DID? The authors quote a review (Vincent 1988) that found only eight cases in the literature of childhood DID up to that time, and quote Putnam (1993, p. 39) as observing that only in the last few years had even a "handful of cases . . . entered the clinical literature." The authors have taken these words somewhat out of context, however, and fail altogether to cite another article, coauthored by Putnam (Hornstein et al. 1992), which reports the examination of sixty-four children and adolescents diagnosed with dissociative identity disorder, according to NIMH criteria.

After critiquing one of the earliest cases in the literature (Janet 1889/ 1913), which the authors feel they convincingly demonstrate to have been the product of suggestion—an arguable point, in my opinion—Piper and Merskey's final argument in part I is to point to the implausibility of the numbers and the bizarre varieties of so-called "alter" personalities in the literature. There is no gainsaying the fact that the frequency of diagnosis of dissociative identity disorder in the 1980s increased exponentially, compared to previous decades of the twentieth century. I find no reason to counter Piper and Merskey's skepticism about the validity of many of those diagnoses, during that period of time, and I have no reason to doubt that mistakes continue to be made in making this diagnosis. I believe, however, mistakes can be made in *either* direction, resulting in underdiagnosis as well as overdiagnosis. The fact that studies on the reliability and validity of the diagnosis are not persuasive to those requiring objective certitude, and that there is only anecdotal information about the nature, severity, and duration of childhood trauma to account for DID, does not in itself invalidate the diagnosis. Fewer people would dispute, for example, that the diagnosis of posttraumatic stress disorder points to an authentic disorder than they would DID, but the same questions that are largely unanswered in the diagnosis of DID are problematic in that diagnosis as well (Neilssen 2008).

Piper and Merskey do not address the concept of dissociation per se, either as a defense or as the hallmark of other disorders; their focus has always been specifically on dissociative identity disorder. However DID does not exist in some separate psychiatric universe, unrelated to any other syndrome. The DSM IV defines dissociative disorders as a separate category, distinct from anxiety disorders, mood disorders, and so forth, although often appearing in conjunction with these other disorders. In addition to dissociative identity disorder, it lists four separate diagnostic syndromes: depersonalization disorder, dissociative amnesia, dissociative fugue, and dissociative disorder NOS.

When one considers some of the criteria required for the diagnosis of the other dissociative disorders, the symptoms of DID do not seem quite as singular. Such criteria include: feeling detached from one's mental processes or body, as if an observer (depersonalization disorder); loss of autobiographical memory and personal identity, even though able to learn new information and perform everyday tasks (dissociative amnesia); and confusion about personal identity or the assumption of a new identity (dissociative fugue).

Many authors (Draijer and Boon 1993; Ellason and Ross 1997; Steinberg 1991; Steinberg and Schall 2001) consider dissociative symptoms to exist along a severity continuum, which can be accurately assessed through an assessment instrument, the Structured Clinical Interview DSM-IV Dissociative Disorders-Revised (SCID-D-R), or by a formal questionnaire, the Dissociative Experience Scale (Bernstein and Putnam 1986). Indeed, Steinberg et al. (1990), using the earlier DSM III-R version of the structured interview, demonstrated that the ratings of dissociative symptoms—amnesia, depersonalization, derealization, identity confusion, and identity alteration—could distinguish between normal controls, mixed psychiatric disorders, and dissociative disorders, in ascending order of severity.

Piper and Merskey, nevertheless, have repeatedly questioned whether even the formal inquiry about dissociative symptoms might not induce a factitious syndrome, which led Putnam (1995) to ask:

> Why should suggestion effects be unique to MPD? We do not believe that asking about hallucinations produces them in a patient. Why should asking about the existence of "other parts" of the self produce alter personalities? What is so magical about the question? (p. 960)

Piper and Merskey's response is to say that concerns arise not from proponents' inquiries about "other parts," but rather from interventions that are "considerably more muscular" (op. cit., p. 678). They go on to quote at length from the DID literature on treatment in which therapists "access," "call out," "let out," and insist on talking with the various "alters." They conclude: "One cannot reasonably doubt that such interventions lie some distance beyond merely asking about 'other parts,' and that their suggestive nature is likely to both encourage and reinforce displays of multiplicity" (p. 679).

It seems reasonable to agree with the authors that suggestion can sometimes play a role in the behavioral manifestations that lead to the diagnosis of DID (see below); however, in their specific rebuttal of Putnam's rhetorical question, it should be noted that they conflate diagnostic assessment with treatment. Putnam's point is that diagnostic inquiry about "hearing voices," amnesic episodes, reports by others of the patient not "being herself," and so forth, are no more likely to induce a diagnosis than inquiry into possible symptoms of major depression would induce that condition. "Calling out parts" is quite another matter, referring to what some clinicians may feel is required in the ongoing *treatment* of such patients.

Piper and Merskey summarize:

> We believe the foregoing discussion should make it apparent that DID—with manifestations that are visible to only some clinicians and on only some occasions; with symptoms that cannot be distinguished from other psychiatric disorders or from malingering; with unacceptably vague diagnostic criteria; and with patients who initially deny their symptoms, show no previous signs of the condition's essential feature, and know nothing of either their traumatic histories or the presence of alters—simply cannot be reliably diagnosed. (p. 680)

and:

> We expect that the condition will revive momentarily and die several times before it finally ceases to be a ripple on the surface of the psychiatric universe. In the end, it is likely to become about as credible as spirits are today. . . . [W]e trust that we have shown sufficient evidence

to predict a steep decline in the condition's status over the next 10 years
and a gradual fall into near oblivion thereafter. (p. 682)

What can my experience bring to bear on the issues that Piper and Merskey have raised? To begin with, these authors might properly pose the
question I myself have raised earlier: Did I not play a significant role in
bringing about the appearance of "Joe" in my first encounter with an
alternative sense of self? Would I have ever seen these alternative presentations of self had I not insisted on talking with a different "part" of
Sandy? Let me say first that there was simply no clinical evidence that
Sandy consciously or unconsciously wanted the transformation that took
place in my office to happen. There is not a shadow of doubt in my mind
that Sandy was frightened of "her people," and particularly that they
should "come out." Obviously, this is a subjective opinion, lacking any
means of objectification. As for me, prior to treating Sandy, I had been
neither frightened by nor interested in dissociative identity disorder; I
simply didn't believe it existed. Thus, the appearance of an altered sense
of self was not among the possibilities I envisioned when I pressed Sandy
to tell me more.[2]

One can turn Piper and Merskey's concern, with equal legitimacy, on
its head, and wonder if contrary behavior on my part might have prevented the emergence of a huge sector of the patient's experience of her
life. Goldberg (1999) has pointed out that

> therapists may find themselves seduced into ignoring issues that might
> otherwise be a focus of attention. . . . This collusion of the therapist in
> what is essentially a repetition of a developmental state is not to be
> thought of as belonging only to the patient or brought about only by
> the patient; rather, it is an adaptation to the particular readiness, or
> perhaps I should say capacity, of a particular therapist, to cooperate in
> the alliance of this form of pathology. (p. 87)

I might well have conducted this therapy in such a manner that other
senses of self, even though a real part of the patient's life experience,
would either never have taken form in my office, or would have done so
despite *my* disavowal that such a thing was actually happening. In fact, I
am sure of it—because it had already happened to me earlier in my
career.

Almost two decades before treating Sandy, I treated a woman in her
late thirties, divorced, with symptoms of major depression. She was a
dangerously isolated person, living alone, without family or friends. One
day she told me of her puzzlement and discomfort at frequently finding
things "rearranged" in her apartment. That is to say, she would find
items of clothing strewn about the floor, with no memory of having either
worn them or put them there. She would find an unwashed coffee cup in
the sink, with coffee grounds still in the coffeemaker even though she
rarely drank coffee. Even furniture would be rearranged.

Apparently most of these events occurred at night—or perhaps that is the time construct into which I put them. In any case, I attributed them to somnambulistic states. She did not feel that this was the explanation, but couldn't elaborate. As weeks went on, my patient, in sessions, would sometimes demonstrate markedly different affect, demeanor, and inter-action, than her usual self: at times childlike, at other times dependent and weepy, and at still others, seductive and sexually provocative. One day—the first session following a three-week break due to my vacation—the patient took umbrage at something I said, and stormed out of the session. I was not taken aback, since I thought I understood what had happened. Also, it had happened before. I would call, urging her to re-turn for her next session so that we could talk about what had transpired, and, after some angry protest, she would do so.

Following this session, however, the patient did not respond to my voice messages, and did not appear for her next scheduled session. I wrote her a letter (these were the days before email), explaining what I *thought* had happened between us—namely, that I had not been suffi-ciently sensitive to her feelings about the break—and urged her to call to make a new appointment. A few days later, I received an envelope in the mail containing my letter, torn to shreds, and a handwritten note that said:

Dear Dr. Moline,
    We thought you were different than the others. But it turns out you're just like all the rest.
    Roselyn, Rose, Ann, Annette, Mary

I think it safe to say that I never assimilated the data this case provided. The denouement had remained isolated in my mind as a singular, bizarre event, not requiring me to rethink the theoretical premises that underlay my clinical practice.[3]

Returning to Piper and Merskey: several of these authors' arguments strike me as *ad hominum,* and based on little more than their skepticism and incredulity. For example, in considering the seeming paucity of re-ported cases to be found in the literature prior to the 1980s, they state:

> *It does not seem that* children in the developed world are more bizarrely mistreated now than in the past. . . . *It seems unlikely that* so many clinicians would so often have made erroneous psychiatric or neuro-logical diagnoses in the patients, or in other words, that only those clinicians who diagnosed DID *were clear-sighted enough* to make the correct diagnosis. (p. 596, italics mine)

I agree with Piper and Merskey that the question of childhood trauma is very complex, and troublesome. The fact that claims, or suggestions, of childhood abuse regularly arise during therapy obviously proves only their psychic reality, and nothing about actual childhood history. In Sandy's case, as I have described, there is a particular narrative, created over the course of the therapy, that I find very plausible, namely: during her fifth or sixth year of life, Sandy was molested by people outside her family, who lived between her home and the school she attended. If, by some miracle, however, we could know the exact details of Sandy's life during those years, it would not surprise me if the truth would look very different from this picture. Nevertheless, the disparate pieces of information that emerged during this treatment cry out for an economical explanation, and it seems to me far more plausible than implausible to conclude that *something happened,* and the data that emerged in the therapy seemed best explained by the narrative we devised. Piper and Merskey would almost surely disagree. The therapeutic approach to accessing such memories, and the implications of doing so, will be discussed at greater length in chapter 14.

Fraser (2005), in a reply to Piper and Merskey, said: "Patients with DID already suffer from a dearth of therapists who are willing to work in this area of psychiatry. This article will do little to encourage young therapists to keep an open mind, when presented with symptoms suggesting a dissociative disorder" (p. 814). I could not agree more.

I think it possible that the explanation for Piper and Merskey's decades-long attack on the concept of DID, as well as for the widespread skepticism of psychiatrists about this diagnosis, may be fundamentally philosophical, rather than scientific. As I have earlier suggested about psychiatric critics in general, what may disturb these skeptics most is the fact that this diagnosis, perhaps more than any other in the nomenclature, integrally involves *process.* It is not a diagnosis reached alone through an objective listing of signs and symptoms, but involves in addition *a particular kind of relationship at a particular point in time.* The idea that mental disorders may reflect *adaptations*—or *maladaptations*—to interpersonal environments is an idea that has been divorced from the putative medical model of psychiatry, and relegated to clinicians whose central focus is not simply diagnosis and psychopharmacological treatment: psychologists, psychoanalysts, social workers, and, alas, fewer and fewer psychiatrists.

There is a further issue to be reflected upon when considering the skepticism—even hostility—manifest in the psychiatric world toward the diagnosis of dissociative identity disorder: namely the issue of sociopolitical movements, and reactions against them. No thorough discussion of the disorder, even if focused on a single case study, can avoid reflecting upon the role of feminism in the changing status of this diagnosis in the twentieth century, and of the politics of illnesses that predominantly affect women. I have earlier referred to the disappearance of the diagnosis, hysteria, from twentieth-century taxonomies; but the topic of hysteria itself has continued to the present day to be intriguing in certain literary and psychoanalytic circles. The *Times Literary Supplement* has even called hysteria the "postmodern malady *par excellence*" (Showalter 1997, back cover review). In the psychoanalytic world, the concept has most notably been resurrected by the French psychoanalyst, Jacques Lacan.[4]

Many observers have credited feminism, as a movement, with bringing the reality of child abuse into modern consciousness, and to the forefront of social issues on the American scene today. In our current era, child abuse no longer implies abuse only of females, as is evidenced by the Catholic Church scandal, but this was not true at the beginning. To quote Herman (1992):

> Not until the women's liberation movement of the 1970s was it recognized that the most common post-traumatic disorders are not those of men but of women in civilian life. . . . The psychological syndrome seen in survivors of rape, domestic battery, and incest are essentially the same as the syndrome seen in the survivors of war. (p. 28)

Hacking has pointed out that there has been a trajectory in the very idea of child abuse—it is not a transparent idea that has always been with us, that we all understood as soon as we thought about it, noticed examples of it, or recalled having experienced it. An attitude that one can imagine was not uncommon just decades ago would be absolutely politically incorrect to verbalize today, across the entire political spectrum: "What's the big deal?"

Showalter, a feminist scholar, in her controversial book (op. cit.) has described a series of twentieth-century syndromes as hysterical epidemics: chronic fatigue syndrome, Gulf War syndrome, recovered memories, multiple personality disorder, satanic ritual abuse, and alien abduction. It is not surprising that many people were outraged by her publication; individuals who are undergoing profound suffering, and often intense despair, from a variety of disorders, are put into a continuum with people who believe they were sexually tampered with by little grey aliens in spaceships. Nevertheless, Showalter has many pertinent insights into how people develop symptoms that are a kind of communication about things they feel powerless to put in words. As she puts it, hysteria through the ages has served as a form of expression, a body language, for people who otherwise might not be able to speak or even admit to what they feel. She and others have pointed out that this understanding is not limited to women—soldiers in all wars have developed hysterical symptoms—but as the origin of the word ("the wandering womb") indicates, this type of syndrome has been closely associated with the female gender. Diane Price Herndl (1988) has written that hysteria "has come to figure as a sort of rudimentary feminism, and feminism as a kind of articulate hysteria" (p. 75).

Showalter states that hysterical epidemics require three ingredients: physician-enthusiasts and theorists; unhappy, vulnerable patients; and supportive cultural environments (1997, ch. 2). She and Hacking are in agreement that child abuse provided an important theoretical base for multiple personality disorder, and a group of clinicians provided the medical imprimatur—beginning, according to Hacking (1995), at a historic dinner in a New York restaurant in 1983, when a group of MPD therapists decided to found the International Society for the Study of Multiple Personality and Dissociation (p. 52). What they needed then were more patients—and as has been noted previously, they soon found them. As to the cultural environment: American society proved more than receptive to the ideas encompassed in what these authors call the multiple personality movement.

As a psychoanalyst trained in a Freudian institute, the concept of childhood sexual abuse as a causative factor in adult psychopathology—and its controversies—were hardly novel ideas to me, but my unquestioned presumption that such a relationship could exist, when Sandy first presented me with her dream painting, perhaps reflected the zeitgeist of the times as much as it did my professional training. (May it be stipulated that this strong suspicion of a causal link was initially in relation to her sustained depression, well before I had any inkling of dissociative identity disorder in the patient.) Given Showalter's identification as a feminist scholar, it was surprising to me that she goes on to raise the question of whether stories—even memories—of childhood sexual abuse might not be factitious in patients diagnosed with MPD, serving to enlist the therapist's sympathy and concern for a "poor victim." Here is her statement concerning the plausible reasons about how this might come about:

> Some [of the answers] come from the structure of therapy itself, from a combination of suggestibility and social coercion. Some of them come from the availability of this explanation for a variety of anxieties and discontents in women's lives. Claudette Wassil-Grimm [concludes that] a woman may search for them because she has become isolated and depressed due to current life problems, and an honored authority told her repressed memories of incest are a common source of deep unhappiness. (op. cit., p. 147)

I find this paragraph unexpected and even astonishing, given its author's credentials, in that it seems to caricature women in very traditional terms. The first explanatory proposal is plainly put: women are so suggestible! Second: it is an "easily available" explanation for the sorts of anxieties and discontents that vex women in their everyday lives—certainly, by implication, not the sort of explanation that a *thinking* person would readily accept. Finally: the female patient accepts the idea because her beloved doctor told her so!

Strikingly absent from Showalter's broad categorization of so many modern syndromes as "hysterical" is any consideration of the hallmark defining characteristic of an hysterical symptom, according to no less an authority than Charcot: *la belle indifference*—the peculiar "indifference" hysterical patients seem to show toward their quite striking symptoms. A recent epidemic of an apparently hysterical syndrome was widely publicized in the United States: tic-like and erratic motor behavior among teenage girls in the town of Le Roy, New York, beginning in the winter of 2012. A journalist investigating this phenomena, in interviewing one of the afflicted girls noted: "Lydia, her arm swinging steadily, spoke in a low, almost disinterested, monotone."[5]

This is typical of what characterizes hysteria, as it has commonly been understood since the nineteenth century. It is distinctly *not* what clinicians have observed in sufferers of several of the syndromes described in Showalter's book, including chronic fatigue syndrome, Gulf War syndrome, or multiple personality disorder.

Both Hacking and Showalter have made reference to patients suffering from DID as, basically, "unhappy people." Is it simply my affection for Sandy that leads me to hear this appellation as condescending and covertly diminishing? One can be unhappy, after all, because of a bad marriage, or withholding parents, or simply a run of bad luck. Is that all there is to the pain of patients with dissociative identity disorder? Are they in fact just ordinarily unhappy people, who happen to be easily influenced and with a propensity toward the dramatic? That is how, at least to me, it sounds, when I read these words. The description is being presented as an adequate representation of individuals who do not simply make suicide threats, but who make serious, actual suicide *attempts*; who do not simply scratch themselves, but cut deeply into their flesh; and who do not simply hit themselves, but flagellate themselves to the point of bruising and bleeding. Unhappy people? Well I suppose that will do, if one also defines schizophrenics as people whose thinking is just a little peculiar.

Even leaving aside the harshest, most emotional skeptics of DID like Piper and Merskey, when I read the works of more thoughtful, philosophical critics like Hacking and Showalter, the most compelling realization that emerges for me is this: I simply do not find my patient. She is not there—not in descriptions, not in attributed motivations, not in her relationship with me, not in her conduct with others. Perhaps it is always thus: the healer, faced with a suffering patient in his consulting room or hospital ward, faces a different reality than the philosopher, thinking about the meaning of larger patterns, in his or her book-strewn academic office. But I find the gap, in this instance, extraordinary.

NOTES

1. It is a surprising oversight, since Bliss also reports treating some DID patients who he believed had been abused emotionally but not physically, and still others who

were not mistreated at all, but seemed to be "sensitive" or highly "imaginative" (1986, p. 137).

2. The academicians who I have quoted at length would, I presume, find this very hard to believe. In their immersion into the phenomena, they have found descriptions, discussions, and debates about MPD everywhere, in the 1980s and 1990s. In their view, every American was intimately familiar with the phenomenology of the disorder, down to the very sorts of altered selves "multiples" presented. Perhaps it was because I had my hands full taking care of a unit full of acutely psychotic patients, during most of those years, with only a part-time office practice, that MPD was not part of my psychiatric world.

3. Interestingly, I had some follow-up about this patient. A clinical social worker had occasion to tell me, a few years ago at an informal gathering, that she was seeing this same woman in psychotherapy, and that my name had come up. She said that the patient remembered me with fondness, and had good feelings about our therapeutic work together. The social worker had never been aware of any dissociative phenomenology.

4. I will confess that I have never read Lacan, know very little of his ideas. For that reason, I have not provided a reference.

5. Susan Dominus, "What Happened to the Girls in Le Roy," in the *New York Times Magazine*, March 11, 2012, p. 38.

TWELVE

The Syndrome II

The "personality" of an MPD patient is the sum and synergy of the system of alter personalities.

—Putnam (1989, p. 123)

Humphrey and Dennett (1998) provide one of the more thoughtful considerations of the diagnosis of multiple personality disorder. They posit a list of criteria they concluded would be necessary to consider the diagnosis valid, which implicitly involve dynamic intrapersonal and interpersonal factors. They are:

1. The different selves would have different "spokesmen," whose access to the memories and thoughts of one another is the same as that which the mind of one human being has to the mind of another.
2. Each self will claim to have conscious control over the subject's behavior.
3. Each self will be convinced of its own rhetoric.
4. This self-rhetoric will be convincing to others.
5. Different selves will be distinctive.
6. The "splitting" into separate selves will have occurred before treatment.

These authors found no case that met, to their satisfaction, all these criteria, and concluded: "'a candidate phenomenon' exists without any scientific proof" (p. 45).

Let me briefly summarize the data that I propose demonstrate that Sandy met these criteria:

1. There were several such "spokesmen": Joe, Sam, Sandra Ellen, Sandy 2, and others. Joe often clearly knew what was inside the mind of Sandy, thus failing to meet Humphrey and Dennett's first

115

criterion. The others, however, clearly did not, and Sandy, as her-self, rarely professed to know the motivations of other senses of self. For the most part, the alternative senses of self viewed Sandy "from the outside," as it were, attributing her behavior to weak-ness, dependency, self-pity, and so forth, much as might any criti-cal lay person, in reaction to some of Sandy's conduct.

2. "Sandy couldn't do it so I *did*," was a basic claimed motivation by various senses of self.
3. "Do not mistake me for Sandy! I am not her!" was the *raison d'être* of the alternative senses of self.
4. I have quoted the skeptics, who presumably would not have found the self-rhetoric of alternative selves convincing. For the most part, I did. Sandy's husband, Craig did; various others—for example, strange men, negotiating a sexual encounter with a seductive woman who suddenly and inexplicably became confused and frightened—apparently did.
5. Distinctive is hardly the word.
6. This is the criterion that is crucial to feeling confident of this diag-nosis and is the criterion, I strongly suspect, which is most com-monly not met by reported cases of DID. Does the data Sandy's case provides meet this requirement?

There was no question that family and friends alike agreed that Sandy acted very differently at different times—on occasion, astonishingly so. She explained to me that the other "selves" had always operated covert-ly—that is to say, they did not identify themselves to others, and did not reveal the different names by which Sandy knew them. Sandy's husband, with whom I obviously had considerable contact, told me that, in retrospect, he thinks he married Sam. The woman he married had aggres-sively pursued a sexual relationship with him, and engaged in a variety of sexual activities—of which, Craig reported, she least preferred actual vaginal sexual intercourse.

Craig said that he had always been puzzled that Sandy, at times, seemed markedly different from this self-confident, worldly woman. After marriage, she would often avoid sex, sometimes seeming afraid of the prospect. She often would relate to him in ways that seemed striking-ly "out of character"—sometimes cool and distant, at other times clingy and depressed. At still other times, they had had fights in which Sandy had been as physical, and as rough, as he had been. Most remarkable to him was the fact that when Sandy was in her attractive, seductive mode, she could drink heavily without getting inebriated, whereas at other times she would get dizzy on two cocktails. In one mode she would order certain drinks and food; in another mode she would have entirely differ-ent preferences. It was only after the diagnosis of dissociative identity

disorder emerged from the treatment that Craig found a rational accounting for these strange discrepancies.

These are some of the things Sandy has said about her life before
treatment: first, she remembers little of it. She had spent her lifetime
pretending to remember events, inventing connecting links, and avoiding
certain people and topics. I have mentioned earlier her evident tennis
skills at an earlier age, of which she has no memory. The details are these:
at a high school reunion some years before therapy, a woman approached her, eager to reminisce about their triumphant capture of the
girls' doubles tennis tournament in their senior year. Sandy remembered
neither the woman, nor ever having participated in a tennis tournament.
She had always considered herself a poor tennis player. She finessed the
situation with the woman, changing the subject as soon as she could, to
their current lives.

I hope it is the reader's sense, as it surely was mine, that in telling me
this anecdote, Sandy was not trying to convince me of anything, except,
perhaps, how difficult her life had been. In regard to this incident, she
added that she "knew" Joe was an excellent athlete, and she suspected
that "he" played in the tennis tournament. She did not "know" this,
however; she could only speculate.

When she thought about her childhood more generally, Sandy reported that it was as if she was remembering different childhoods. There
was a tomboy, adventurous and assertive. Memories of this child seemed
unrelated to other memories, those of a student—a shy, serious, book-
worm. There were still other memories, which felt unrelated to either of
these, of a vivacious, outgoing girl, interested in boys.

It would be close to a mischaracterization to say that she remembers
"herself" in these various personality presentations. It comes closer to her
subjective experience to say that she remembers *a* tomboy, *a* shy student,
a girl interested in boys, and so forth. Are any of these configurations of
memory more "her" than others? Perhaps. She can only think of herself
as having been shy and withdrawn—one might say: *self*-effacing.

For as long as Sandy could remember—as was described in chapter
1—her thinking processes took the form of conversations, or discussions.
Different voices took different positions, often arguing, to reach decisions. *Her* voice often counted for little in these debates. The voices were
distinctive; again, as long as she could remember, she could picture quite
clearly the individuals to whom they belonged. It was her constant, lifelong experience that *she* did not reach decisions; decisions *were reached.*

Sandy had long believed that "her people," as she called them, at
times took over her life. She would repeatedly have the experience of
"finding herself" in situations which she felt were not of her making, and
which she felt unequipped to handle. Not all such experiences were sexual in nature. There had been times when Sandy would find that she had
apparently made an outstanding presentation at a job interview—of

which she would have little or no memory—only to find herself employed at something for which she felt totally unqualified.

A seemingly minor, but perhaps important, slightly discrepant aspect of the dissociative phenomenology Sandy demonstrated was the way in which she seemed to both know and *not* know about her dissociation. For example, as I have just outlined, she was quite clear about the people in her head: their voices, and their appearance. But she seemed to be continually surprised—and horrified—when "they" entered into the external world. That she was horrified is understandable. But what was there to be surprised about?

For example, as previously mentioned, there were many distinct and separate wardrobes in her closet. She had always been upset and puzzled by this. How could it be, she wondered? And yet, given everything that she had said to me and that she knew about herself: How could it *not* be? She would "awaken" in a strange place. She would think: *My God, how did I get here? What has happened?* Such occasions obviously would be terribly upsetting for anyone; but it is not her dread and anxiety to which I am now referring, but her surprise and puzzlement. Neither at the time, nor in the telling, did there seem to be *a sense of familiarity* with this recurrent pattern. There seemed to be no recognizant: *But of course! It's happened again, just like so many times before!* These episodes had occurred over and over in Sandy's life; but in the telling, it was as if each time was the first time.

These observations, it seems to me, could plausibly support the skeptic's view that the DID phenomena were of a hysterical, or manipulative, nature. Did they not reflect a certain wish to exaggerate, or dramatize, the phenomena being presented to the therapist? I never either confronted Sandy about, nor explored with her, her reactions and behaviors in this regard. But if I had forthrightly addressed these apparent inconsistencies, the serious critic might ask, might it not have led to an unraveling of the whole elaborate schema?

I have raised an issue I cannot put to rest, with either data or an irrefutable explanation. My understanding stems from the conviction that Sandy had no sense of ownership about these untoward behaviors at all. She lived with the vain hope—even belief—that by sheer willpower, she could prevent such things from happening again. She had her own version of *never again,* which could be taken to be the *raison d'être* of the major alternative senses of self. When something would happen—new clothes in her closet, finding herself walking at night along a street she did not recognize, awakening in her own bed with a sore anus, her shock and dismay was not, *Oh my God, I did it again!* But rather, *Oh my God, it has happened again!* Yet once more, she had been unsuccessful in preventing one of "them" from doing something she abhorred. By the next day, there would be new resolve—*That's never going to happen again, I won't let it!*—with the consequence that, sometime later, she would yet again find herself shocked, dismayed, and surprised.

It is possible also that the element of shock and surprise has something to do with how dissociative processes are encoded in the brain. Neurobiological considerations of this disorder will be considered in later chapters.

Let us consider the prototypical scene of Sandy's bar experiences in more detail. Both before and after her marriage, Sandy would at times go to a bar, hoping to pick up someone, almost purely out of a needy dependency. Sometimes, this would later be repressed, or dissociated, but not always. Even if she were later amnesic for this behavior, she would, in the telling of it, have an embarrassed sense of why it had happened. She believed that this sort of neediness belonged to "the other Sandy"; but it seemed clear that this was something that she *wanted* to believe—the episodes reflected needs and behaviors that she did not want to own, that were completely unacceptable to her. It was I—not Sandy—who chose to call this aspect of her "Sandy 2, or Sandy, too." Serious critics, again, may propose that I thus invented, or created, an altered sense of self. I, on the contrary, felt that I was bridging motivations that Sandy disowned and attributed to "someone else," by forging a link: Sandy-self and Sandy too—it was all Sandy.

In these situations, the patient would often be successful in eliciting the interest of a man. The man would presume that the woman was looking for a sexual liaison. Sandy 2 was not; she was desperate to be cuddled, caressed, and admired. Things would progress; Sandy 2 would become terrified, and in an instant, the fear and neediness would be replaced by a seductive but also "take-charge" attitude, known to Sandy and me as "Sam." Whether or not sex took place, the situation would be "handled," and for a period of time there was apparently a sense of being in control. Sometime during this course of events—usually but not always before an actual sexual act—Sandy would "awaken," horrified and humiliated at what had transpired or was about to transpire—which, most often, was anal intercourse. How did she know that Sam had taken over? The description repeatedly offered by her husband, and occasionally by other men, matched her inner picture of this sense of self. (Why would "Sam" maintain control on some occasions through the actual sexual encounter, and why at other times would she give way to a terrified Sandy, before actual physical contact? God only knows.)

Still, one need not necessarily postulate "altered personalities" to make psychological sense of these scenarios. Could not one imagine a so-called borderline, or hysterical patient, describing just this sequence of events, without benefit of "Sandy 2" or "Sam"? Of course one could—taking note, however, that the therapist would be filling in some major gaps for which the patient was amnesic (presuming of course, that the therapist "believed" in amnesia) and would lack an explanation for the radically different appearance and behavior of the patient at such times, according to witnesses. Could it be, however, that *acting* like a different person, consciously or unconsciously, was simply a way of disowning conflictual impulses?

Let us leave the bar scene, and consider other situations. How to account for the alternative behaviors in situations in which she exhibited exceptional competence, such as on the tennis court or in the workplace? In the former, presumably the worst-case scenario would be that she was revealed to be a poor tennis player. In the workplace, it might become apparent that she was not a superlative interviewer, or prospective employee. Certainly these are circumstances that can provoke intrapsychic conflicts with which any psychoanalytically oriented therapist is familiar: patients who "inexplicably" are threatened by their success, as well as those who in similar mysterious fashion perform far below their obvious capacities. The conflicts we ordinarily uncover in such cases, however, are hardly so overwhelming, so threatening to the patient's very sense of self, that the result is amnesia, or an attribution of the conduct to someone else entirely. Clearly, these defenses, if that is how to characterize them, go beyond rationalization, or denial, or even splitting, in the sense in which we usually use the term in the treatment of borderlines. One can even question whether these psychological events *are* defenses. Defenses against what?

This, then, was Sandy's life. As I have indicated, she was very resistant to the idea that her "people" ever escaped the confines of her head, and took over control of her whole being-in-the-world; she was, in fact, horrified at the idea. Is there a better way, however, to conceptualize this information? What is unaccounted for, what is lost, by accepting the reality of the phenomena subsumed under the diagnosis, dissociative identity disorder? It seems to me that the primary loss is to the therapist's—or critic's—equanimity, when faced with human conduct that seems to belie one's customary and comfortable view of identity and sense of self.

Perhaps there is no possible theory, no accumulation of data, which can prove compelling to someone who is, in good conscience, skeptical of such dramatic, even theatrical, symptomatology. Perhaps it can only be compelling to the individuals—patient and therapist—who have experienced it. Simpson (1995) has said:

> There's a phoniness and a strong flavor of ham acting about the portrayals one is shown. . . . So many of the alters I have been shown on videotape . . . as well as some of those I have watched perform in embarrassing performances on public television have seemed crude and unconvincing—amateur theatrics. I do not say this as a pejorative comment, but as a carefully considered, scientific description of phenomena I am being urged to take seriously. (p. 121)

Nothing could have been further from the subjective truth of my encounters with "Joe," "Sam," "Vicki," the nameless child with the razor, or the mutilator. For me, these encounters gave rise to a rapid pulse, dry mouth, and uncanny visceral sensations. I believe the same would have been true for Simpson, and it is difficult to imagine his "carefully considered, scientific description" of such presentations of self not being significantly impacted by the experience.

THIRTEEN

The Syndrome III

> The problem is not having more than one personality; it is having less than one personality.
>
> —Spiegel (1993)

The nature of the pathology in dissociative identity disorder leads to a question both peculiar and unique to the treatment of this disorder: Who is the patient? Putnam (1989) states, "The 'personality' of an MPD patient is the sum and synergy of the system of alter personalities" (p. 123). Most of the early experts in the identification and treatment of this disorder (Braun, 1984; Kluft, 1984, in addition to Putnam) were convinced that no one "alter" in the personality system of this disorder was more "real" than any other. It is a view with which I am in basic disagreement, which I will address below.

The reality of the person, according to Putnam (1989), lay in the system as a whole, and the "host personality" was nothing more than "the one who has executive control of the body the greatest percentage of time during a given time period" (p. 107).

Putnam makes quite clear that, "Whatever an alter personality is, it is not a separate person" (p. 103). However, he goes on to say:

> I have seen a number of therapists struggling implicitly or explicitly with the question, "Who is the patient?" while working with their first MPD cases. In such an instance, the "patient" in the therapist's mind is originally the host personality, who presents for treatment. . . . The therapist must come to recognize that the patient really is a multiple and that the therapeutic work involves the whole personality system. (p. 109)

Putnam's view of treatment derives from his understanding of the developmental basis of the disorder. In a more recent book (1997) he has said:

[T]he identity fragmentation seen in MPD and other disorders associated with childhood trauma is not a "shattering" of a previously intact
identity, but rather a developmental failure of consolidation and integration of discrete states of consciousness. In particular, it is a profound
developmental failure to coherently bind together the state-dependent
aspects of self experienced by all young children. (p. 126)

Elsewhere, in a case discussion (1992), he has elaborated:

We are not born into the world with a single, unified personality. . . .
[W]e may view [the patient] as someone who has failed to complete the
developmental work of integrating a more-or-less continuous sense of
self. (p. 101)

According to this perspective, in the treatment of Sandy, all the "alters"
were my patient(s). It followed that I would need to have a relationship
with all of them, to the degree possible, and treat them as equals within
the system. "They" would ultimately determine whether or to what extent integration would occur, not the therapist and the "host" personality. Putnam warns (1989), "Before a therapist performs a partial or final
fusion, the therapist should try to determine whether the alters are ready
for such a fusion" (p. 306).

In the object-relations sector of psychoanalysis, there is a long tradition of viewing the self as discontinuous, but it suggests a different
understanding of its origin and meaning. Ferenczi (1933), who preceded
and anticipated this particular psychoanalytic framework, described various kinds of splits in the personality as "all the different fragments, each
of which behaves as a separate personality" (p. 165). He also linked this
sort of disorder to childhood sexual trauma. Decades later, Winnicott
(1960) identified what he called a "false self," which was a socially compliant presentation of self different from the "true" self, and brought
about by primary caregivers who would not tolerate a "misbehaving"
child.

In the 1940s and 1950s, Fairbairn (1952), working with psychologically
damaged children as well as adults, postulated that early trauma leads to
the splitting off of separate egos from the *central* ego, leaving the central
ego impoverished and fragile. He spoke of the split-off antilibidinal ego,
which relates to the object in a rejecting, hateful way; and the libidinal
ego, which is seductive, attention-seeking, and desperate for attachment.

These early psychoanalytic theorists posit a core sense of self which,
when exposed to severe psychological trauma, reacts with extreme measures affecting sense-of-self and sense-of-other, that include a defensive
function. This contrasts with Putnam's view, which posits no such function, but rather a failure to be able to incorporate trauma-related discrete
behavioral states into a coherent sense of identity.

Some contemporary psychoanalytic theoreticians have questioned the
very concept of a unitary self, and considered whether multiplicity might

e of keeping in mind: a) the *pathological and function-*
avioral states that are not being consolidated and
rent sense of self and b) the need to search for, and
ntary healthy organized self, however fragile. In
e self was fragile indeed, and perhaps, as she herself
ven evident outside my office walls. It is true that
f self, in Sandy's case, seemed more functional than
nstrating coping skills, social competencies, and
But they were born of trauma, and seemed to me
time, despite the passage of decades and the accu-
ts that had occurred "on their watch," so to speak.
rnative presentations of self all seemed to represent
means of controlling, denying, or overcoming un-
tion, betrayal, abandonment, and pain.
ctive, then, the "host personality" is not simply one
ileged as "the patient" no more and no less than any
it is the self which holds whatever healthy experiences of
raction preceded the patient's traumatic experiences, and
led by dissociation, has continued that interaction in
clusively have the traumatic abuse as their core. Vir-
nical descriptions of DID patients describe the "host
ever identified, as enfeebled, vulnerable, and de-
however, that very characterization reveals them to be
ls the "central ego." *They have no identifiable defensive*
ly can't cope.
g the human personality as composed of many dis-
warz (1995) says:

o say that one part functions as the creative part, and
protector part. Each part is capable of functioning in
capacity. . . . Each part is unique and has a full range of
onal responses and functions. (p. 29)

ely sums up the point about which I am in disagree-

y *potentially* had/has the full range of healthy emotional
nctions, but these, because of dissociative reactions to
of trust, assault, betrayal, and seduction, among others,
e to develop. In contrast, I do not believe that Joe, whose
e was, *"Never again"* (to be forcibly and helplessly pene-
le), could have developed the capacity to accept the un-
lnerability of being in a loving relationship—without,
g Sandy. Nor that Sam could ever have relinquished total,
trol of sexual encounters, thus allowing for the vulner-
der. It is simply not what they were about; it is not why
s world.

in fact be normative. Presaging their ideas in certain respects, Harry Stack
Sullivan, in the 1950s, postulated an interpersonal approach to psychotherapy in which he conceptualized the "self" as in fact an interpersonal
"self-system," the primary function of which was to avoid the anxiety
inherent in interpersonal relations (Sullivan, 1953). At times, he went so
far as to question whether in fact an individual self can exist other than as
a self-system in relationship with other self-systems (Sullivan, 1950). Unlike contemporary psychoanalytic theorists, however, Sullivan's ideas
were based on a pragmatic operationalism, focusing on what people actually do with each other. It is a view of self as action, and the therapist
was presumed to have a privileged position from which to objectively
assess interpersonal action patterns.

A further bridge to modern psychoanalytic theories was provided by
Janine Lampl-De Groot (1981), in which she hypothesized that multiple
personality is a pathological manifestation of a basic phenomenon of normal mental functioning. Davis (1996) provides a more recent formulation
of this idea:

Here I wish to go one step further and suggest that this aberration of
psychic structure, which reveals itself so clearly in true cases of multiple personality disorder and severe dissociative pathology, is, in fact,
only the severe, pathologically induced exaggeration of what I believe
to be a more accurate rending of unconscious psychic structure. I suggest that dissociation, even when conceived of as the overarching organizational mental process, always exists in a state of intimate tension
with association processes. Such an organization of self, and of the
multiple selves that comprise "mind," implies the finely tuned maintenance of an optimal tension state between the primarily, memory-
based connections that hold us together and the dynamic processes
that threaten to fracture our organizations—a kind of counterbalancing
of centrifugal and centripetal forces. . . .

Within such a system, any psychic distress, be it internally or externally derived, can potentiate a "fracturing" of integrative processes—a
splitting apart along what might be considered structurally normal
"stress points" or "fault lines." (pp. 564–65)

This view of psychological structure is shared by many current psychological and psychoanalytic theorists (Bromberg, 1980, 1991, 1993, 1996;
Davies and Frawley, 1994; Hermans et al, 1992; Slavin and Kriegman,
1992; Spillius and Feldman, 1989), and may be characterized as a "postmodernist" perspective. Bromberg (1996) states:

[A] discernible shift has been taking place with regard to the psychoanalytic understanding of the human mind and the nature of unconscious
mental processes—away from the idea of a conscious/preconscious/
unconscious distinction per se, toward a view of the self as decentered,
and the mind as a configuration of shifting, nonlinear, discontinuous

states of consciousness in an ongoing dialectic with the healthy illusion of unitary selfhood. (p. 512)

Elsewhere (1993), he echoes Putnam's view of the normal development of self:

[S]elf-experience originates in relatively unlinked self-states, each coherent in its own right, and . . . the experience of being a unitary self is an acquired, developmentally adaptive illusion. (pp. 162–63)

Goldberg (1999) from a self-psychology standpoint, similarly reflected that,

It may not always be felicitous to say that one self is true and one is false, or to say that one self is in touch with reality and the other is not; rather, it should be noted that they exist in different worlds at different times and for different purposes. (p. 56)

Slavin and Kriegman (1992) reach similar conclusions from an evolutionary biology perspective:

Multiple versions of the self exist within an overarching, synthetic structure of identity . . . which probably cannot possess the degree of internal cohesion or unity frequently implied by concepts such as the "self" in the self psychological tradition, the "consolidated character" in Blos's ego psychological model, or "identity" in Erikson's framework. . . . Although the coexistence of "multiple versions of the self" that we observe introspectively and clinically may thus represent crystallizations of different interactional schemes, this multiplicity may also signal the existence of an inner, functional limit on the process of self-integration. (pp. 204–5)

Mitchell (1992), however, has expressed doubts about including multiple personality disorder on a continuum with normal multiplicity of self. He points out that:

Despite the discontinuities [in my sense of self], I still recognize all these differences as versions of a more or less invariant "myself." I do not, even for a moment, consider the possibility that I actually have awakened as someone or something else. (pp. 204–5)

He says also:

Kohut was getting at something very important in the analytic process that tends to be overlooked in perspectives that emphasize the multiplicity of self. What distinguishes multiple personalities from the rest of us is precisely that in multiple personalities, there is no sense of continuity from one self-organization to the next, no recognition of a continuous, enduring subjectivity. The discontinuities are too discontinuous. Kohut was addressing the sense of self as integral and continuous. . . . The central thrust within mind is viewed as integrative, and that continuous line of subjective experience forms the core of the self. (p. 108)

My patient could no
attunement in her ch
her mother would no
ful, and family life i
Alcott. There was no
mother's words, a "g
have recounted, earlie
idyllic journal of an ea
the occasional episodes
turn on her with a fie
misattunements continu
her extreme sense of d
brought her a large box
that the patient was con
not, in any case, particula

As a consequence—or
oped, quite early on, an in
ly she became compliant,
ingly a perfect example o
contained her sadness, lon
to think that these self-state
themselves to be distinctive

This state of mind, how
susceptible to the seduction
struction, initially expresse
around six years of age, offe
her prettiness and charm. W
touching, and then outright s
fractured, like a crystal han
there was *no* caretaker attune
one, apparently, was the wisel

Sandy is reluctant to blan
thing, but she will readily ac
interactions with her mother, a
by her. The mother's efforts a
and she is reduced to futile att
latter blames herself for the pat
spective, one has to wonder wl
mother who seemingly failed to
in a state of terror, often staying
baseball bat to protect herself fro
door.

From the single case study tha
doubt unwise to overgeneralize a
ciative identity disorder. Still, my

toward the importanc
al nature of those beh
integrated into a cohe
privilege, the rudime
Sandy's case, this cor
suggested, was not e
some altered senses
Sandy herself, dem
even social histories
essentially frozen in
mulation of life eve
Ultimately, these al
compartmentalized
bearable overstimul

From this persp
more alter, to be pri
other alter. Rather,
attachment and inter
which, though crip
ways that do not e
tually all of the cl
personality," how
pressed. Perhaps,
what Fairbairn ca
function. They sim

In characterizi
crete identities, Sc

It is incorrect
another as the
more than one
possible emoti

This quote preci
ment.

I believe Sand
responses and fu
relational issues
had not been abl
entire *raison d'êt*
trated as a fema
certainty and v
that is, becomin
deliberative cor
ability of surrer
they were in thi

I felt some clinical validation of this perspective on one occasion, late in therapy, when Sandra Ellen was making frequent appearances. Of all the alternative senses of self, Sandra was one of the few who could lay claim to "having a life." There was continuity in her professional accomplishments, she had often been responsible for managing the children (who were apparently none the wiser), and she regularly interacted with Craig. She related to me in a warm if slightly distant manner, and was reflective, as well as cognitively analytical.

Sandra Ellen, in fact, made it clear to me that she felt *she* was the "person" I should be talking to most of the time, and who I should regard as the central self. She of course could see no particular reason why she should be in *therapy*, per se, but she enjoyed talking with me. Why, she asked one day, did I prefer Sandy, who was such a mess, to her? I took up the challenge, in a way that, earlier in the therapy, undoubtedly would have had very negative consequences. I answered that it was not a matter of preference, but simply a matter of fact. However fragmented and vulnerable Sandy was, there was a completeness to her life experience that Sandra Ellen and the others lacked. I understood she would feel offended by that view, but I thought I could prove it to her.

"How?" she asked.

"By this observation," I replied. "You *do not exist* from the neck down."

Sandra paled, and looked frightened. Moments later, she faded. She had understood, I believe, exactly what I meant: she achieved her self-assurance, analytic ability, and freedom from troubling emotions solely through denial that she had a body, which could respond to sexual stimulation, could be (and had been) raped, and could be seductive. I explained to Sandy what had happened, which left her as disconcerted as it did relieved.

Aside from whether or not I "proved" my point to Sandy, one may certainly wonder whether this intervention was empathic, interpretive, or merely grandstanding. But it leads to the thorny, complex question: How ought one conduct a therapy with these patients? What should one do?

FOURTEEN

Treatment: Nonpsychoanalytic Techniques

> We must try to go as fast as we can and as slow as we must, at the same time.
>
> —DID patient, as reported by Marmor (1991, p. 686)

To reflect on this long and intensive treatment is an extraordinary experience. I am a psychoanalyst, after all, as I occasionally have had to remind myself as well as the reader; but as I read over the various interventions, techniques, and actions in which I engaged during this therapy, it gives new meaning to the word "parameters" (Eissler 1958). It reveals, among other things, a therapy "frame" (Langs 1978) in tatters.[1]

The fact of the matter is that this treatment, at one point or another, violated the principles of every theoretical framework for the treatment of severely disturbed patients with which I am familiar. Consider the clear guidelines offered by one of the most prominent experts in the field of dissociative identity disorder, Colin A. Ross, as reported by Cohen et al. (1995):

> The therapist is neutral with respect to the reality of any given memory. . . . The therapy must have healthy boundaries and usually involves one to three hours a week of therapy. . . . The vast bulk of the therapy, consisting of a rational, adult conversation, is conducted in a working, problem-solving mode, and involves a blend of systems, cognitive, and psychodynamic techniques. (p. 414)

I believe my therapy with Sandy qualifies only for the last phrase of the last sentence.

Below are further excerpts of Ross's theory of treatment for DID patients:

The treatment of DID is much more like the cognitive-behavioral treatment of depression, or treatment of panic disorder through systematic desensitization. It is detailed, based on a clear treatment rationale, and involves specific steps and techniques. . . . One might compare the treatment of DID to the manufacture of a jet aircraft. (p. 416)

By far the most common and entrenched transference problem is the effort of the patient to place the therapist in the rescuer role, while the host personality becomes the victim, and the perpetrator role is projected onto the persecutor alters internally. (p. 420)

One of the key interventions . . . is making friends with persecutory alters. Too often these alters have been rejected, devalued, and hurt by the host personality and [previous] therapists. . . . As quickly as possible, we move to form a treatment alliance with the key persecutor personalities involved in the presenting problem. (p. 430)

In the above excerpt, Ross has certainly pegged what was a transference-countertransference pitfall for me, namely falling into the rescuer role, to the patient's victim role. I can only admire the resolve it must require to respond neutrally, when the voice of a persecuting sense of self, at the other end of a phone, tells the therapist that she is about to put an electric fireplace-starter up the patient's (her) anus. If the therapeutic boundary included absolutely no phone calls, this particular situation, of course, would not arise; but quite obviously, such threats can be made in the consulting room as well as on the telephone (as with the razor cutting, in my office)—eliciting, almost surely, inevitable countertransference-laden responses.

The treatment of dissociative identity disorder has become quite standardized by now, along the lines indicated in the Ross quotations above. There is a DD Psychotherapy Training Program provided by the International Society for the Study of Trauma and Dissociation (ISSTD), which is described by Brand et al. (2009) as follows:

As described by the Treatment Guidelines, the first stage of treatment involves developing safety of self and stabilizing self- and other-destructive behaviors, about their diagnoses and symptom management, and developing a good treatment alliance. When DD patients are able to stabilize and develop a good working relationship with their therapist, they can proceed to the next stages of treatment (that were identified in this study as stages 2–4) that entail identifying, accepting, and talking about their histories of abuse and trauma; cognitive processing of trauma-related themes and misattributions (e.g., believing that they were and are "bad" and that the childhood maltreatment was deserved); emotional processing, including the grieving of related losses (such as the loss of innocence, loss of potential); and creating a cohesive rather than a disjointed and dissociative narrative. Over the course of treatment, patients become increasingly aware of their tendency to disin fact be normative. Presaging their ideas in certain respects, Harry Stack Sullivan, in the 1950s, postulated an interpersonal approach to psychotherapy in which he conceptualized the "self" as in fact an interpersonal "self-system," the primary function of which was to avoid the anxiety inherent in interpersonal relations (Sullivan, 1953). At times, he went so far as to question whether in fact an individual self can exist other than as a self-system in relationship with other self-systems (Sullivan, 1950). Unlike contemporary psychoanalytic theorists, however, Sullivan's ideas were based on a pragmatic operationalism, focusing on what people actually do with each other. It is a view of self as action, and the therapist was presumed to have a privileged position from which to objectively assess interpersonal action patterns.

A further bridge to modern psychoanalytic theories was provided by Janine Lampl-De Groot (1981), in which she hypothesized that multiple personality is a pathological manifestation of a basic phenomenon of normal mental functioning. Davis (1996) provides a more recent formulation of this idea:

> Here I wish to go one step further and suggest that this aberration of psychic structure, which reveals itself so clearly in true cases of multiple personality disorder and severe dissociative pathology, is, in fact, only the severe, pathologically induced exaggeration of what I believe to be a more accurate rending of unconscious psychic structure. I suggest that dissociation, even when conceived of as the overarching organizational mental process, always exists in a state of intimate tension with association processes. Such an organization of self, and of the multiple selves that comprise "mind," implies the finely tuned maintenance of an optimal tension state between the primarily, memory-based connections that hold us together and the dynamic processes that threaten to fracture our organizations—a kind of counterbalancing of centrifugal and centripetal forces. . . .
>
> Within such a system, any psychic distress, be it internally or externally derived, can potentiate a "fracturing" of integrative processes—a splitting apart along what might be considered structurally normal "stress points" or "fault lines." (pp. 564–65)

This view of psychological structure is shared by many current psychological and psychoanalytic theorists (Bromberg, 1980, 1991, 1993, 1996; Davies and Frawley, 1994; Hermans et al, 1992; Slavin and Kriegman, 1992; Spillius and Feldman, 1989), and may be characterized as a "postmodernist" perspective. Bromberg (1996) states:

> [A] discernible shift has been taking place with regard to the psychoanalytic understanding of the human mind and the nature of unconscious mental processes—away from the idea of a conscious/preconscious/unconscious distinction per se, toward a view of the self as decentered, and the mind as a configuration of shifting, nonlinear, discontinuous

states of consciousness in an ongoing dialectic with the healthy illusion of unitary selfhood. (p. 512)

Elsewhere (1993), he echoes Putnam's view of the normal development of self:

[S]elf-experience originates in relatively unlinked self-states, each coherent in its own right, and . . . the experience of being a unitary self is an acquired, developmentally adaptive illusion. (pp. 162–63)

Goldberg (1999) from a self-psychology standpoint, similarly reflected that,

It may not always be felicitous to say that one self is true and one is false, or to say that one self is in touch with reality and the other is not; rather, it should be noted that they exist in different worlds at different times and for different purposes. (p. 56)

Slavin and Kriegman (1992) reach similar conclusions from an evolutionary biology perspective:

Multiple versions of the self exist within an overarching, synthetic structure of identity . . . which probably cannot possess the degree of internal cohesion or unity frequently implied by concepts such as the "self" in the self psychological tradition, the "consolidated character" in Blos's ego psychological model, or "identity" in Erikson's framework. . . . Although the coexistence of "multiple versions of the self" that we observe introspectively and clinically may thus represent crystallizations of different interactional schemes, this multiplicity may also signal the existence of an inner, functional limit on the process of self-integration. (pp. 204–5)

Mitchell (1992), however, has expressed doubts about including multiple personality disorder on a continuum with normal multiplicity of self. He points out that:

Despite the discontinuities [in my sense of self], I still recognize all these differences as versions of a more or less invariant "myself." I do not, even for a moment, consider the possibility that I actually have awakened as someone or something else. (pp. 204–5)

He says also:

Kohut was getting at something very important in the analytic process that tends to be overlooked in perspectives that emphasize the multiplicity of self. What distinguishes multiple personalities from the rest of us is precisely that in multiple personalities, there is no sense of continuity from one self-organization to the next, no recognition of a continuous, enduring subjectivity. The discontinuities are too discontinuous. Kohut was addressing the sense of self as integral and continuous. . . . The central thrust within mind is viewed as integrative, and that continuous line of subjective experience forms the core of the self. (p. 108)

My patient could not count on, and it seems did not receive, adequate attunement in her childhood. From a very early age, she had realized that her mother would not countenance negative affects. Life was to be cheerful, and family life in particular was to be a page out of Louisa May Alcott. There was no unhappiness, no psychological trial, which, in her mother's words, a "good roaring fire" in the fireplace wouldn't cure. I have recounted, earlier, Sandy's reaction of incredulity at her mother's idyllic journal of an early family vacation. At another time, she recalled the occasional episodes when her mother would suddenly, unexpectedly, turn on her with a fierce rage that devastated and shocked her. Such misattunements continue to the present; Sandy reported sadly, one day, her extreme sense of discomfort and conflict when mother, on a visit, brought her a large box of chocolates. Mother had every reason to know that the patient was constantly concerned with gaining weight, and did not, in any case, particularly like chocolate.

As a consequence—or, if you will, correlated with this—Sandy developed, quite early on, an inner sense of herself and an outer self. Outwardly she became compliant, even-tempered, and apparently happy—seemingly a perfect example of Winnicott's false self (1960). Her "inside" self contained her sadness, loneliness, and guilt. There is no reason, however, to think that these self-states constituted different senses of "I," which felt themselves to be distinctive. Both were aspects of Sandy.

This state of mind, however, almost surely made her extraordinarily susceptible to the seductions of the perpetrators who, in our joint construction, initially expressed great delight with Sandy when she was around six years of age, offering her cookies and milk while they extolled her prettiness and charm. When these adults turned affection into erotic touching, and then outright sexual abuse, her already fragile sense of self fractured, like a crystal hammered along preexisting fault lines. And there was *no* caretaker attunement after the fact—she told no one and no one, apparently, was the wiser.

Sandy is reluctant to blame her mother—or anyone else—for anything, but she will readily admit that she has no warm memories of interactions with her mother, and, to this day, cannot bear being touched by her. The mother's efforts at empathy leave the patient shuddering, and she is reduced to futile attempts at reassuring her mother when the latter blames herself for the patient's problems. From the therapist's perspective, one has to wonder what was going on intrapsychically with a mother who seemingly failed to notice that her six-year-old daughter was in a state of terror, often staying up at night crouched in a closet with a baseball bat to protect herself from a vicious lion that stalked outside her door.

From the single case study that comprises much of this book, it is no doubt unwise to overgeneralize about all patients diagnosed with dissociative identity disorder. Still, my experiences with Sandy seem to point toward the importance of keeping in mind: a) the *pathological and function-al nature* of those behavioral states that are not being consolidated and integrated into a coherent sense of self and b) the need to search for, and privilege, the rudimentary healthy organized self, however fragile. In Sandy's case, this core self was fragile indeed, and perhaps, as she herself suggested, was not even evident outside my office walls. It is true that some altered senses of self, in Sandy's case, seemed more functional than Sandy herself, demonstrating coping skills, social competencies, and even social histories. But they were born of trauma, and seemed to me essentially frozen in time, despite the passage of decades and the accu-mulation of life events that had occurred "on their watch," so to speak. Ultimately, these alternative presentations of self all seemed to represent compartmentalized means of controlling, denying, or overcoming un-bearable overstimulation, betrayal, abandonment, and pain.

From this perspective, then, the "host personality" is not simply one more alter, to be privileged as "the patient" no more and no less than any other alter. Rather, *it is the self which holds whatever healthy experiences of attachment and interaction preceded the patient's traumatic experiences,* and which, though crippled by dissociation, has continued that interaction in ways that do not exclusively have the traumatic abuse as their core. Vir-tually all of the clinical descriptions of DID patients describe the "host personality," however identified, as enfeebled, vulnerable, and de-pressed. Perhaps, however, that very characterization reveals them to be what Fairbairn calls the "central ego." *They have no identifiable defensive function.* They simply can't cope.

In characterizing the human personality as composed of many dis-crete identities, Schwarz (1995) says:

> It is incorrect to say that one part functions as the creative part, and another as the protector part. Each part is capable of functioning in more than one capacity. . . . Each part is unique and has a full range of possible emotional responses and functions. (p. 29)

This quote precisely sums up the point about which I am in disagree-ment.

I believe Sandy *potentially* had/has the full range of healthy emotional responses and functions, but these, because of dissociative reactions to relational issues of trust, assault, betrayal, and seduction, among others, had not been able to develop. In contrast, I do not believe that Joe, whose entire *raison d'être* was, "*Never again*" (to be forcibly and helplessly pene-trated as a female), could have developed the capacity to accept the un-certainty and vulnerability of being in a loving relationship—without, that is, becoming Sandy. Nor that Sam could ever have relinquished total, deliberative control of sexual encounters, thus allowing for the vulner-ability of surrender. It is simply not what they were about; it is not why they were in this world.

sociate and the functions that dissociation and their dissociative states of mind or self-states served in the past and in the present. *Patients develop more awareness of their inner states and what is usually a conflicted agenda among them and learn to develop internal dialogue and cooperation.* As this process continues and deepens over the middle states, it results in less amnesia between the disparate parts of self and as these self-states increasingly understand the similarity of their motivations and become more accepting of each other, they begin to blend and integrate. Not all DD patients can manage the intense work involved in the middle and later stages of treatment and some choose not to integrate. In the last stage of treatment, self-states continue to be integrated, patients learn to cope with stress and emotions without dissociating, and they work to develop healthy relationships, an enhanced ability to work, and an increased sense of purpose in life. (pp. 159–60, my italics)

It all sounds quite straightforward and unexceptionable, and these authors claim a high success rate of ultimate integration in patients treated according to this format. One would not have a clue, however, from this description, about the inevitable intense emotional interchanges between a therapist and his DID patient, nor the role such interchange may play in the course of the treatment. It all sounds quite . . . rational.

I would suggest, also, that there is not as seamless a continuum in treatment techniques, in this approach, as the description would seem to indicate. There is a turning point, the introduction of something singular, in my view, in the sentence I have italicized. While the treatment up until then seems to be an amalgam of commonly accepted therapeutic techniques including empathy, support, education, and cognitive-behavioral interventions, the therapy is now described as having alternate senses of self increase their dialogue with one another. As I have indicated throughout this book, this is where my therapy with Sandy differed from the ISSTD paradigm: I did not attempt to contact every altered sense of self, and develop an ongoing dialogue with each of them, or they with each other.

I am hardly unique in taking this position in the treatment of DID; one need not reject the entire construct of multiple personalities to decide on principle not to regard alternative presentations of self as equivalent to the "host" personality. Segall (1995, p. 396) attributes to Orne (1991) the fear that interacting with split-off ego states will only increase dissociation, and to Yalom (1989) the concern that the depleted presenting ego state will feel further neglected and weakened if the therapist attends to a more dramatic and interesting emergent ego state. This principle leaves unanswered what the therapist, then, *does* when confronted with an alternative sense-of-self. I will address the issue at greater length below.

Given the premise that the personality of the DID patient is the sum of each of the alters, and that the "host" personality has no more standing in reality than the other presentations of self, the "end game" of therapy, as described by the authors using the ISSTD paradigm, bears no relation to that which occurred with Sandy. The end stage in their model is described more extensively by Putnam (1989), and consists of bringing about what he calls *fusion*: "Before a therapist performs a partial or final fusion, the therapist should try to determine whether the alters are ready for such a fusion" (p. 306).

How? By asking them, and exploring their willingness to "give up" their autonomous standing, and "blend" with others:

> [Alters are read for fusion when] they begin to accept each other and to develop a sense of mutual self-identification. . . . The next step usually involves a ceremony or ritual, frequently augmented by hypnosis. . . . Most ceremonies involve the use of visual imagery and metaphors, and are generally performed while the alters are in a trance. (p. 307)

Apparently, this formulaic denouement is not always successful. Putnam states that Braun often said in workshops, "The first fusion *isn't!*" (p. 309). Kluft (1988), in a follow-up of ninety-one patients whose "personalities" were therapeutically blended into "unification," found that almost 95 percent required additional therapy, usually including renewed efforts at fusion. The psychoanalyst is reminded, first, of Freud's return rate, when his topographical theory of the mind, and its consequent definition of treatment as "making the unconscious conscious," failed to produce lasting change in his patients. This led to his development of the structural model of the mind and a consequently more prolonged therapy approach involving what he called "working through." Second, the analyst is reminded of Kohut's comparable response to orthodox theory when patients with narcissistic problems (including, most notably himself), failed to achieve lasting change. Putnam et al. concluded that failure to work with the problematic character traits of the unified individual resulted in a very high relapse rate back into dividedness (op. cit., pp. 224–27)—as opposed, it seems to me, to another possible explanation: a faulty theory of treatment.

In my therapy with Sandy, the transition toward a unitary sense of self seemed to occur through a variety of processes. I have previously described Sandy's report, well into the therapy, of being "present," even while Sandra Ellen was conducting the business of living—a spontaneous and unsolicited description of "blending." I have described her looking in the mirror, one day, and seeing herself as having breasts and curves—which felt to her like a revelation. The most common change, however, as Sandy became a whole person, consisted of altered senses of self simply not taking form in my office anymore. This was correlated with Sandy's reports of the conversations in her head becoming less insistent, less dialogic, even less loud.

A rather remarkable, albeit completely subjective, point of transition happened one evening when I was yet again talking to Sandy 2 on the telephone, at a point in time when, in my office, I had not witnessed an altered sense of self for some weeks. These conversations invariably were ended by me—sometimes tactfully, sometimes abruptly—when it became apparent that Sandy 2 was, in a needy and desperate fashion, trying to stay on the line as long as possible, and well after the crisis of the moment had become manageable.

On this occasion, I noted with surprise that Sandy 2 repeated what I had been saying about that evening's crisis, as though truly absorbing it. "Yes," I said, after her summary, "that's exactly what I mean."

She next, with what I took to be deep sadness in her voice, indicated that there didn't seem to be anything further that needed to be discussed. I agreed. "Well . . . okay," she said. "I guess then I'll just say goodbye," and hung up. As soon as the receiver was on the hook, I had a powerful sense that this goodbye had not simply been about ending the phone call, but about her very sense of self. I felt, further, that I would never see or hear from her again. I was right.

Bliss (1986) is among those who consider dissociated states, intrusive visions, body memories, and so forth, all as examples of spontaneous self-hypnosis, and further, as evidence that the patients are excellent candidates for clinical hypnotic therapy. He understands hypnotic states to be based on the ability of the reticular activating system of the brain to hyperattend to the inner operations of the mind, and particularly to some perceptual or remembered information at the expense of others. This focus, sharp and unwavering, can create a sense of realism that can, in turn, deprive the mind of reality testing. The behaviors emerging from unconscious memories, Bliss points out, can be compelling (pp. 116–30).

Bliss might well regard the first appearance of an altered sense of self—Joe—in my office as hypnotically induced, even if inadvertently, by my intoning the words that the patient had previously provided me. However, elsewhere in his book, Bliss provides an additional, or alternative, explanation that I find more compelling: "The 'spontaneous' transformation of the alert patient into a personality usually occurs when the patient encounters a stress with which he or she cannot cope. The switch can be rapid, almost instantaneous, but the repetitive explanation by patient and personalities is simply that the patient 'disappears' when the alter ego assumes the body" (p. 125). There can be no question that, in my insistence to Sandy that she provide more information about her evening experiences of a demanding voice, I had produced considerable stress—from which, she may have also felt, there was no escape.

I have earlier provided references to the considerable literature advocating the use of hypnosis in treating DID. Kluft (in Cohen et al. 1995) has gone so far as to say: "It often is possible to treat DID patients without ever inducing hypnosis, but it is completely impossible to treat them without hypnosis" (p. 370). He goes on to explain his view that dissociative behaviors are self-hypnotic phenomena, and that, therefore, "the decision to abjure [clinical hypnosis] deprives the physician of the opportunity to help the patient restructure his or her autohypnotic proclivities and patterns toward therapeutic ends, and leaves the patient's psychopathologies with an often insurmountable home field advantage" (p. 371).

When I proposed hypnosis to Sandy, sometime during the first two years of therapy, she was terrified at the prospect, for reasons not so dissimilar from her reluctance to take medication: loss of control. How could she not, given that throughout much of her life she felt that she was not *in* control? She did not disagree with my aim, however, which was to stop the seemingly relentless self-mutilation. Clearly, the cutting, and the overdoses, were a direct consequence of what had been triggered, or invoked, by the therapy; but the motivations involved had been so radically disavowed by Sandy as to be experienced as belonging to someone else, and I felt desperate to access that "part" of her, however defined, which had access to them.

As described earlier, I was unsuccessful in inducing a hypnotic state in Sandy. It is certainly possible that I spent insufficient time exploring the patient's fears about hypnosis; on the other hand, perhaps Sandy was the exception that proves the rule. In my attempt to induce a hypnotic state, it is clear, retrospectively, that I was *shown*, rather than told, several things: 1) the means of self-mutilation were readily at hand, whether I liked it or not (the razor in the purse), 2) their use potentially could be averted, without recourse to a technique like hypnosis, and 3) if it was my wish to be in direct contact with the part of her that produced the self-mutilation, this, too, could be accomplished without hypnosis. In choosing to apply a treatment *technique*—an action—rather than remain in an intersubjective, empathic and exploratory mode, Sandy responded in kind.

The use of EMDR seems to me a more complicated story. The use of this technique hinges on a premise that is itself controversial. In the treatment of patients with a history of childhood abuse—let us assume that the evidence was convincing that the painting, the nightmares, dissociation, self-abuse, and so forth, were related to things that the patient had experienced as a child—is it necessary to revisit the original events? Is a primary aim of the treatment to help the patient "remember" what had happened to her? Most authorities in the field would answer in the affirmative; Marmer (1991), from a psychoanalytic perspective, puts it thus:

> The hermeneutic school of Schafer (1976, 1983) and Spence (1982) teaches us that one of the ways therapy changes people is to rewrite their biographies. . . . We are powerless to change the historical truth of the patient's traumatic past, but we are capable, together with the patient, of writing a narrative truth that transforms the meaning of the unchangeable events. (p. 688)

The obstacles to achieving such an aim are particularly formidable, however, in the case of suspected childhood sexual abuse, because the stakes are extremely high. More than in most therapies, it is of exceptional importance that the narrative truth bear some real correlation with the historical truth, not least because of the legal implications. Brenner (2001) points out that there may be a variety of psychological factors at work that lead to distortion, beyond the unreliability of perceptual registration. There are the problems of: "distinguishing repressed memories from unconscious fantasy, a perverse and negotiable attitude toward reality, the role of suggestion, a disturbance in the barrier between wakefulness and REM sleep in traumatized individuals, and the dreamlike secondary revision quality of dissociative content" (p. 47). These presumed attributes of patients with dissociative disorders can only add to the uncertainty of normal memory, which, studies in psychological, sociological, and legal fields of investigation (Hedges 1994; Loftus 1993) consistently demonstrate, is an unreliable descriptor of past events. Current theories of memory, in fact (Lenzinger-Bohleber and Pfeifer 2002) suggest that memories are not fixed or stored structures, but rather are active products, regularly constructed anew.

For a patient suffering from DID, whose life has been characterized by a kaleidoscope of disparate, seemingly unrelated islands of memory, it would seem all the more important to develop a narrative (this will be explored in a later chapter). As Marmer (op. cit.) further points out: "The therapist carries the narrative for the patient in the early stages of therapy. For the patient, the knowledge of the therapist and the experience of the therapy may be the first event shared by all the alters" (p. 680).

There is often an exquisite paradox for the therapist in constructing this narrative for the patient suffering from dissociative identity disorder, or from other sequelae of childhood abuse. The common worry, of fellow professionals and lay people alike, is that the therapist will be too gullible, accepting at face value the memories that the patient tells. The problem in therapy often is the opposite. Patients like Sandy *deny* that anything happened to them; they insist that the horrendous symptoms are not evidence of a traumatic history, but are evidence of personal weakness and perversity.[2] The therapist has his own doubts; and yet he must come to *believe* in the history of abuse, if the patient is ever to risk an entirely different construction of her sense of self and how she came to be who she is.

How then, to develop a coherent, plausible narrative, grounded not only in psychic but material reality? I have spoken previously of my rationales for using eye movement desensitization and reprocessing. My temporary abandonment of an analytic, intersubjective therapeutic paradigm reflected not only my anxiety over the uncertain progress of the treatment and a wish to somehow hasten the retrieval of early childhood memories, but also a genuine theoretical quandary.

It did not seem unreasonable to think that, through the analytic relationship, the patient eventually could reexperience, and come to understand, the needs and desires that had led to many of her encounters with men, as well as the inhibitions, displacements, and other ways of coping that these relationships reflected. I could imagine as well the therapeutic relationship itself providing the soothing, mirroring, tension-regulating functions that the patient could, over time, internalize (although, in my frequently beleaguered state, the plausibility of this therapeutic rationale was severely tested). But what was the patient to do with those behaviors and experiences, both mental and physical, about which she felt no sense of ownership? How to come to terms with these emboli, which coursed like calcified foreign bodies through her veins, and surfaced, seemingly at times with the least of triggers, into painful awareness? Is something different from the empathic, intersubjective psychoanalytic paradigm required in treating dissociation? My sense was that, without some narrative of her childhood that claimed some objective reality, a corrective emotional experience within the therapeutic relationship would not ultimately change her basic sense of herself as someone who had been inexplicably perverted and despicable from an early age. But how to arrive at that narrative?

EMDR is a technique that consists of several steps (Parnell 1999). First, there is a *preparation* phase: one provides the patient a description of the technique, and its rationale. One also makes clear that the patient may stop the process at any time, by raising her hand, and that there are no expectations about what ought to happen, no right or wrong feelings.

Next is an *assessment* phase. The therapist helps the patient identify and focus on a target related to the trauma. Several questions are asked in this regard: "What picture represents the worst part of the incident?" "What words best go with the picture that express your negative belief about yourself now?" "What would you like to believe about yourself when you bring up the image?" Finally, the therapist asks the patient what *emotions* she feels when she brings up the picture with the negative cognition. For each of these questions, the patient is asked to do a SUDS (Subjective Units of Disturbance Scale, Wolpe 1991), rating: a ten-point scale rating the degree of subjective disturbance the patient feels in regard to the picture.

Then comes the *desensitization* phase. The patient is asked to bring up the disturbing image, together with all its emotions, body sensations, and negative cognition, and to follow the therapist's fingers with her eyes, letting whatever comes up come up without censoring it. After about twenty-five right-left movements, or when there is an apparent change, the therapist stops and instructs the client to "let it go and take a deep breath." The therapist asks, "What do you get now? After the patient reports her experience, the therapist says, "Go with that," and begins another set of eye movements. Throughout this process, the therapist takes frequent SUDS ratings. As the process is repeated several times, according to Parnell, the imagery disturbs the patient less and less. When the image gets a rating of only 0 or 1, where 10 is maximally disturbing, the patient is invited to recall the positive cognition that was earlier elicited—or to create a new one.

There are two more stages in this treatment protocol, which I will not describe, because Sandy never got to them—perhaps because, as I have said earlier, I did not follow this protocol rigorously. The rationale I gave Sandy for the procedure, namely suggesting that it might evoke more memories or images that would help her make sense of her experiences, was different than that of usual EMDR protocol. I did use the specific technique of finger movement, and Sandy cooperated, following my finger with her eyes. I did not ask Sandy to provide "negative cognitions," and "positive cognitions." I did not ask her for any cognitions at all.

Also, I never did SUDS ratings—although I have no doubt that, at the end of our experimentation with EMDR, Sandy's SUDS ratings would still have been high for the imagery we evoked, albeit perhaps less than when we began. The very idea that, through imagery and eye movement, Sandy would have become "desensitized" to imagery that she could not bear to identify as "real," that came unbidden, and that had terrified her for as long as she could remember, seemed to me implausible.

What happened during the EMDR was, first, that Sandy saw specific, graphic imagery—whole pictures—that connected and made sense of disparate bodily sensations and glimpses of images she had had throughout her life, and second, that it conveyed to her that something horrendous had, in fact, happened to her as a child. It was as much as I had hoped for.

I can only consider the prescribing of medications—or more precisely, my urging the patient to take them—to have been an unempathic, and untherapeutic, act. Sandy, at best, was very ambivalent about medication; she felt in some way lessened by the idea that a drug would affect her mind, and prevent her from doing what she needed to do "on her own." It is almost surely the reason she was unable to tolerate doses generally considered efficacious. My urging medications upon her came out of my desperation to put a floor under her depression and despair, together with the belief that it was my duty as a physician to provide whatever aid was at my disposal to lift her out of her suicidal depths. Not an unreasonable aim, surely. But what did it mean that, in the interests of treating the patient's suicidality, I provided her pills with which at various times she tried to kill herself? Let me even postulate the worst-case possibility: stretched to the limits of my endurance, was I *trying* to kill her?

Such an impulse is outrageous and unthinkable; but as any psychoanalyst knows, neither of those attributes makes it impossible. The most I can say is that I didn't think so, before or after the fact, and neither did Sandy. The problem with this interpretation of the countertransference is less that the impulse is so unthinkable and unacceptable, than that it is too specific. The relationship reflected in the act of prescribing medication was often, if not invariably, an enactment of some sort, and the motivational system activated in me often did include anger, even rage— but not *only*, and not *primarily*, anger and rage. Rather the emotional impetus for these interventions seemed, then and now, to be rooted in fear, anguish, and a sense of therapeutic impotence. The enactment seemed to be akin to an interaction between a drowning victim and helpless rescuer: "Help! I am sinking!" was Sandy's cry. "Here! Grab hold of this lifeline, this life raft!" was my agitated response, in writing the prescription. But no: the life raft did not reach, or it had a leak, or it in fact was weighted, rather than buoyant. Or perhaps: the water was not as deep as it seemed, and the patient had more capacity to swim than either of us was acknowledging.

At the time of my offering prescriptions, of course, I did not think I was being unempathic; I framed the issue—and genuinely meant it—as simply an experiment: we would see, together, whether or not the medication helped her, and if it did not, she of course would stop it. Wasn't that reasonable? How could she disagree? The point is that she *did* disagree, reasonable or not; and I wrote the prescriptions anyway. In the long course of this therapy, I prescribed a variety of antidepressants, occasional anxiolytics, and several hypnotics. None of them helped in any significant way. In retrospect, I would not have given her any medication.

The sustained efforts at empathy, the failures thereof and subsequent efforts at repair, the self-disclosures, affective exchanges, and attempts to understand them—all characterize, however competently, a treatment informed by self psychology, intersubjectivity, and social-constructionism. But EMDR? Meetings with the patient's family? A virtual pharmacopoeia of medications? All these interventions require further scrutiny, to determine whether they are compatible with an empathic-introspective therapy, or were in fact antithetical to its very premises.

At a surface level, one can describe the various parameters identified above as "doing something" to the patient, as opposed to a psychotherapy that is empathic and reflective. At a deeper level, however, this is an insufficient distinction. When we offer a tentative interpretation to a patient, speak with affect, pose a question, we are also "doing something"— often with greater impact than any medication or hypnotic suggestion. The difference, rather, it seems to me, lay in the fact that the "doing" of some of the therapeutic endeavors in which I engaged did not arise out of an authentic response to the patient's subjectivity at that point in time; it was not an attempt to understand what the patient had been saying about her life, or what had just happened in the therapeutic interaction. It was rather as if I had called a "time-out" to the basic analytic process.

Can such an interruption ever be an *appropriate* intervention, rather than a deflection by the therapist of the hard work involved in entering into, and understanding, the patient's despair and hopelessness? Kohut (1984) has said, "My inclination is to respond with the old adage that they should get out of the kitchen if they cannot stand the heat" (p. 182). Is this essentially what I had unconsciously done?

From a self-psychological, intersubjective, or social-constructivist perspective, the answer is not simply to be found in the mind of the observer. It can only be found in the intersubjective events that led to the extra-analytic interventions, and the meanings attributed to the intervention by both individuals before, during, and afterward. Trying to understand the meanings of these various interventions from any and all of these perspectives leads, in my retrospective opinion, to a mixed and complicated picture. There is some reason, however, to think that I indeed was getting out of the kitchen.

In discussing an earlier version of this book, Sandy expanded on her experience during the session, following her having brought in her painting, in which I had crudely blurted out my frustration at her responses. As I earlier said, the center of my interest at the beginning of that session basically wasn't on the *patient,* but rather on her painting. Thus it was, that I hadn't even noticed that she had sat in a different chair—one closer to mine—than usual. (My office was so arranged that there were several seating options, in the service of seeing couples and families, which had also been part of my practice.) Sandy explained that she felt she had taken an enormous risk by moving closer, and that it had reflected her tentative increase in trust, as well as her attachment to me. All the worse, of course, that this move was met with an expression of anger—even notwithstanding the possibility that the totality of her conduct may have unconsciously set up a reenactment of early rejection.

I asked Sandy, in this same discussion of my book, what thoughts she had at this point about the use of EMDR. Here is her reply:

> The EMDR was initially challenging for reasons that you probably wouldn't even suspect. It terrified me to have you move across the room and sit so close; I had an extremely hard time focusing on the movements that I was supposed to focus on when I knew your focus was on me—what I was looking like, experiencing, etc. I was very skeptical about all of it; so the fact that whatever the repetitive movement does to the brain actually overcame the resistance and fear I had is pretty remarkable.

In other words, Sandy makes clear that EMDR did not represent a "time-out" from the transferential/countertransferential relationship at all—it just moved it out of my view.

She went on to say this about the EMDR:

I don't think the EMDR changed my understanding of the problems
that I had; I think that it made whatever happened more real; what was
very vague and very "physically" experienced became more visually
real as well as physically intense. . . . [W]hat I mean is that imagery
became sharper rather than diffuse . . . still not saying it right. . . . I
could "see" things that I hadn't "seen" before; what had been imagery
of shades of darkness/light evolved more into actual discernable/tan-
gible "things": table, door, cabinet, window, even people. I probably
don't remember as much as you might hope that I would about the
intensity. I would imagine maybe it's like "labor"—it's beyond belief
when one is going through it but later and after the fact, it doesn't seem
so bad.

To this day, Sandy cannot say she fully "believes" that she was the subject of childhood abuse—by which she seems to mean that she continues
to both know and not know it. She explains further that she can *remember*
going to the lake with her family, graduating from grade school, getting
together with a childhood friend, and so forth; but she cannot *remember*
the events of her abuse in the same way. Rather, she *experiences* them, and
"sees" them, without the sense of objective reality that ordinary memory
provides.[3] It is paradoxical that the childhood sexual abuse is both less
real and *more* real than such ordinary memory.

It was perhaps as important, or even more important, for the dissociated senses of self to bear witness to what had happened, as the experien-
tial memories emerged, as it was for Sandy in her normal state. It was,
after all, "they" who claimed she was simply an inexplicably depressive,
ineffectual wimp. I have a progress note in my records, from this period
of time, that reads: "Sandy reports that Joe is thinking hard about things,
reevaluating old assumptions. She added that she somehow wishes she
could put her arms around him; ask him why he hates her so."

NOTES

1. Psychoanalytic perspectives will be considered in the next chapter, but Mitchell's observations on boundaries, and limit setting, from a contemporary psychoanalytic point of view (1993), are pertinent here: "It is apparent that one person's 'firmness' is another's rigidity, and that one person's flexibility is another's 'caving in.' Both
firmness and flexibility are important and should be among the considerations of any
clinician struggling with these situations. But I do not believe either of these positions
provides a terribly reliable or helpful guide. . . . The problem with the principle of
standing firm is the assumption that it must mean to the patient what the analyst
wants it to mean" (p. 194).

2. Stolorow and Atwood (1992) point out, "Even if able to remember the traumatogenic experiences, the child may remain plagued by tormenting doubts about their
actuality, or even about the reality of his experience in general, an inevitable consequence of the absence of validating attunement that . . . lies at the heart of psychic
trauma" (p. 55).

3. "Normal" memory may involve considerable left-brain organizational and linguistic contributions. Valent (1988) has proposed that early trauma may be deeply remembered in later life not in verbal explicit memory but in the form of disconnected physiological responses and emotions. Joseph (1982) states that early emotional learning occurs in the right hemisphere unbeknownst to the left, and may later be completely inaccessible to the language centers of the brain.

FIFTEEN

Treatment: Psychoanalytic Perspectives I

Recapitulation of the abuse usually occurs on at least two levels: within the personality system, and within the therapy.
—Putnam (1989, p. 178)

Saks (1999) has stated that a therapy is psychoanalysis if: 1) it purports to work via beliefs; 2) the beliefs include propositions about what kind of a person one is; 3) the beliefs include propositions about one's conscious and unconscious mental states; 4) the beliefs include propositions about mental states that play a causal role in one's behavior (pp. 44–45).[1] Certainly much of this therapy—but hardly all—fits this definition.

One of the hallmarks of a psychoanalytic treatment is the attention given and importance accorded to the cognitive-affective interaction within the therapeutic relationship. In the treatment of DID, it is virtually impossible to avoid such considerations, regardless of orientation. Almost all therapists, of whatever theoretical persuasion, report intense personal reactions in these therapies, however they choose to use these feelings in the service of the therapy. Consider the following quotes from widely disparate theoretical points of view.

Putnam (1989), advocating a standardized, methodical approach to treatment has said:

> The desperate quality of the host's struggle to maintain control and the apparent frailty of this control are often mirrored in the therapist's feelings of loss of control over the treatment process. (p. 171)

> Multiples push against every traditional therapy boundary and can cause discomfort in therapists wedded to a particular theoretical orientation or therapeutic stance. Such therapists often find themselves

145

caught between their pragmatic observations of what works with an MPD patient and the dictates of their professional training. (p. 189)

Bliss (1986), an advocate of hypnotherapy, states:

> Therapy can be a long, tough, precarious climb. Misadventures do oc-
> cur, and trust wavers. It is an elemental relationship with the omni-
> present threat of crises, if not disasters. (p. 201)

> Every form of transference may occur, particularly when patients enter
> trance states. . . . I have made home visits when crises occurred; tele-
> phoned and insisted on further therapy when patients refused to re-
> turn; and embraced patients when they were distressed—I think in a
> fatherly fashion. (p. 203)

Parnell (1999), describing EMDR treatment of a patient with a history of severe childhood abuse, reports:

> One woman began to cry in panic during EMDR processing and
> slipped off of the couch onto the floor. She was then overtaken by
> spasmodic jerking, simulating orgasm. In her case, the therapist got
> down on the floor near her and gently encouraged her to continue with
> the eye movements [!], following the therapist's fingers until the body
> reaction subsided. The therapist and the client were exhausted by the
> experience. (p. 54)

Psychoanalysts who view DID within the context of classical psychoanalytic theory—that is, as representing a particular configuration of libidinal and aggressive intrapsychic conflicts—describe intense countertransference feelings. Gedo (2000) reports:

> One day, several months into the treatment, [the patient] was unchar-
> acteristically spacey and out of touch. A growing sense of passivity,
> helplessness, and dyscontrol overwhelmed me. . . . I felt like I might
> lose my mind and go crazy. (p. 612)

Brenner (2001), from a similar theoretical framework, reports what would seem to be intense but unacknowledged countertransference on the part of a therapist under his supervision, with a consequent disruption of treatment:

> The patient was found in a comatose state and reported a near death
> experience. But by this time there was an almost complete rupture of
> trust, and her doctor told her that he could not work with her anymore
> if she continued to deceive him and act on her suicidal wishes. She was
> transferred to another facility. (pp. 58–59)

Mitchell (1993) has aptly summarized the theoretical position of those contemporary psychoanalysts who focus more on the meaning of the co-constructed dyadic pattern in therapy than on intrapsychic conflict:

> I view the psychoanalytic process as one in which the analysand is created through an intersubjective process. . . . Analysis is not simply a method of uncovering the hidden; it is more importantly a process of creating an analytic subject who had not previously existed. (p. 34)

Therapists working from this theoretical perspective are especially open to identifying their emotions and reactions, both in their writings and with their patients. Mitchell, referring to psychoanalytic therapy generally, has further said:

> A central consequence of the analyst's personal stake in the efficacy of his own understanding is that periods of impasse in analyses are likely to disrupt the analyst's own personal equilibrium, awakening the analyst's own dreads, and challenging the analyst's hopes not only for the patient but for himself as well. (p. 214)

Within such a framework, Davies and Frowley (1994), in their work with sexually abused patients, have been particularly frank about their reactions:

> We have felt inexplicably nauseous, terrified, bigger, or smaller, have had tingly skin, numbness of an extremity, headaches, dizziness, vaginal pain, or contractions, or have experienced states of sexual arousal, all of which were disorienting and alien to a normally functioning ego. (p. 151)

In summary, the experiences of therapists treating sexually abused patients, and dissociative identity disorder patients in particular, seem remarkably similar regardless of theoretical therapeutic approaches. I have taken pains in this work to include examples of such intense emotional interchanges, because I believe it was through the accumulation of these reactions, counterreactions, and consequent efforts at understanding, that the most therapeutic change took place in my treatment of Sandy. I am distinguishing such efforts from therapeutic interventions that seek to fully know all the disparate senses of self, that seek primarily to create a coherent historical narrative, or that seek to provide a complete catharsis of childhood trauma.

Kohut (1971, 1977), to my knowledge, was the first theoretician to emphasize the importance of empathic failures in the vicissitudes of self-development, labeling the healthy, structure-promoting episodes of such failures "optimal frustration." In his words, "Tolerable disappointments in the pre-existing (and externally sustained) primary narcissistic equilibrium lead to the establishment of internal structures which provide the ability for self-soothing and the acquisition of basic tension tolerance in the narcissistic realm" (Kohut, 1971, p. 64).

Stolorow et al. (1987) later challenged this concept, emphasizing the importance of the *responsiveness* of the primary caretaker/therapist to empathic breaks. They objected to that aspect of Kohut's concept that retained a "quantitative," or "economic" metaphor, which they attributed to holdovers from drive theory. In their words:

> We are contending here that it is not solely or even primarily the "quantity" of the accompanying depressive affects that determines whether they will be experienced as traumatic and self-disintegrative or as tolerable. . . . We believe that what is crucial to the child's (and patient's) growing capacity to integrate his sadness and his painful disappointments . . . is the reliable presence of a calming, understanding caregiver, irrespective of the "amount" or intensity of the affects involved. (p. 75)

In previous chapters, I have described the evidence suggesting that Sandy lacked a responsive caretaker in her earliest life. The quintessential traumatic experience for Sandy, however, was a *sequence* of interpersonal events: first, finding herself appreciated and cared about by an adult (in this sequence, her chronological age was of no consequence), who seems to hold the promise of meeting an intense and unfilled need; second, allowing herself to trust the person(s), and to begin to develop hope that perhaps she could, after all, be loved; and third, a totally unexpected and violent disillusionment in the people who seemed to promise so much. The fourth and final part of the sequence, both in her early experiences and in subsequent enactments, was a reaction of self-hatred and humiliation for having been such a fool as to think she could allow herself hope, which often would lead to self-destructive behavior.

It is apparent that this sequence can define the experience of a needy child turning to a parent who holds out the promise of reliable soothing and caretaking, but who, at crucial moments, rejects the child. What proved devastating for Sandy, however, was that the sequence culminated in violent sexual abuse. Thus it developed that subsequent enactments of the modal scene, in which the assaults were almost always psychological, were experienced by Sandy as physical, sexual assaults. It is a sequence that occurred countless times in Sandy's outside life and many times within the therapy.

If one accepts this sequence as plausible, it invites further questions about how to characterize it. A classic self-psychological perspective might propose that the sequence begins with a break in empathy—a misperception of what the patient was trying to convey, and what she needed at that point in time. This rupture in the selfobject relationship initiated a disintegration of the self, an experience that brought back with extreme intensity previous, highly traumatic, episodes of empathic rupture. Goldberg (1990) offers an additional perspective:

> If the analyst is to realize the transference with [such a] patient, it may, or perhaps must, be done in the form of a mutual enactment. . . . We once again wonder if a successful treatment requires that some of these transferences be actualized in behavior. (p. 132)

The classical self-psychology understanding of the sequence beginning with a break in empathy begs the question of whether such a break is itself, in some way, unconsciously induced by the patient. This question in turn, however invites, if not an infinite regress, at least a regress going back to the beginning of the therapeutic relationship. The point may be moot. In Bromberg's words (1996):

> As an enactment begins, an analyst will inevitably shift his self-state when the patient shifts his, but the phenomenon is always a two-way street. An enactment can just as easily begin with the analyst. . . . Thus, when an enactment begins (no matter by whom it is initiated), no analyst can be immediately attuned to the shift in here-and-now reality, and he inevitably becomes part of the dissociative process, at least for a period of time. (p. 527)

However the sequence begins, when the therapist reacts out of his own needs and unreflectively, it is traumatic to the patient. Schore (2003b, p. 86) has stated that the patient who receives an unmodulated stressful communication from the therapist becomes psychophysiologically dysregulated in a repetition of her early history of such events. A representation of "dysregulated-self-in-interaction-with-a-misattuning-object" is activated, triggering an expectation of imminent self-disorganization.

The first major empathic break in my therapy with Sandy, clearly, was my unbidden and impulsive reaction when I experienced her as not addressing the feelings connected with having brought in her dream painting, in the previous session. My attack was psychological, an accusatory riposte; her experience was of a physical as well as psychological attack, sexual and overwhelming, and led directly to repeated and extended cuts on her abdomen.[2]

It may be useful to point out that the patient had been able to bring in her anxiety-laden painting in the first place only because of more than a year of "good enough" empathic therapy, and, consequently, the beginning of a trusting relationship. Indeed, this is a necessary first step in the enactment. To take some of the mystery out of my subsequent unempathic criticism, or attack, it seems plausible to me that I had simply not attended within myself to how hard-won and costly my empathic efforts had been, over the previous many months. I had accepted consciously that my intense efforts might take a very long time to produce a mutuality that would reflect progress (and, I might add, personal competence). When, however, I heard the all too familiar, "Fine," following what had seemed to me a breakthrough session, I was caught completely off-guard, and responded with a level of frustration I didn't know I had. I thus entered into a major reenactment of Sandy's trauma — what Lichtenberg (1989) refers to as the reconstruction of a "modal scene."

I do not believe that Sandy's reexperience of her modal trauma in this instance, and my subsequent efforts at empathy and understanding, were reparative; regretfully, the entire sequence of transactions was much closer to the original, overwhelming experience, than to Kohut's model of "optimal frustration." It was only from my subsequent understanding of what had taken place that subsequent empathic ruptures and reenactments were attenuated, could be grasped more quickly, and the therapeutic relationship reestablished more readily.

A second example of a reenactment involving an unempathic response on my part concerned the issue of hospitalization. In reading the clinical material, it would be understandable if the reader found him/herself disturbed that I did not unequivocally insist on the patient's hospitalization many more times, and then follow through. It is certainly my reaction in reviewing the treatment.

Again, Sandy and I were coconspirators. She, through her actions and presentation of self, would convey that she could not be trusted to keep herself safe; I would then raise the necessity of hospitalization, at times quite vigorously. (Whether she could have been committed against her will at these times, under Illinois law, is open to question.) There would follow a dramatic reversal in her apparent ego-strength (seemingly without dissociation). As we approached the reality of taking action, she would make a compelling case that hospitalization would, after all, be extremely disruptive and damaging to her family and business life, and she would propose some other way to address the dangers of outpatient work—involvement of her husband in oversight, scheduled phone sessions, "contracts" not to hurt herself, and so forth. I would find my resolve evaporating—wholly aided and abetted by my reluctance in the first place to hospitalize her.

I nevertheless count our exchanges over this issue as ultimately contributing to the strengthening of Sandy's sense of self. Early on, it would be apparent after the fact that it frightened her that she could manipulate me, in both conveying a desperate need for hospitalization, and then an apparent capacity to convince me otherwise. As these episodes recurred, however, their intersubjective meaning seemed to shift. Initially, the sequence was: a) empathic concern, b) a shift in the patient's apparent ego strength, c) unempathic confusion on the part of the therapist, infused with self-interest, and d) anger, on the part of the patient, but accompanied often with an apparent diminution of self-destructiveness,. The sequence later became something healthier. In the postargument we would have after an aborted hospitalization, she would remonstrate that, by having let myself be talked out of hospitalization, I had not really protected her (even though nothing catastrophic had subsequently happened). I would get defensive; I would counterargue, insisting she look at the facts as they had presented themselves to me. She would in turn counter with a deconstruction of my rationalizations.

After one such session, exhausted and annoyed that I had been outargued, and left confused as to whether, a) I had been negligent in protecting her from harm, b) had followed a proper therapeutic course, or c) had simply fallen victim to my own countertransferences, it occurred to me that our argumentative discussion had been, for all the world, like an unremarkable fight with my wife! That is to say: we were two adults, equal and ordinary, having a fight about something that touched on each of our self-esteems. Neither of us was "crazy," in making our case; but neither of us was free of defensiveness and rationalizations. If the content could have been disguised, no outside observer would have realized one person was a psychoanalyst and the other a patient. (I am not terribly good at winning arguments with my wife, either.)

A third example of an ostensible break in the empathy seems to me to have been clearly reparative. In chapter 2, I have described the appearance one day in the session of a child sense of self, who had hidden behind my chair and begun cutting him/herself. I felt I had no choice but to be intrusive. Davies and Frawley (1994) have said, "We believe the patient's behavior and her unconscious fantasy invite certain activity by the analyst, particularly the kind of penetrating, overstimulating activity the patient is most hypervigilant to" (p. 122). This was certainly true in the first example, likely true in the second, and perhaps in this one as well. On this occasion, however, my countertransference did not lead to sudden, unintended action.

When I realized that the patient was harming herself, I forewarned her that, since she would not give me the razor voluntarily, I was about to violate her space and take it from her. I told her that I regretted having to take that action, and I repeated this regret after the fact. Then, when the patient repeatedly corrected me about "his" age and gender, I would not be dissuaded from continuing to address our affective exchange, indicating that my basic concern was for the patient's safety and *feelings*, not the "persona" which was the scaffold around them. "Whatever," was my response—meaning, of course, "Whoever"; an intuitive effort on my part to declare my priorities and what I regarded as most important to the patient—her safety—even if it was not manifestly empathic with the "little boy" in front of me.

It is possible that this particular sense of self lost its *raison d'être* with this unempathic/empathic intervention—the discovery that there was an adult in this world who would not stand idly by while a child was being hurt. In any case, I never saw her/him again.

NOTES

1. I am indebted to Arnold Goldberg for bringing this reference to my attention in his book, *Misunderstanding Freud* (2004).

2. Very late in the therapy, Sandy volunteered that the cutting of her abdomen had actually been a substitute for cutting herself "down below." I suspect this awareness came about as a result of the therapy, and that it originally was a manifestation of what Freud described as "displacement upwards" — that is, was unconscious.

SIXTEEN

Treatment: Psychoanalytic Perspectives II

Working-through requires many skills on the part of the patient and the therapist, and in some ways remains as mysterious as the capacity to develop MPD in the first place.

—Marmer (1991, p. 686)

There is an early and interesting contribution to the literature on the treatment of multiple personality disorder describing the psychoanalysis of a patient with this disorder, by Marmer (1980). A notable aspect of the case described is that the patient underwent psychotherapy for symptoms of MPD fifteen years *before* Marmer's treatment—which would have been in the 1960s. There are several interesting aspects of this earlier treatment, not least being its time frame: the patient was exhibiting MPD symptoms, and received psychoanalytically oriented treatment for her condition, at least two decades before the syndrome became generally familiar to the lay public and diagnosed with increasing frequency by psychiatrists. (But not, the ever-alert skeptic will point out, before the publication of *The Three Faces of Eve*.)

It is also of interest that her symptoms of dissociative senses of self cleared up, in this earlier treatment, and the patient was free of them for many years—reappearing again only after a major psychological stress that led her to Marmer's office. Now, however, her alternate presentations of self were somewhat different from those she reported had earlier been the case. In the previous treatment, she stated, the alternate selves had been identified by colors: she had described to her previous therapist "red person," "green person," and "yellow person." Now, she said, they actually had names: Jane, Child, and Witchy.[1]

Marmer's treatment was apparently successful, although he does not describe in detail the outcome. The final aspect of the case report I find interesting is its overall format and description: it is a classic psychoanalytic case study, focused entirely on the patient's symptoms, transference developments, and progress, with the analyst dimly seen as a neutral authority, simply observing and interpreting the data with which he is presented. This was in keeping with decades of strict adherence to so-called neutrality—at least in psychoanalytic writings –following Freud's disapproval of Ferenczi's claim that some patients required active evidence of the analyst's caring.

Despite major revisions in understanding the nature of the analyst's contribution to psychoanalysis since Marmer's paper, the classical perspective continues to have adherents, however, even in the treatment of patients who were the victims of sexual abuse. Thus, in Cruz and Essen's consideration of the possible causes of premature termination (1994), the analyst, presumably neutral and self-contained, is entirely absent:

> Throughout treatment there is always a risk of the patient interrupting the process, whether because of negative transference, insurmountable resistance, a flight into health, a decrease in motivation, or numerous other factors [lack of ego resources, external events, etc.]. (p. 71)

The authors seem to assume that the well-analyzed psychoanalyst, like a well-tempered clavier, will be an instrument of exquisite sensitivity and perfect pitch:

> A show of authentic interest in the patient and his or her problems should be complemented by a consistent, congruent, and reliable therapeutic atmosphere. (p. 53)

> Therapists must avoid responding with shock or surprise to the adult survivor's disclosures or descriptions of how they have dealt with abuse. (p. 61)

Perhaps such characterizations of the analyst's role should not be surprising. Mollon, in 1996, suggested that there continued to exist a "code" as to what is and is not "psychoanalytic":

> To accept the patient's perception [of childhood abuse] is to risk shame in analytic circles. We may be seen as no more than an empathy-ridden counselor. Unless we are decoding and revealing a hidden text, at odds with the patient's conscious account, we perceive ourselves as analytically impotent. In this way we strive to view ourselves as master (mistress) of the analytic theatre. (p. 55)

Winnicott (1960, 1992, 1996) was the first widely read psychoanalytic theorist after Ferenczi to consider what, beyond neutrality, the analyst may need to provide to successfully treat certain patients. He suggested the idea of the analyst providing a "holding environment," as a necessary precondition to interpretation. In his view, this aspect of the relationship did not constitute a reliving of a previous relationship—that is, a classical transference, but a new experience, or, as Balint (Kahn 1969) put it, a "new beginning." Modell (1968) also discussed the noninterpretive mutative functions the analyst provides. Gedo and Goldberg (1973), and Gedo (1973), within the context of a comprehensive developmental schema, described the need of some patients with early developmental disorders for "pacification," serving to promote control and diminishment of over-stimulation, and "unification," serving to promote cohesion and integration of self.

Beyond very general prescriptive guidelines, however, these writings gave little indication of: a) how the analyst should actually conduct himself or herself in order to create these therapeutic benefits, b) how the demands for meeting these needs might intersect with the average expectable strengths and limitations of a therapist, or c) how the ongoing interaction between therapist and patient might alter and influence the therapeutic intentions of the therapist. It was not until the past few decades, when contributors such as Kohut, Goldberg, Stolorow, Atwood, Gill, and Hoffman began to look at the therapeutic relationship itself that these issues began to be addressed. Within this more recent literature, empathic failures, whether or not designated "countertransference," were acknowledged to be unavoidable and inevitable, and consideration was given to their role in the therapeutic process.

The clinical section of this book amply reveals empathic failures, and I have given them theoretical consideration in the previous chapter. If the reparation of empathic breaks is crucial to the enterprise, however, as these modern theorists have postulated, then surely there has to be a solid base of empathic immersion into the patient's subjectivity in the first place, to sustain the therapy. In this chapter I wish to consider those less dramatic aspects of the therapy that I believe provided the firm ground on which we stood, during rocky times.

The first, and perhaps most crucial, therapeutic intervention was my recognition early on that the patient was deeply troubled, and in need of intensive therapy. She did not come to me seeking therapy for herself, and in agreeing to enter into individual treatment, did not identify something she "wanted to work on"—that is, there was no "therapeutic contract" (Ross 1989). Rather, there was my intuition that behind this woman's façade that everything was now "fine" following our short-term couple therapy, there were hidden depths of sadness and a covert willingness to uncover her demons (little did I know!). I took as supportive evidence her agreement to enter into three-times-a-week psychotherapy.

Ross (op. cit.) talks about the usefulness, particularly in the therapy of DID patients, of "chatting." In his words: "Chatting is good not just for a minute or two at the beginning of a session, but as a normal experience for the patient. . . . It gives the patient the experience of being regarded as a normal human being" (p. 308).

I would go beyond Ross to say that chatting was crucial to Sandy's therapy. In the early months, chatting occupied more than half of most sessions, allowing the patient to feel sufficiently comfortable and safe for me to ask finally about her unhappiness. For example: she was raising adolescent children; I was doing the same, a couple years ahead of her. I could empathize and commiserate, and we could compare notes. (If there are experts in providing advice on how to live contentedly with adolescents, I am not among them.) We had traveled to some of the same vacation destinations; we could talk about those experiences. Sandy might venture to talk of some extreme discomfort or embarrassment in business gatherings; I could share similar experiences in professional meetings. To a degree far greater than I even imagined at the time, Sandy experienced these as the most "normal" conversations she had ever had in her life.

Virtually all authors who write about the treatment of severely disturbed patients cite the extreme importance of therapists being authentic and honest. Renik (1999) has said, "A willingness to self-disclosure on the analyst's part facilitates self-disclosure by the patient, and therefore productive dialectical interchange between analyst and patient is maximized" (p. 65). Mitchell (1993), however, adds the important caveat that, "Authenticity in the analyst has less to do with saying everything than in the genuineness of what actually is said" (p. 146).

Orange et al. (1997) define the intersubjectivist stance in regard to the issue:

> Although recognizing that the analyst is constantly unwittingly revealing his or her psychological organization to the patient, the methodology of empathic-introspective inquiry does not prescribe deliberate self-disclosure by the analyst. Instead . . . it enjoins the analyst to make specific decisions about self-disclosures on the basis of his or her best understanding of the likely meanings of such disclosures for the patient and analyst, and on his or her assessment, arrived at with varying degrees of collaborative input from the patient, of whether such interacting meanings are likely to facilitate or obstruct the analytic process—the unfolding, exploration, illumination, and transformation of the patient's subjective world. (p. 44)

Over time, as Sandy became more comfortable and then more intensely involved, she became as adept at reading my facial expressions and subtle mood variations as I was of hers.[2] She would ask, "Is something wrong?"—often before I was even aware that I was having a troubling thought. I would think about it, and answer—more often than not very directly, although, if it involved my personal life, I would say so and indicate it was not something I wished to talk about. She would invariably understand, and back off.

Occasionally, even if the issue on my mind *was* personal, I would share it—for example, some *contretemps* with one of my kids. The choice of what and whether to share was based on my assessing whether the issue at hand was something Sandy also struggled with, and whether it was something the sharing of which would not risk leaving *me* feeling so vulnerable that the patient would feel the need to take care of me. It was not exactly modeling—unless what I was modeling was, for example, the occasional befuddlement and feelings of helplessness engendered by raising teenagers.

Thus, the personal reflections I shared were, to my knowledge, never for me at the expense of the patient—I was not attempting to work out a problem, or covertly asking for help, or taking up time that the patient needed in order to talk about *her* problems. I emphasize that I was *unaware* of ever doing so; it is certainly possible that I did—even in which case, however, I am not sure Sandy would regard it as having been detrimental to her therapy. Presuming I am correct that there was no egregious overstepping of bounds in this particular regard, I suspect that, as the social-constructivist perspective has alerted us (Hoffman 1983, 1992, 1998), Sandy sensed *my intention* in purposeful sharing, and this, beyond the content, contributed to her sense of being respected. I hoped, in accordance with the authors I have referenced, that Sandy would take from these exchanges how very much alike we were as human beings, with strengths and weaknesses. I count this, too, an essential part of the therapy, with someone who regarded herself as grotesque, perverse, and less than human.

"Respect for the patient" would hardly seem to require elaboration in discussing a psychotherapy case. With the DID patient, however, this becomes a rather tricky business. How do you maintain your sense of respect when challenged with intensely provocative behavior both within and without sessions, and how does respect for one presentation of self interweave with respect for other presentations of self?

Ross (op. cit.) gives the following anecdote:

> The adolescent came out in a session at my request and made it clear that there was nothing I could do to ensure that the patient made her appointments. I therefore stopped making appointments with the host personality altogether and said I would only make appointments with the adolescent, at her request. The host personality thought this was very unfair—"Why should *she* have the appointment and not *me*? *I'm* the one who's in therapy!" I replied that it was too bad, but that was how I was going to handle it. (p. 255)

At first reading, one might be inclined to consider Ross's action disrespectful, and feel that the patient (the "host" personality) was exactly right—who is in therapy here, after all? However, the patient was, in fact, missing sessions, apparently because the "adolescent alter" would take control and prevent her from coming. Which was more empathic: respecting the expressed (conscious) wishes of the "host" personality (while she continued, seemingly helplessly, to miss sessions), or dealing with what can be regarded as a resistance, through an active, directive intervention that might enhance the likelihood that the patient would come for her sessions? Even if one declines Ross's views of co-equal personalities, it is still possible to interpret this intervention as empathically accepting the patient's ambivalence toward the therapy, allowing that aspect of self containing her suspicion and anger to be present in the room. It seems also clear that Ross's declaration was clear, authentic, and genuine.

What it does *not* do, of course, is acknowledge and *explore* the patient's resistance from an empathic introspective stance. But that's the rub with dissociative identity disorder patients: the patient does not *experience* the behavior—even, it would seem, at an unconscious level—as her own resistance. In circumstances such as Ross describes, the therapist can't empathize with the hidden fear of, or anger about, sessions, in the hopes of making the unconscious conscious, because, in a very significant sense, those feelings are not there. One cannot, following accepted psychoanalytic technique, lift the repression barrier by empathic immersion in the hidden anxieties and sensitive interpretation of the resistance, because they are not repressed—they are dissociated.

Ross is among those many authors to whom I have previously referred who state flatly that the treatment of MPD necessarily involves getting in touch with and relating to all the dissociated alters. In Ross's words: "It is impossible to treat MPD without mapping the system. . . . A full map includes the name, age, time of appearance, function, degree of amnesia, position in the system, internal alliances, and any other relevant traits of each alter personality" (p. 235).

Ross further thinks that this requires no particular therapeutic sensitivity or advanced training: "Calling out alter personalities is a skill that could be easily learned by all medical students in a two-month rotation if there was enough opportunity" (p. 229).

My eventual view of what empathy for the patient meant precluded such an activity. I am not sure how many altered senses of self Sandy actually possessed; I am not sure I ever met all of them, and a few I met only once. It seems to me possible, however, that, if a therapist has a very explicit, self-assured protocol of how to proceed in therapy—a procedure which includes mapping the altered senses of self—it may not necessarily be experienced by a patient as disrespectful, but rather: "This is just how it's done." Like going to a dentist.

I am puzzled, however, by how it is possible to truly empathize with and respect the so-called "host" personality when that very nomenclature reveals your view of the patient as simply one among many. Sandy once told me, as I have earlier mentioned, that the Sandy I saw in my office did not exist outside my door—as soon as she entered the real world, other "compartments" took over. That, to me, did not make Sandy any less my "real," and only, patient. I reframed her description with the metaphor that, as soon as she left my office, it was necessary to put on one of several uniforms, to present to the world a competent façade—and when she did so, she temporarily became what the uniform signified. Without these uniforms, she felt naked and completely vulnerable.

Another attribute of an effective therapist is the elusive quality, "caring"—a slippery slope, most therapists would agree, but one which is even more essential and even more problematic with DID patients than others. Dissociative identity disorder patients tend to be chronic suicide risks, and repeatedly engage in actual and threatened self-destructive behaviors. How far can one's "caring" go? Again, Ross: "The therapist who is desperate to 'save' the patient and is incessantly worried and frightened won't be able to tolerate the work" (p. 258).

I partially agree, and believe that if I were to treat another DID patient, I would be less vulnerable to falling into "saving" behaviors. I believe, however, as I have tried to make clear through narrating my own experiences as well as quoting extensively from the literature, that it is virtually impossible not to get tangled in such feelings with these patients, however one chooses to deal with them. We are, first of all, merely human—however self-possessed, well analyzed, or immersed in the medical model we may be. When our patient in session or on the phone is threatening self-harm, with a proven track record, it is almost impossible not to react emotionally. Whether we try to empathize, become firm, plead, interpret, or even yell in frustrated rage at the patient, our reaction is almost inevitably an expression of concern. In Davis and Frawley's words (op. cit.):

> Here, as therapists, we dance on the head of a pin, caught maddeningly
> between the dangers of under- and overreaction to the patient's violent
> behavior. We assume . . . that we will fall prey to both extremes of the
> countertransferential valence. It is only as we fail the patient that we
> enable her to rework the dissociated matrices of relational paradigms
> that have become her unique legacy. (p. 146)

Clinical wisdom or rationalization? Ultimately, it may be impossible to decide which is the prevailing truth, in any given therapy with DID patients; that it is common clinical *experience*, however, there can be no doubt. Mitchell (1993) summarizes the issue this way:

> In my view, what is most important is not what the analyst does, as
> long as he struggles to do what seems, at the moment, to be the right
> thing; what is most important is the way in which analyst and analy-
> sand come to understand what has happened. What is most crucial is
> that, whatever the analyst does, whether acting flexibly or standing
> firm, he does it with considerable self-reflection, an openness to ques-

tion and reconsider, and most important, with the patient's best interests at heart. (p. 195)

I agree.

NOTES

1. Has our skeptic's voice grown louder? Had the patient in fact read about the "three faces" of Eve, and developed her own "three faces" accordingly? (Of course, there would have been *four*, counting the core personality.)

2. I am indebted to those authors (Aron 1991; Gill and Hoffman 1982; Hoffman 1983, 1998; Joseph 1989; Sandler 1987) who have alerted us to the reality that patients are "reading" us just as we are "reading" them, often with great accuracy. Armed with this awareness, I endeavored to make it acceptable to Sandy to share her observations.

SEVENTEEN

Narrative

> There seems no doubt but that a well-constructed story possesses a
> kind of narrative truth that is real and immediate and carries an impor-
> tant significance for the process of therapeutic change.
>
> —Spence (1982, p. 21)

Hacking, in his book on multiple personality disorder from which I have
quoted extensively (1995), sums up his views of its treatment in this way:

> [Some] fear that multiple personality therapy leads to a false conscious-
> ness. Not in the blatant sense that the apparent memories of early
> abuse are necessarily wrong or distorted—they may be true enough.
> No, there is the sense that the end product is a thoroughly crafted
> person, but not a person who serves the ends for which we are persons.
> Not a person with self-knowledge, but a person who is the worse for
> having a glib patter that simulates an understanding of herself. (p. 266)

What is Hacking getting at here? The simplest reading would be that he
is critical of those cases in which patients, in true hysterical fashion, can
rattle off stories about their traumatic childhoods as explanations of their
entire lives with little affect, and conveying little sense of authenticity. I
have no idea if this description characterizes most such individuals, a
great many, or a few. Perhaps this author believes it is true of many, but
he seems to be making a generalization beyond statistics.

Hacking may rather be getting at something more profound, which
goes to the heart of modern psychotherapeutics—at least those of a
psychodynamic orientation, as well as those concerned with the treatment of dissociative identity disorder, namely: the role of historical narrative, as it relates to psychopathology in the adult, and to successful
treatment. Are the general assumptions made about the correlation between plausible narrative, psychiatric symptoms, and positive outcome
justified?

161

Interestingly, this is less problematic for classical psychoanalysis than its contemporary versions. Classical analysis also develops a narrative, over the course of the treatment, but the story has much less to do with the alleged truth of events in the patient's childhood than in the patient's intense feelings and fantasies about the important people from that period in her life.[1] What unfolds, and is revealed, in the psychoanalysis is less "what happened" to the patient, than who the patient felt herself to be in relationship to those who created her childhood, her yearnings and fears in regard to them, and her interpretations of their intentions and involvements. Spence, in the book from which is taken the quotation that introduces this chapter, makes the case that "narrative truth" is a more accurate and compelling description of what a psychoanalyst provides his patient than "historical truth."

In the treatment of serious disorders of the self, however—borderline personality disorders, narcissistic disorders, and dissociative disorders (some would also still include certain psychotic disorders)—the understanding of *what happened* seems like important and necessary data, over and above a patient's fantasies, internal conflicts, and instinct-driven elaborations and distortions. It does not feel sufficient to say, of the patient who makes a serious suicide attempt after her abusive boyfriend walks out on her, that she is, in the language of psychoanalytic ego psychology, simply revealing an "ego weakness," or that she has excessive dependency needs. One wants to know: *why* did the patient place such unrealistic hopes on such an unlikely prospect? *Why* does loss of such an object lead to feelings that life is not worth living, rather than, alternatively, anger? *Why* is she so impervious to the interpretations and insights the therapist tries to provide her? The dynamics of sado-masochism, wishes for dependency gratification, and primitive instinctual rage, all feel like insufficient explanations to many contemporary psychoanalysts. The sense is, rather, that these patients did not have childhoods and parental caretaking that were anything like what most of us experienced.

The problem, however, as Spence has so articulately elaborated, is that we almost always are without means of accurately determining *what happened.* We have the patient's memories, dreams, snippets of past reality in the form of photographs, diaries, and so forth, and transference distortions. And it is not enough to make us *sure.* Freud likened the practice of psychoanalysis to the profession of archeology: the analyst is unearthing actual past events, and is essentially putting together shards of broken vases to create a whole picture of what previously existed. Spence makes clear how inaccurate this metaphor is. The patient gives us verbal translations of visual impressions, which themselves are only fragmentary, and which only point to, rather than capture, the visual; to this the analyst brings his own imagery—derived from theory, intuition, life experiences, and so forth—and rewords what the patient has said. The patient adds more words, in response, and those words have as much or more to do with how the patient is feeling about the analyst—whether she is wanting to please him, placate him, challenge him, seduce him, whatever—as with the resonance of the analyst's remarks to the original visual impressions. From this, the analyst is supposed to arrive at a historical truth.

Spence does not, as a consequence of his views, dismiss the entire psychoanalytic enterprise as rubbish, à la critics like Frederick Crews (2006); rather, he proposes a different understanding of what constitutes a compelling and therapeutic psychoanalytic interpretation: namely, that it is a statement that captures a *narrative* truth—which feels meaningful, aesthetically pleasing, and synthesizing—rather than necessarily a historical truth. He attributes to Viderman (1979) the view that the psychoanalyst is more like a poet than a historian, and gives a lovely vignette illustrating Viderman's thesis. In the example (Spence, op. cit., p. 178) a patient presents the following dream to Viderman (the analysis is conducted in French): "My father and I are in a garden. I offer him a bouquet of six roses."

Viderman has an intuition that the dream is about the patient's ambivalent feelings about his father, who died of cirrhosis of the liver, due to alcoholism. His response takes advantage of the phonetic similarity, in French, between "six roses" and "cirrhosis," and thus he replies, in French: "Six roses ou cirrhose?" The author explains that the interpretation is designed to open up new possibilities, to bring new ideas together in a new and potentially evocative combination. He has done so in a clever, aesthetically pleasing way, raising a pithy question the patient will not soon forget. It has no clear reference to a past historical reality, and indeed does not require an actual historical antecedent. What matters is the future—what the patient will do with this interpretation.

To the therapist treating someone whose life, or at least whose physical integrity and well-being, seem to be hanging by a thread, such interpretations sound like they belong to a whole other genre of therapy—playful, creative, inviting of dialogue in some transitional space. When the therapist is confronted with a patient in a truly existential crisis, however, he is looking rather desperately for an interpretation that says something like: *Look! Stop! You need not do what you are doing! You are reacting to thus-and-so event in your past, not to what is happening in the here and now!*

This was certainly the spirit in which, first, I identified in Sandy a sequential reaction: a) trusting me, b) interpreting my conduct as betraying that trust, c) experiencing a physical sensation of fullness and severe pain in her pelvic area, together with disorientation and shock, and d) wanting to punish herself in some way—and second, interpreted this sequence to her as a recapitulation of childhood sexual abuse. Was my interpretation one of historical truth—which Spence, among others, would claim is highly unlikely—or one of narrative truth? Or did it have any truth value at all? I have an answer for the last question, at least: despite having no immediate efficacious effect, nor eliciting an "ah-ha!" response, it did seem ultimately meaningful to Sandy.

I have already spelled out the narrative of her childhood that I co-created with Sandy, namely that, between the ages of five and six, she was cajoled into entering a house, located near her school, where she was treated to milk and cookies, extravagantly praised for her prettiness and charm, petted, and otherwise treated with warmth and appreciation by a small group of people who thus met an emotional craving that was a consequence of a self-absorbed mother and distant father. This attention was deliberate, manipulative, and in the service of perverse sexual proclivities on the part of the adults, who, once feeling certain of the neediness and compliance of the child now in their control, turned their attention to fulfillment of their desires, in the process transforming the child into a dehumanized sexual object. Narrative, or historical?

I find the story compelling. Sandy finds it anxiety provoking, but believable. Spence, however, is right: there are innumerable places, in the construction of this story, that I have brought my own intuitions, theories, and predilections to bear, in ways that I cannot rationally defend. Here are some examples: I have mentioned that Sandy's seminal painting of the recurrent dream that plagued her life featured a large male face in the middle, facing outward. I have reported Sandy as having said that, in the original painting, family members had told her that the face resembled her grandfather. She didn't think it should look like him, and re-painted the face.

I have not previously mentioned—or perhaps did so in passing—that the painting also featured a large sofa-arm. Sandy told me that the sofa portrayed was a sofa in the home of her grandparents. Elsewhere, I mentioned, also in passing, that at a particular point in time, Sandy brought in drawings of stick figures: girls, with objects being thrust into them sexually. In several, the figures were bent over a sofa. Finally, I have described to the reader a hallucination the patient would sometimes have, while conversing with a man, of an erect penis, surrounded by white pubic hair.

I have just presented the reader with enough data to suggest the possibility that another narrative of sexual abuse—modifying, or even replacing, the narrative I have presented—could be constructed, which featured her grandfather as abuser. I will also tell you that this is an avenue of exploration that I never pursued with any vigor—although I did not neglect it entirely. I raised some questions that pointed to the possible implication of Sandy's grandfather, but in response to her firm negative responses, I dropped the matter. Did I thereby miss the "real" history of Sandy's childhood abuse? Was the whole improbable narrative about neighbors, in a house on a street near her school, a ruse, a displacement from something closer to home? I continue to think not; there were too many disparate pieces of evidence, seemingly not initially connected in the patient's mind, to suggest an elaborate fabrication. Still: might it not be the case that the patient's grandfather was also an abuser? If you ask me why I did not pursue this possibility more vigorously, my only answer is that I sensed that, *for whatever reasons,* Sandy simply would not go there. At the same time, the need to have some sort of plausible, satisfying story of something having happened felt imperative, and the bits and pieces of data pointing to the narrative we created felt compelling.

I have made only relatively brief mention of another narrative—this one buttressed by a diary—that seemed to point to other experiences of painful, if not traumatic, betrayal by an adult, namely the patient's relationship with a minister, Reverend Pete, during her adolescent years. For a considerable period of time in the middle of therapy, this part of her life history preoccupied us, as she struggled to remember events reported in her diary and to make sense of inchoate feelings of anguish and guilt in relationship to Reverend Pete. There were many other fleeting images, feelings, and quasi memories from her adolescence, sexual in nature, that we tried—mostly unsuccessfully—to weave into a coherent narrative. After the material pointing toward much earlier trauma began to emerge, we dropped this narrative altogether, and never returned to it. Was it relevant? Was it crucial to an overall, ultimate understanding of Sandy's story? I have no idea. At what point does one stop trying to weave the infinite events of a life into a plausible narrative that accounts for the major facets of who one has come to be, as an adult? By what criteria does one differentiate between "significant" and "insignificant" life experiences?

Earlier, I have quoted Murphy (op. cit.) as claiming that much of what is given as fact, in the DSM classification system, amounts to nothing more than "folk psychology," and is without established scientific foundation. Certainly this is even more true of psychotherapy. What counts as evidence that childhood events have led to adult psychopathology? Merskey and Piper want to start with objective, eyewitness confirmation of the allegedly pathogenic childhood events. Hard enough to find even when the abuse has been overtly violent and sexual; impossible if the pathogenesis is alleged to involve a disengaged, or unreliable, or double-binding mother. Some therapists, as I have discussed, simply take at face value what their patients tell them about their unhappy childhoods, and take it as a given that the patient has put her finger on the problem; or, they believe they find the historical truth revealed in dreams and associations. Psychoanalysts of all varieties find the transference relationship compelling: the patient who experiences gentle inquiry as a sadistic intrusion, or who demands complete attention, with no interest in what the therapist has to say, seems to be distorting the reality of the current, adult-to-adult relationship, in accordance with unconscious expectations, or needs, or experiences from another era. But however the evidence is gleaned, however plausible it may seem to the therapist, is it truly necessary to make a story of it? Does "cure" *require* that the patient have a new historical narrative of her life, different from that with which she began therapy?

Hacking seems to be questioning this, at least for DID patients. His concern would seem to be that the stories we, as therapists, develop, together with our patients, may at times be reductive, and diminish the richness and complexity of what it is to be human, rather than enhance it. I understand the point; it is not uncommon to meet someone, either a patient or acquaintance, who defines himself almost entirely in terms of the twelve-step program with which he is involved: he is a "recovering alcoholic," and in his telling, addiction, or recovery from it, accounts for every aspect of his life that bears mentioning.

One of the fascinating aspects of Sandy's case is that she fiercely resisted being reduced to a story about childhood abuse. I trust I have made clear the defensive aspects of this stance: if something had been done to her, that meant it could not be *undone*; she could not, through discipline and perfectionism, become someone different than a person who had been seriously wounded—or so, at least, she feared. Beyond her defenses, though, it seemed to me that she simply was unwilling to define herself as a "victim." Perhaps it speaks to some of the good things that she got from her early parenting that, even in her worst moments, she almost never gave up the belief that she could ultimately prevail— even if that belief was, for a time, being held by an alternative sense of self, rather than by her depleted core personhood.

Here, however, is an example of how complicated, how confusing, how imprecise, the interweaving is of our actual past, our memories, and our present. At the end of chapter 5, I quoted Sandy's answer to my question: what would you lose if you accepted the reality that you were sexually abused as a child, by a group of adults? Her answer was that it would mean the whole event meant . . . nothing. That she was just a gullible little kid who had been raped. That's all. Previously, I commented on the poignancy of her response. What I would like to point to now is that, in her answer, she is acknowledging *that there was, in fact, an event—* the only thing that she seems to be changing is what the event *meant*. In other words, she is acknowledging that some things took place, with a group of people, at a particular time and place, that included sexual activity—whereas what she had previously been adamantly claiming was that she had no memory of any such event, only peculiar, isolated images and "body-memories." At what point had she in fact a memory of actual people, in whom she had placed a desperate hope that they love and appreciate her, and who betrayed her? Moments before, after I'd asked the question? In the course of our work together in the previous months? For years? Could it be that she herself could not have answered the question in a way that was historically accurate?

There are different ways of viewing one's life as having been difficult, and Sandy's way is not the way that Hacking worries about. I believe, today, she would say of her past life that it was difficult—even horrendously difficult—but, even accepting the reality of childhood traumatic abuse, and of a mother who often seemed oblivious of her needs, she would not define the difficulties as someone else's fault. It is rather as if she viewed her life as a path that was strewn with huge obstacles, including razor-sharp rocks, and she had to use every means at her disposal to continue on, and ultimately prevail. To change metaphors, it was the hand she was dealt, and to complain about the cards has never made any sense to her.

Therapy is not science, and I think Sandy has been happy to move on, to leave the past behind her, and to flourish, without further asking for a comprehensive accounting of how she came to have the problems she had. As I have indicated, I don't think the childhood sexual abuse theory entirely satisfies her; and in truth, it doesn't entirely satisfy me. Without adopting the rejectionist stance of Merskey and Piper, there are, it seems to me, things we are missing, and, aside from neurobiological considerations, they surely involve the vexed sociocultural factors that are such a point of controversy.

For decades, I have supervised psychiatric residents at an urban university on their patient caseloads, a major percentage of which reflect a lower socioeconomic population of African Americans and Hispanics. I have heard countless stories of childhood physical and sexual abuse, largely at the hands of relatives—without doubt, well over 75 percent of the cases I have supervised. During that time, I have heard about, or helped a resident make a diagnosis of, dissociative identity disorder, only a handful of times, the majority of which I have described in chapter 9. How to account for this discrepancy?

My experience is not unusual, as evidenced both by studies of social dysfunction in lower socioeconomic groups and of the demographics of dissociative identity disorder. Virtually every study of the characteristics of DID patients have demonstrated, as I have noted, that the typical patient is female, Caucasian, and with some college education. What was there about Sandy's white, upper-middle-class upbringing that made her more susceptible to developing dissociative identity disorder than so many poverty-level ethnic minority patients who seemed to have a similar history of childhood sexual abuse? I have conjectures; I have, however, no evidence to support them, either from the clinical or the scientific literature. One of them has to do with isolation.

I will limit my remarks to American culture. No subculture, to my knowledge, countenances childhood sexual or physical abuse. "Spare the rod, spoil the child," to be sure, among certain conservative religious groups; but broken bones, burns, facial trauma, and so forth, are beyond the pale even for these subcultures, not to mention sexual involvement with a child. Let me borrow from Murphy's concept of "folk psychology"—meaning psychological understanding that is so commonly shared that its truth is not generally challenged even by professionals—to propose a concept I shall call "folk knowledge." By this I mean knowledge that one knows, and that one knows that everybody else knows as well—but here, I mean to refer to knowledge within a subculture. The knowledge is experience-near, not experience-distant. The reality of voodoo, in the sub-culture of Haitians in America, might be such an example.

My thesis—or hypothesis—is that, in the lower socioeconomic classes of this country, there is folk knowledge of incest, and childhood abuse, that is different in kind from the knowledge of the middle class—or at least this was true until only very recently. It seems to me that, until recently, most middle-class people knew about child abuse only from the media. (Let us leave aside people who are only one generation removed from poverty, and let us leave aside race, which may reflect nothing more than the lopsided proportion—again, until only quite recently—of Caucasians, compared to minorities, in the middle class.) They did not know a cousin, or a friend, or a neighbor, who was either abused or designated an abuser. I am suggesting that, if you were a poor female child in a single-parent family, living in a ghetto, by the time you were a teenager you had folk knowledge of such phenomena. And by that time, as well, you might have had a rather desperate need to put into some kind of context what had happened to you, at the hands of your mother's boyfriend, before you were even pubescent. I am not suggesting that such experiences were not traumatic. I am raising the question of what may lead to posttraumatic stress symptomatology, versus what may result in dissociative identity disorder.

The skeptics have suggested that TV talk shows and soap operas made knowledge of multiple personality disorder ubiquitous in the 1980s and 1990s, and that hysterics (particularly of the white, middle-class variety) began to flock to gullible doctors, saying: Me too! Again: I have no doubt that this happened, and that some such cases could be counted as "false positives" in any scientific study. The point I am raising is that it might be the case that many such cases were in fact genuine, and in part a consequence of having been raised in a culture where such traumas as violent sexual abuse simply "didn't happen." That is, where the victim had no folk knowledge to counter the overpowering feeling that they were like no one else they knew of, and where they thus felt that they were, in fact, uniquely chosen, uniquely debased, uniquely evil. I propose, then, that, for many such individuals, the talk shows did not contribute to the creation of their syndrome, but revealed—alas, too late to be in the service of prevention—that they were not alone.

Part of this story certainly fits Sandy. She felt utterly, ashamedly, despicably unique. There was nothing about her life story that she felt matched some narrative, shared by others, of parental misattunement, childhood wounds, and extreme coping mechanisms. On the other hand, what she lacked in terms of folk knowledge was *not* later compensated for by public knowledge—she did not tune into the media coverage of the disorder from which she suffered and thereby find herself comforted to be among fellow sufferers.

I have another thought—hypothesis would be too strong a word— that is even more speculative than the above. Let me provide some context.

In the 1980s, I headed a group of researchers at the Illinois State Psychiatric Institute that attempted to replicate some significant findings regarding the relationship of family expressed emotion to relapse in schizophrenic patients (Moline et al. 1985). The original findings had come out of research in Great Britain. The British studies, in brief, had found significant and replicable correlations between the level and sort of emotions expressed by family members in relation to a schizophrenic member of the family, and relapse of that member. High levels of criticism, and/or of "infantalization" of the patient-member of the family, were correlated with relapses requiring hospitalization. My group's intention was to determine whether a lower socioeconomic group of American subjects reflected a similar correlation: that is, whether diagnosed schizophrenics, predominantly of ethnic minority heritage in an American urban setting, were also more likely to relapse if they returned to live with families with high levels of expressed emotion, as defined by the research criteria established in the British studies.

A colleague, Mr. Sant Singh (a psychiatric social worker) and myself, under the tutelage of the original British investigators, learned to conduct the structured family member interview which formed the heart of the research, and to achieve reliability on the instrument. In brief, our findings replicated those of the original studies, but with one interesting caveat: the cutoff level at which family criticism was correlated with patient relapse, in our cohort, was two points higher on the rating scale than any of the British studies, all of which clustered around the same cutoff level. In other words, our American schizophrenic subjects appeared to be able to tolerate higher levels of criticism from their family members, without ill effect, than was true of their British counterparts, at least as measured on this instrument.

I was not surprised. I had lived in Chicago for decades, and taken an elevated transit system to and from work daily, during much of that time, whose riders were predominantly non-Caucasians of lower economic class. I had long ago discovered that what sometimes sounded to me like an alarming escalation of rhetoric and volume between two or more of my fellow riders, was met with apparent indifference and equanimity by the other riders. And they were right: virtually never did a situation that I thought would lead to violence actually escalate into something to be concerned about.

My speculation, in regard to DID, flows from these observations. Rage, rejection, criticism, and certainly abuse, can surely be traumatic and consequential to any child. But might it be the case that children, fairly early in life, learn to identify, and in a sense, comprehend, such behaviors, when they are transparent and overt, and that their intuitive assessment of such behaviors render them less traumatogenic? Might it be that there are *other* sorts of parental interactions—less obvious, less identifiable, more confusing—that lead a child to be more vulnerable to fragmentation as a consequence of *subsequent* physical or sexual abuse? I am speculating, in other words, about a kind of parental pathology that may be more commonly found in the psycho-social milieu of the middle class and that may contribute to the higher rate of DID in that socioeconomic sector. I am speaking of the sort of family pathology Linehan (1993), a cognitive-behaviorist, postulates as etiological in the development of borderline personality disorder, such as the "perfect family," which cannot tolerate negative affects (Sandy's mother comes immediately to mind), or the "typical family," referring to families that supersubscribe to the American ideal of self-reliance, independence, and competitive success.

Tolstoy famously said that all happy families are the same, but unhappy families are each unhappy in their own way. Perhaps the same may be said of the myriad ways in which a parent or caretaker can cocreate a child with vulnerabilities that leave her uniquely prone to the sort of fragmentation that characterizes DID, when exposed to subsequent physical or sexual abuse. Certainly the psychiatric profession has not thus far been very successful in identifying the environmental contributions to other psychiatric disorders, in ways that can be reliably demonstrated, much less to DID. We seem to be a far way still from being able to meet Engel's ideal of a biopsychosocial formulation of any mental illness, in which we can have strong confidence.

NOTE

1. This follows, of course, from Freud's famous—or infamous (Masson 1984)—conclusion that neurotic disorders were not due to childhood traumas, as he had originally thought, but to instinctual conflicts and fantasies.

EIGHTEEN

Neurobiological Considerations

The more I know about how we are designed to function—what neuro-physiology, infant research, affect theory, cognitive psychology, se-mantics, information theory, evolutionary biology, and other pertinent disciplines can tell me about human development—the better I am prepared to be empathic with a patient's communication at a particular time in his or her treatment.

—Basch (1995, p. 372)

We are in fundamental disagreement with Basch's belief that psycho-analytic explanations must be grounded in a knowledge of brain func-tioning. We contend that brain functioning does not even fall within the domain of psychoanalysis.

—Stolorow et al. (1987, p. 6)

When interest in dissociative identity disorder peaked in the 1980s, there were, not surprisingly, a number of investigations into the neurobiology of the disorder. (See, as examples, Flor-Henry et al. 1990; Matthew et al. 1985; Ross et al. 1989. See also Putnam et al. 1990 for an extensive list of research references.) Most such studies reported some abnormal neuro-biological findings, but finding a reliable distinguishing biological mark-er for the condition proved as elusive as finding such a marker has been for any other psychiatric disorder. Also, isolated abnormalities often ei-ther could not be replicated or remained as singular contributions to the literature.

Recently, there have been more promising studies specific to the understanding of dissociative identity disorder. Reinders et al. (2003, 2006) examined eleven DID patients, each of whom exhibited what the authors termed "traumatic identity states" (TIS), who claimed awareness of traumatic memories, and "neutral identity states" (NIS), who did not. They exposed these different self-states to both a neutral and a trauma-related script, then compared sensorimotor, cardiovascular, and regional cerebral blood flow (via positive emission tomography) measures between them. The two groups of distinctive self-state demonstrated significant differences in all three parameters, with different neural networks associated with different processing of the neutral and trauma-related memory script of NIS and TIS.

In another recent study, Sar et al. (2007) investigated regional cerebral blood flow in twenty-one drug-free DID patients compared with nine healthy volunteers. The controls had to be without a history of childhood trauma and without any depressive or dissociative disorder. Regional cerebral blood flow (rCBF) was studied with single photon emission computed tomography (SPECT). Compared with findings in the control group, patients with dissociative identity disorder showed a lower rCBF ration in the orbitofrontal region bilaterally, and a higher rCBF ratio in median and superior frontal regions and occipital regions bilaterally.

Vermetten et al. (2006) noting that smaller hippocampal volume has been reported in several stress-related psychiatric disorders, including posttraumatic stress disorder, borderline personality disorder, and major depressive disorder with early abuse, used magnetic resonance imagining (MRI) to measure the volumes of the hippocampus and amygdala in fifteen female patients with dissociative identity disorder and twenty-three female subjects without DID or any other psychiatric disorder. They found that hippocampal volume was 19.2 percent smaller, and amygdalar volume 31.6 percent smaller, in the patients with dissociative identity disorder, compared to the healthy subjects.

Kelly (2001), hypothesizing on the neurobiological etiology of dissociative identity disorder, proposed what he called an "orbitalfrontal" model, integrating and elaborating on theory and research from four domains: the neurobiology of the orbitalfrontal cortex and its protective inhibitory role in the temporal organization of behavior, the development of emotion regulation, the development of the self, and experience-dependent reorganizing neocortical processes. He proposed that early abusive environments, characterized by discontinuity on the early affective interactions between the infant and the primary caretaker, markedly disrupt the experience-dependent maturation of the orbitalfrontal cortex, and may be responsible for a pattern of lateral inhibition between conflicting subsets of self-representations which are normally integrated into a unified self.

Whether such neurophysiological studies and theorizing have or ought to have any relevance to clinicians treating dissociative identity disorder is, as the quotations given at the beginning of this chapter indicate, a matter of controversy. Ever since Freud abandoned the "Project for a Scientific Psychology" (1957d), psychoanalysis has had, at best, an uneasy relationship with the more objective sciences. For the most part, psychoanalysts have abandoned Freud's hope that psychoanalysis itself could become the means toward an objective science of the mind. An enterprise variously described as self-psychological, intersubjective, social constructivist, or narrative-creating, has come to bear an evermore uncertain relationship to objective knowledge.

However, few psychoanalytic theorists find such knowledge completely irrelevant to the psychoanalytic enterprise. Indeed, what is any theory, even a theory of intersubjectivity, but an attempt to form objective hypotheses about certain kinds of data? The intersubjective theorists extensively quote not only from researchers of infancy such as Emde (1988a, 1988b), Beebe and Lachmann (1988a), and Sandler (1985), all in Stolorow and Atwood (1992), but also from cognitive psychology (Piaget 1954, in Stolorow et al. 1987, p. 36),[1] and even from the sociology of knowledge (Mannheim 1936, in Orange et al. 1997, p. 72). Further, these theorists, like all psychoanalytic clinicians, must ask themselves: How do we judge what interpretations, or understandings, are more compelling, more accurate—more "true," if you will—than others?

One answer, from an intersubjective perspective (Stolorow et al. 1987), is that: "psychoanalytic interpretations must be evaluated in light of distinctly *hermeneutic* criteria" (p. 8). Such criteria, however, include:

> the logical coherence of the argument, the comprehensiveness of the explanation, *the consistency of the interpretations with accepted psychological knowledge,* and the aesthetic beauty of the analysis in disclosing previously hidden patterns of order in the material being investigated. (Atwood and Stolorow 1984, pp. 5–6, my italics)

The idea that psychological knowledge in itself is in any way *objective*, is one that intersubjectivity theorists, as well as many self psychologists, either question or reject outright. In the words of one of these theorists, Stolorow et al. (1987): "[W]e do not believe that the analyst possesses any 'objective' knowledge of the patient's life or of human development and human psychological functioning" (p. 6). This view has many ramifications, for example Orange et al. (1997) claim: "We must insist . . . that there are no mental structures without intersubjective context" (p. 86) and Stolorow and Atwood (1992) claim: "Within the myth of the isolated mind, the world is viewed as having a definitive existence of its own; its experienced substantiality thereby becomes transformed into a metaphysical absolute" (p. 24).

Given this deep suspicion of reification, of mechanistic postulates, and of the objectification of subjective knowledge, it is not surprising that most intersubjective theorists, following upon Kohut in this regard,[2] consider neuroscience as fundamentally irrelevant to an empathically based psychotherapy. The studies cited above, however, seem to point at least to an interrelationship between the psychology of severe disorders of the self, such as DID, and neurobiological changes and deficiencies. I agree with Schore's observation (2003b) that, "When self psychology, like

psychoanalysis in general, discards the biological realm of the body—
when it overemphasizes the cognitive and verbal realms—it commits
Descartes' error, [separating] the most refined operations of mind from
the structure and operation of a biological organism" (p. 111).

The neurobiological studies that seem most relevant to the understanding and treatment of DID are those that address more broadly the
development of self, and its derailments. Travarthen, a researcher of infancy, stated in 1990 that: "The intrinsic regulators of human brain
growth in a child are specifically adapted to be coupled by emotional
communication, to the regulators of adult brains" (p. 357). Similarly,
Buck (1994) stated: "[S]pontaneous emotional communication constitutes
a *conversation between limbic systems* . . . the individuals in spontaneous
communication constitute literally a *biological unit*" (p. 266).

Schore (op. cit.), summarizing a plethora of recent studies, under-
scores the fundamental principle that the baby's brain is not only affected
by interactions with the caretaker, its growth *requires* right brain-right
brain interaction and occurs in the context of an intimate positive affective relationship. In his summary, he states, "attachment is, in essence,
the right-brain regulation of biological synchronicity between organ-
isms" (p. 41).

In short, what contemporary neuroscience investigations are revealing
about normal human development is that the interaction between mother
and infant is crucial to the development of the right brain—which is
equivalent to saying that it is crucial to the development of the self, exactly as self psychology and intersubjectivity have postulated. Indeed, Devinsky (2000) has said that the very function of the right hemisphere "is
to maintain a coherent, continuous, and unified sense of self" (p. 64). I
referred earlier to the cognitive mental structures which have been eluci-
dated by Piaget; one might suggest that the Piagetian cognitive structures
are predominantly products of the left brain and depend rather less on
interpersonal factors, whereas affective structures are predominantly
right brain, and depend almost completely on intersubjective experience.

Schore refers to several authors who have postulated that there are
direct parallels between the attributes of an effective therapist and the
characteristics of the psychobiologically attuned intuitive parent (Dozier,
Cue, and Barnett, 1994; Holmes, 1993; Sable, 2000). He characterizes their
viewpoint in this way:

> Empathic resonance [in the therapist] results from dyadic *attunement,*
> and its [*sic*] induces a synchronization of patterns of activation of both
> right hemispheres of the therapeutic dyad. *Misattunement* is triggered
> by a mismatch, and describes a context of stressful *desynchronization*
> between and destabilization within their right brains. Interactive *reat-
> tunement* induces a resynchronization of their right brains. (p. 51)

Schore is thus providing a psychobiological explanation of the inevitable, repeated, and painful experiences of a therapist treating a patient with a disorder of the self: periods of empathic resonance, marred by ruptures in empathy, followed by efforts to repair the sense of connectedness.[3]

A further implication of these findings is that both the core of the problem in disorders of the self, and also the core of the therapy of these conditions, involves affective structures that, being in the right corticoid-limbic system, are essentially *nonverbal*. Obviously, as two adults, patient and therapist are thinking, reflecting, and, to a greater or lesser degree, analytic, beings. We do not sit in our offices cooing at our patients. Nevertheless, this research suggests that, in the treatment of disorders of the self, our words are as much, if not more, in the service of affective regulation, as they are in the service of insight. A further implication is that, in our attempts to write about or describe our therapeutic efforts, we are essentially trying to capture intersubjective events that are, "beyond interpretation" (Gedo, 1979).

Consider the following exchange, which occurred long after Sandy had stopped dissociating into alternative senses of self: in an unplanned phone call, Sandy reported with an affect of depression and fear that she "couldn't move." She was faced with a huge number of things that had to be done, under time constraints: work presentations, preparing to sell her house, moving to a new condominium three hours away, and so forth.

I listened for a while, with calm empathy and occasional supportive remarks, until I suddenly noticed that something was happening to me internally. My stomach had begun to churn; I felt anxious, and in some undefined way, threatened. There was an urge to get away. I realized—or at least strongly suspected—that I was feeling what Sandy was feeling.

Presumably, the most empathic form of relating at that point would have been to continue to provide a "holding" environment, and to reflect an understanding of her pain and sense of being overwhelmed. I couldn't do it—or more precisely, I experienced pain and frustration at not know-ing *how* to do it. It felt to me as if staying in a receptive, empathic mode would be like holding the hand of a drowning woman, as we sank be-neath the surface together.

What I *did* do was say, "You know what, Sandy? You need to get out of the house. You need to get up and go for a long walk!"

I immediately felt better (of course!). I listened closely, though, for Sandy's reaction. There was silence; I became alarmed that she had expe-rienced me as having just abandoned her, emotionally. However, she began to talk again, sounding pretty much as she had previously; I sensed she either didn't see the point of a "walk," or couldn't imagine mobilizing for it. I nevertheless persisted. I said that I knew she couldn't imagine leaving the house when there was so much to be done; but the point was that she wasn't getting any of it done, anyway. She needed to clear her head, get some air—get moving again, literally and physically.

Sandy emailed me that evening, saying the following:

> Just wanted to thank you again for listening to me today. It's the most
> hideous thing in the world when that hits like that; I want some kind of
> instant cure, which doesn't exist, I know; or I don't think it exists. I am
> terrified that I'll fall off the edge; that I won't be able to hold out until it
> ends or that it won't end but just keep coming back with shorter and
> shorter intervals in between.
>
> I feel a little better now. I did go for a walk; not hugely long but I
> did get out.

These remarks quite obviously can be taken to support the view that
what really mattered, in this interaction, was the therapist's receptive,
empathic listening stance. I think, however, that one can add to this
understanding. I believe that, while Sandy did not articulate my contribution beyond the fact of my listening, my intervention consisted of a
more complex *affective* communication, in which I conveyed to her that,
having briefly been with her in her depths of despair and immobilization,
I could envision and *experience* a way out—and that if I could, she could.
For sure, not an instant cure, but a good-enough way of muddling
through a difficult life moment. Most important, perhaps: even as I
moved away from empathic identification with her, I did not leave her.

Carpy (1989), likening this sort of basically nonverbal intervention to a
mother-infant interaction, says:

> The normal infant needs to be able to sense that her mother is strug-
> gling to tolerate her projected distress without major disruption of her
> maternal function. The mother will be unable to avoid giving the infant
> indications of the way she is affected by her infant, and it is these
> indications which allow the infant to see that the projected aspects of
> herself can indeed be tolerated. (p. 287)

Schore (op. cit.) describes such phenomena from a neurobiological framework:

> The right hemisphere is dominant not only for processing negative
> primary emotions but also for mediating pain and pain endurance and
> modulating distress states via a right-brain circuit of inhibition and
> emotion regulation. This right-lateralized regulator maneuver facili-
> tates the therapist's countertransferential modulation of sensed nega-
> tive affect; that is to say, it allows for the countertransference to be not
> "grossly" but only "partially" acted out. But this "partial acting out" is
> critical to the patient's implicit learning of a corrective emotional expe-
> rience. . . . [It] represents an important opportunity for the patient to
> perceive (in real time) that the therapist is affected by the patient's
> projected communication, that he struggles to tolerate the negative af-
> fect, but, ultimately, he manages to contain it without grossly acting it
> out. (p. 98)

Bowlby, in 1969, described two different responses by infants to attachment ruptures: protest and despair. Schore states that the extreme forms of these responses, neurophysiologically, are, first, hyperarousal, and subsequently, dissociation (pp. 67–68). Hyperarousal is characterized physiologically by a high level of sympathetic nervous system arousal and, behaviorally, by crying, followed by screaming, in an intense bid for interactive regulation. If the caretaker does not soothe the infant, or even engages in a mutually escalating arousal, a second, longer-lasting reaction is seen: dissociation, characterized by a sudden intense parasympathetic response *added to* the intense sympathetic arousal. High levels of behavior-inhibiting cortisol are released, as well as pain-numbing endogenous opioids. Behaviorally, the infant disengages from the external world, staring into space with a glazed look. Schore postulates that the developing brain of an infant who has had to take recourse to the primitive avoidant strategy of dissociation will have permanent brain alterations, thereby increasing the use of dissociation in later life.

It is less clear how dissociation, in response to traumatic misattunement, leads to dissociated senses of self. Dissociation as a primitive, fundamentally neurological, coping mechanism, seems beyond psychological explanation; only its precipitants would seem to lend themselves to this sort of understanding. But what of psychologically differentiated presentations of self? Can they truly be explained in psychological terms? In earlier chapters, I have attributed specific defensive functions to different senses of self: Joe as personifying a rejection of female sexual and physical vulnerability; Sam as acknowledging her femaleness but focusing, almost to the exclusion of other dimensions of life experience, on the control of sexual interaction with men; Sandra Ellen as virtually denying entirely the life of the body, in the service of competent performance; and so forth. But other self-representations seemed less clear-cut. In attributing defensive functions to these behavioral phenomena, have I psychologized phenomena that are actually better accounted for neurobiologically?

However one chooses to look at it, the neuroscientific information I have summarized suggests to me that the psychoanalytic theorists who have dismissed such data as "logical-empiricist," and incompatible with a depth psychological understanding, have been premature in their dismissal. Hoffman and others may well be right that, in the clinical setting, our so-called objective knowledge may do more to obstruct than enhance a deep understanding of what is going on in the patient's mind and in the interaction between us. But no analytic theorist denies that we are all *informed* by theories of all sorts that provide a rough framework within which we try to help our patients. I would put it this way: our theories help us stay in our chair, when a more natural reaction to the pain, helplessness, and confusion that patients engender in us would be to end the endeavor.[4]

The fact that these psychophysiological theories correspond persua-
sively with the psychoanalytic theories are a great reassurance to me. I
consider it useless to challenge whether such information and hypothesizing is "necessary" in an empathic, exploratory psychotherapy with a
patient. Where does one draw a line between what is useful and what is
not, or when knowledge helps and when it gets in the way? Is knowledge
of Freud's theorizing necessary and useful? Fairbairn's? Bowlby's? Kohut's? As I have said earlier, any and all theorizing is an attempt to
objectify experience and data. To rule out whole bodies of knowledge on
philosophical grounds seems to me to impose pointless limitations on
one's efforts at understanding.

This neurobiological model lends support to my belief that, beyond
(or beneath) multiplicity, dissociation, unawareness, and so forth, the
patient *fundamentally* has only one unconscious. There are reasons to say
otherwise, of course. One sense of self seems to know things that another
does not—what is unconscious to one is conscious to another. However,
to what degree a defense is conscious or unconscious has long ceased to
be an important question, in psychoanalytic theory and practice; what is
central and core is what they are defending against (or in language more
congenial to self psychology and intersubjectivity, what is threatening the
patient's sense of cohesive well-being).

The neuropsychological organism—the patient—either anticipates or
actually experiences, first, interpersonal affective misattunement; and
second, overwhelming dysregulation of the autonomic nervous system.
The organism responds with an extreme psychophysiological state: dissociation. In some yet-to-be-understood fashion, the DID patient moves
out of the fundamental dissociative state of the infant—apathetic, frozen,
immobilized—into a state in which the threatened or actual dysregulation is short-circuited into a subjective and externally perceivable alternative sense of self that allows the patient some measure of control, as well
as the capacity to continue to function in some fashion.

My point here is that it all begins with a patient—one person, one
self—responding to an actual or threatened neuropsychological catastrophe. I was convinced that all of Sandy's dissociated senses of self were
fundamentally elaborated methods of defending against the catastrophic
dangers and fears that she had once experienced—that, in other words,
they all represented means of trying to cope with the same issues and life
events, both consciously and unconsciously.

In Sandy's case, the here-and-now precipitants to these changes, as
well as their antecedents, were unknown to the patient, and for the most
part, to the alternative self-presentations as well. As I pieced these antecedents and precipitants together, I was increasingly able to interpret them
to Sandy, both at times of relatively calm reflection, and during times
when she was undergoing intense neuropsychological dysregulation. Initially, these interpretations helped me more than they did Sandy; feeling

that I understood what was happening, I was able to remain calmer and to respond with less tension and emotion. Gradually, they helped Sandy as well—or perhaps more accurately put, interpretations coming from a better-regulated therapist began to make a difference in her capacity for self-regulation. I will consider the interpretative act *per se* with this patient, in the final chapter.

NOTES

1. It seems a safe generalization to say that psychoanalysts of all persuasions have tended to ignore Piaget, whose theories on the epigenetic development of universal cognitive structures are buttressed by persuasive, objective scientific evidence.

2. Kohut stated (1981), "I do not believe, however hard that it is tried, that there is any possibility to create such a misalliance as psychobiology, or biopsychology, or something of that order" (p. 529).

3. Goldberg (2004) would go further and postulate that this sequence, albeit with the important addition of the cognitive component, interpretation, in fact defines any psychoanalytic therapy, regardless of patient characteristics: "The sequence of understanding, misunderstanding, interpretation, and understanding, defines and delineates the place or form of psychoanalysis as an understanding psychology" (p. 50).

4. It is, of course, possible to end the endeavor without ever leaving the room, through what Plakun (1999) calls the "refusal of the transference." When the therapist, under the stress of unconsciously perceived impending right brain dysregulation, shifts out of the right-brain, empathic connection to his own and to the patient's pain, into a left-hemispheric, rational mode, he is likely to make a verbal interpretation that basically initiates an enactment. He may as well have physically left. And if this is his prevailing response to such stressful moments, he or the patient soon will.

NINETEEN

Conclusion

> Achieving integration is not the end of the therapy. The patient faces the task of living without dissociation.
>
> —Mollon (1996, p. 157)

Can dissociative identity disorder be cured? Tricky terrain, for psychoanalysts, the concept of "cure"; and yet Kohut dared title his last published book, *How Does Analysis Cure?* (1984). There seems ample evidence that the symptoms that characterize the DSM IV diagnosis of dissociative identity disorder can be alleviated and even eliminated (Coons 1986; Kluft 1985b). For a psychoanalyst, however, "cure" is not simply defined by symptom removal. From a self-psychological perspective, it involves the attainment of a more solid sense of self, with healthy ambitions and ideals, sustained by and sustaining life-enhancing selfobject relationships. From all psychoanalytic perspectives, a psychoanalytic treatment is not complete until the patient has acquired greater self-understanding and awareness—insights that in considerable part come about through analytic interpretation.

Goldberg (2004) has delineated three levels of psychoanalytic interpretations:

> The first level has to do with the observations that we make of the patient: his behavior, his character, his transference. We [point these out to the patient sensitively] but "from afar.". . . The second level includes another common kind of interpretation having to do with empathy and one's ability to feel what the patient is experiencing. . . . When [these interpretations] are done to the exclusion of a consideration of the unconscious factors responsible for the ebb and flow of empathy, this second level falls short, much as does the first. . . . [O]nly the third level proposed here, that of verbally interpreting the particular transference configuration with its unconscious roots and configu-

181

ration (that is comprehended by one's empathic connect to the patient),
is the level of interpretation unique to psychoanalysis. (p. 113)

Goldberg's emphasis on the importance of the third kind of interpretation notwithstanding, I suggest that the first level, having to do with
interpretations "from afar" was crucially important for Sandy. Let me
return briefly to the question of, "What can Sandy believe?" During the
time that she was struggling, with enormous ambivalence, to understand
how events in her childhood might help to explain who she was, she
came in one day and made the following summary: There were five
irrefutable facts about her life, from which she wished she could develop
more irrefutable facts. They were: 1) the excruciating pelvic pain, triggered by external situations; 2) the transformations into something hideous; 3) the dream; 4) the early morning terrors; and 5) the image of a child
who cannot close her legs (and accompanying felt terror). There were
other irrefutable facts, of course: her "people," her quasi hallucinations of
erect penises, her masochistic history; all these, however, were attributable in her mind to weakness and/or perversion. These five facts, she felt,
were not fully explained by this self-assessment.

Of course, we could not develop further "irrefutable facts." All of the
above facts preceded treatment and had been a part of experience of
herself for as long as she could remember. Other facts came to light
during treatment: paintings and drawings, more sexual imagery, memo-
ry-like "scenes," and so forth—none of them irrefutable. The stuff, in
other words, of interpretation.

The second level of interpretation was also extremely helpful to
Sandy. For example: once when there had been a misunderstanding between us about the length of a session (see chapter 6), she was stunned
and dismayed when I reminded her that we only had five minutes left. In
trying to understand her extremely intense reaction, in the following session, I suggested that coming to these sessions and taking the risk of
baring her innermost thoughts and feelings, was very much like coming
into a room and taking all her clothes off. Then, to abruptly hear (an
exaggeration to make the point): "Okay—it's over. Put your clothes back
on and leave," was devastating and humiliating. Sandy was stunned
again—this time by how accurately my interpretation captured what she
felt.

It is an interesting twist on Goldberg's emphasis on the third level,
involving the transference and unconscious processes, that some of the
most salient of these interpretations came to be made by Sandy herself.
There came a time when she observed (only slightly paraphrased): "I
have a pattern that I've done with men all my life and now I've done it
with you. Some part of me pushes and pushes a male until I either get
beaten or rejected, or both. I think the closeness begins to feel unreliable,
and scary—and so I put it to the test, and afterwards there's this huge

release of tension, when it turns out nobody has been destroyed." I couldn't have made a more salient interpretation.

There is no question that, at the time our therapy ended, Sandy thought, acted, and felt as one person, and her early question in the therapy, "How do people think?" could, at that point, be answered confidently: "The same as you." Mollon (1996), however, has pointed out:

> [A]nother painful aspect of life which the [newly-integrated personality] has to face is that of loneliness. While he or she was dissociative and regularly hearing the voices of other alters, loneliness was not an emotion commonly felt by the MPD/DID patient. (p. 158)

That was certainly true for Sandy, particularly after her relationship with her husband ended. For several years, the loneliness was mitigated by her relationship with Bill, as described in chapter 7; but I count it a sign of her increasing feeling of wholeness and self-confidence that she was able to attenuate, and eventually end, that relationship, even without another to replace it. Her recent report of having fallen in love with a man she found decent and caring, and that she planned to marry, seems to me not only to strengthen that assessment, but to illustrate the immensely satisfying fact that our patients may continue to grow, long after our therapy has ended.

Both Winnicott and Kohut speak of the infant finding herself in her mother's gaze. Who did Sandy find reflected in her therapist's eyes? Of course, only she could answer the question with accuracy. The Sandy that I believe I reflect is an enormously courageous and decent person; a woman who was forced, from childhood on, to create a life with virtually no "co-creators," and who, almost surely, bore alone the excruciating, traumatic burden of having been sexually abused at an early age. She has survived, and more, has prevailed.

Shortly before terminating our regular contact, Sandy gave me a gift: a black-and-white, photographic portrait of herself. In the picture, she is smiling—but it is not the ordinary "say cheese," smile to be found in most photographs. It is a smile that seems to say: *at last.*

It was some time before I grasped the true meaning of this gift. It was, in fact, the ultimate present that she could have given me. It was a gift that said—that *showed*—"Here I am. This is *me*. This is *my Self*." I am humbled and proud to have played a part in creating that portrait.

Postscript

The meeting over coffee that Sandy proposed shortly before her planned wedding, as mentioned at the end of chapter 7, never took place. I received a subsequent email saying that she had developed Meniere's Syndrome—imbalance and dizziness caused by an inner ear disorder—and was effectively disabled for some period of time. By the fall of 2011, almost two years had passed without further communication, and when, on occasion, I thought of Sandy, I felt some unease. What did it mean, that I hadn't heard anything further about her wedding—or for that matter, her health? With some slight trepidation, I decided to email a Christmas greeting. I received back a heartening reply—happy to hear from me, and happy to report good news on all fronts. She characterized her marriage as constant love, understanding, trust, intimacy, laughter, quietness, and fun. Not without bumps, she acknowledged. In addition, her work was going well, and her kids were thriving.

When, a couple of months later, I received notice that this book had been accepted for publication, I emailed Sandy again, including the following:

I can imagine you have mixed feelings about this news—happy for me, hopeful that my book will be of help to other therapists, treating these enormously difficult problems, but uneasy about having your most personal life put out to the public for all to see. I can only reassure you that, as we talked about a long time ago, and as you read, I have disguised your identity beyond recognition.

I am not sure whether you will want to read the book, and revisit all that awful pain. On the other hand, your life has changed so much, and it is by now— thank goodness—so many years ago, it might be like visiting a foreign country, that you barely remember having visited many years ago.

Sandy replied promptly, saying that, first, she was very excited for me, and indeed hoped my book might help others in her situation, and second, that she did actually have mixed feelings about reading the book— but thought that, bottom line, she would wish to. She would feel honored, she added, if I would sign it for her.

I replied as follows:

Sandy—

I will certainly send you a signed copy. And I will think a very long time about how to inscribe it.

"Dr. M"

References

Aldridge-Morris, R. 1989. *Multiple Personality: An Exercise in Deception*. Hove, UK: Lawrence Erlbaum Associates.

American Psychiatric Association. 1994. *Diagnostic and Statistical Manual of Mental Disorders*. 3rd ed. Washington, DC: American Psychiatric Association.

———. 2000. *Diagnostic and Statistical Manual of Mental Disorders*. 4th ed., textual rev. Washington, DC: American Psychiatric Association.

Ariés, P. 1962. *Centuries of Childhood*. London: Jonathan Cape.

Arlow, J. A. 1992. "Altered Ego States." *Israel Journal of Psychiatry and Related Sciences* 29: 65–76.

Aron, L. 1991. "The Patient's Experience of the Analyst's Subjectivity." *Psychoanalytic Dialogues* 1: 29–51.

Atwood, G., and R. Stolorow. 1984. *Structures of Subjectivity: Explorations in Psychoanalytic Phenomenology*. Hillsdale, NJ: The Analytic Press.

Baer, R. 2007. *Switching Time*. New York: Crown Publishers.

Basch, M. F. 1988. *Understanding Psychotherapy*. New York: Basic Books.

———. 1995. Kohut's contribution. *Psychoanalytic Dialogues* 5: 367–73.

Beebe, B., and F. Lachmann. 1988a. "The Contribution of Mother-Infant Mutual Influence to the Origins of Self- and-Object Representations." *Psychoanalytic Psychology* 5: 305–37.

———. 1988b. "Mother-Infant Mutual Influence and Precursors of Psychic Structure." In *Frontiers of Self Psychology: Progress in Self Psychology* 4, edited by Arnold Goldberg, 3–25. Hillsdale, NJ: The Analytic Press.

Benschoteen, S. C. 1990. "Multiple Personality Disorder and Satanic Ritual Abuse: The Issue of Credibility." *Dissociation* 1: 13–20.

Bergman, R. L. 2008. *Mindless Psychoanalysis, Selfless Self Psychology*. Seattle: The Alliance Press.

Berman, E. 1981. "Multiple Personality: Psychoanalytic Perspectives." *International Journal of Psychoanalysis* 62: 283–300.

Bernstein, E. M., and F. W. Putnam. 1986. "Development, Reliability, and Validity of a Dissociation Scale." *Journal of Nervous and Mental Disease* 174: 727–35.

Bliss, E. L. 1980. "Multiple Personalities: A Report of 14 Cases with Implications for Schizophrenia and Hysteria." *Archives of General Psychiatry* 37: 1388–97.

———. 1986. *Multiple Personality, Allied Disorders, and Hypnosis*. New York: Oxford University Press.

Borch-Jacobsen, M. 1996. "Sybil," *New York Review of Books* (April 14): 60–64.

Boudewyns, P. A., S. A. Stwertka, L. A. Hyer, J. W. Albrecht, and E. V. Sperz. 1993. "Eye Movement Desensitization and Reprocessing: A Pilot Study." *Behavior Therapy* 16: 30– 33.

Bowlby, J. 1969. *Attachment and Loss*, vol. 1, *Attachment*. New York: Basic Books.

Brand, B., C. Classen, R. Lanins, R. Loewenstein, S. McNary, C. Pain, and F. Putnam. 2009. "A Naturalistic Study of Dissociative Identity Disorder and Dissociative Disorder Not Otherwise Specified Patients Treated by Community Clinicians." *Psychological Trauma: Theory, Research, Practice, and Policy* 1: 153–71.

Braun, B. 1984. "Towards a Theory of Multiple Personality Disorder and Other Dissociative Phenomena." *Psychiatric Clinics of North America* 7: 171–93.

Brenner, I. 2001. *Dissociation of Trauma: Theory, Phenomenology, and Technique*. Madison, CT: International Universities Press.

Bromberg, P. 1980. "Empathy, Anxiety, and Reality: A View from the Bridge." *Contemporary Psychoanalysis* 16: 223–36.

———. 1991. "On Knowing One's Patient Inside Out: The Aesthetics of Unconscious Communication." *Psychoanalytic Dialogues* 14: 399–422.

———. 1993. "Shadow and Substance: A Relational Perspective on Clinical Process." *Psychoanalytic Psychology* 10: 147–68.

———. 1996. "Standing in the Spaces: The Multiplicity of Self and the Psychoanalytic Relationship." *Contemporary Psychoanalysis* 32: 509–36.

Buck, R. 1994. "The Neuropsychology of Communication: Spontaneous and Symbolic Aspects." *Journal of Pragmatics* 22: 265–78.

Carlson, J. G, C. M. Chemtob, K. Rusnak, N. L. Hedlund, and M. Y. Muraoka. 1998. "Eye Movement Desensitization and Reprocessing for Combat-Related Posttraumatic Stress Disorder." *Journal of Traumatic Stress* 11: 3–24.

Carpy, L. 1989. "Tolerating the Countertransference: A Mutative Process." *International Journal of Psychoanalysis* 70: 281–93.

Casey, J., and L. Wilson. 1991. *The Flock*. Columbine, NY: Fawcett.

Celani, D. P. 1993. *The Treatment of the Borderline Patient: Applying Fairbairn's Object Relations Theory in the Clinical Setting*. Madison, CT: International Universities Press.

Chodoff, P. 1987. "Multiple Personality Disorder." *American Journal of Psychiatry* 144: 122– 23.

Chu, J. A., L. M. Frey, B. L. Ganzel, and J. A. Matthews. 1999. "Memories of Childhood Abuse: Dissociation, Amnesia, and Corroboration." *American Journal of Psychiatry* 156: 749– 55.

Cohen, L. M., J. N.Berzoff, and M. R. Elin. 1995. *Dissociative Identity Disorder*. Northvale, NJ: Jason Aronson.

Cohen, S. 2002. *Folk Devils and Moral Panics: The Creation of the Mods and Rockers*. New York: Routledge Press.

Conte, J. R. 2002. *Critical Issues in Child Sexual Abuse: Historical, Legal, and Psychological Perspectives*. Thousand Oaks, NY: Sage Publications.

Coons, P. M. 1986. "Treatment Progress in the Treatment of Multiple Personality Disorder." *Journal of Nervous & Mental Diseases* 174: 715–21.

———. 1994. "Confirmation of Childhood Abuse in Child and Adolescent Cases of Multiple Personality Disorder and Dissociative Disorder Not Otherwise Specified." *Journal of Nervous & Mental Diseases* 182: 461–64.

Crews, F. 2006. *Follies of the Wise*. Emeryville, CA: Shoemaker & Hoard.

Cruz, F. G., and L. Essen. 1994. *Adult Survivors of Childhood Emotional, Physical, and Sexual Abuse*. Northvale, NJ: Jason Aronson.

Davies, J. M. 1996. "Multiplicity of Self." *Contemporary Psychoanalysis* 32: 560–71.

Davies, J. M., and M. G. Frawley. 1994. *Treating the Adult Survivor of Childhood Sexual Abuse: A Psychoanalytic Perspective*. New York: Basic Books.

Devinsky, O. 2002. "Right Cerebral Hemisphere Dominance for a Sense of Corporeal and Emotional Self." *Epilepsy and Behavior* 1: 60–73.

DeYoung, M. 1996. "A Painted Devil: Constructing the Satanic Ritual Abuse of Children Problem." *Agression and Violent Behavior* 1: 235–48.

Dozier, M., K. L. Cue, and L. Barnett. 1994. "Clinicians as Caregivers: Role of Attachment Organization in Treatment." *Journal of Consulting and Clinical Psychology* 62: 793–800.

Draijer, N., and S. Boon. 1993. "The Validation of the Dissociative Experiences Scale against the Criterion of the SCID-D, Using Receiver Operating Characteristics (ROC) Analysis." *Dissociation* 6: 28–36.

Eissler, K. 1958. "Remarks on Some Variations in Psychoanalytical Technique." *International Journal of Psychoanalysis* 39: 222–29.

Ellason, J. W., and C. A. Ross. 1997. "Childhood Trauma and Psychiatric Symptoms." *Psychological Reports* 80: 447–50.

Ellis, B. 2000. *Raising the Devil: Satanism, New Religions, and the Media*. Lexington: University Press of Kentucky.

Emde, R. 1988a. "Development Terminable and Interminable: I." *International Journal of Psychoanalysis* 69: 23–42.

———. 1988b. "Development Terminable and Interminable: II." *International Journal of Psychoanalysis* 69: 283–96.

Fahey, T. 1988. "The Diagnosis of Multiple Personality Disorder: A Critical Review." *British Journal of Psychiatry* 153: 97–606.

Fairbairn, W. 1944. "Endopsychic Structure Considered in Terms of Object-Relationships." *International Journal of Psychoanalysis* 22: 250–53.

———. 1952. *An Object Relations Theory of the Personality*. New York: Basic Books.

Ferenczi, S. 1933. *Final Contributions to the Problems and Methods of Psycho-Analysis*. London: Hogarth Press.

Fink, D. 1986. "Psychotherapy of Multiple Personality Disorder: A Case Study." *Journal of Nervous and Mental Diseases* 174: 49–70.

Flor-Henry, P., R. Tomer, L. Kumpula, Z. J. Koes, and L. T. Yeudall. 1990. "Neurophysiological and Neuropsychological Study of Two Cases of Multiple Personality Syndrome and Comparison with Chronic Hysteria." *International Journal of Psychophysiology* 10: 151–61.

Fraser, G. A. 1997. *The Dilemma of Ritual Abuse: Cautions and Guides for Therapists*. Washington, DC: American Psychiatric Association Publishing, Inc.

———. 2005. "Letter to the Editor." *Canadian Journal of Psychiatry* 50: 814.

Freud, S. 1957a. "Beyond the Pleasure Principle." In *The Standard Edition of the Complete Psychological Works of Sigmund Freud*, vol. 18, *1920–1922*, edited by James Strachey. London: Hogarth Press.

———. 1957b. "The Case of Schreber." In *The Standard Edition of the Complete Psychological Works of Sigmund Freud*, vol. 12, *1911–1913*, edited by James Strachey. London: Hogarth Press.

———. 1957c. "The Ego and the Id." In *The Standard Edition of the Complete Psychological Works of Sigmund Freud*, vol. 19, *1923–1925*, edited by James Strachey. London: Hogarth Press.

———. 1957d. "Project for a Scientific Psychology." In *The Standard Edition of the Complete Psychological Works of Sigmund Freud*, vol. 1, *1886–1899*, edited by James Strachey. London: Hogarth Press.

———. 1957e. "Studies on Hysteria." In *The Standard Edition of the Complete Psychological Works of Sigmund Freud*, vol. 2, *1893–1895*, edited by James Strachey. London: Hogarth Press.

———. 1957f. "Three Essays on Sexuality." In *The Standard Edition of the Complete Psychological Works of Sigmund Freud*, vol. 7, *1901–1905*, edited by James Strachey. London: Hogarth Press.

Garvey, Ann M. 2010. *Ann's Multiple World of Personality*. Victoria, Canada: Friesen Press.

Gedo, J. E. 1979. *Beyond Interpretation: Toward a Revised Theory of Psychoanalysis*. New York: International Universities Press.

Gedo, J. E., and A. Goldberg. 1973. *Models of the Mind*. Chicago: University of Chicago Press.

Gedo, M. 2000. "The Treatment of Multiple Personality Disorder." *Journal of the American Academy of Psychoanalysis* 28: 609–19.

Gill, M. M., and I. Z. Hoffman. 1982. *Analysis of the Transference*, vol. 1. Madison, CT: International Universities Press.

Giller, E., B. M. Cohen, and W. Lynn. 1991. *Multiple Personality Disorder from the Inside Out*. Brooklandville, MD: Sidran Institute Press.

Goldberg, A. 1999. *Being of Two Minds*. Hinsdale, NJ: The Analytic Press.

———. 2004. *Misunderstanding Freud*. New York: American Psychoanalytic Association.

Hacking, I. 1986. "The Invention of Split Personalities." In *Human Nature and Natural Knowledge*, edited by A. Donagan, A. N. Perovich, and M. V. Wedin. Dordrecht, Germany: Reidel.

———. 1988. *Mad Travelers*. Richmond: The University Press of Virginia.

———. 1995. *Rewriting the Soul*. Princeton, NJ: Princeton University Press.

Hedges, L. E. 1994. *Remembering, Repeating, and Working Through Childhood Trauma*. Northvale, NJ: Jason Aronson.

Herman, J. L. 1992. *Trauma and Recovery*. New York: Basic Books.

Hermans, H. J. M., H. J. G. Kempen, and R. J. P. van Loon. 1992. "The Dialogical Self: Beyond Individualism and Rationalism." *American Psychologist* 47: 23–33.

Herndl, D. P. 1988. "The Writing Cure." *National Women's Studies Association Journal* 1: 54.

Hoffman, I. Z. 1983. "The Patient as Interpreter of the Analyst's Experience." *Contemporary Psychoanalysis* 19: 389–422.

———. 1988. *Ritual and Spontaneity in the Psychoanalytic Process*. Hillsdale, NJ: The Analytic Press.

———. 1992. "Some Practical Implications of a Social-Constructivist View of the Psychoanalytic Situation." *Psychoanalytic Dialogues* 2: 287–304.

Holmes, J. 1993. "Attachment Theory: A Biological Basis for Psychotherapy?" *British Journal of Psychiatry* 163: 430–38.

Hornstein, N. L., and F. W. Putnam. 1992. "Clinical Phenomenology of Child and Adolescent Dissociative Disorders." *Journal of the American Academy of Child and Adolescent Psychiatry* 31: 1077–85.

Humphrey, N., and D. C. Dennett. 1988. "Speaking for Our Selves." In *Brainchildren: Essays on Designing Minds*, edited by D. C. Dennett. Cambridge, MA: Bradford.

Janet, P. 1889/1913. *L'automatisme Psychologique*, Paris, France: Felix Alcan.

Joseph, B. 1982. "Addiction to Near-Death." *International Journal of Psychoanalysis* 63: 449–54.

———. 1989. "On Passivity and Aggression." In *Psychic Equilibrium and Psychic Change*, edited by M. Feldman and E. B. Spillius. New York: Rutledge.

Kahn, M. 1966. "On the Clinical Provisions of Frustrations, Recognitions, and Failures in the Analytic Situation: An Essay on Dr. Michael Balint's Researches on the Theory of Psychoanalytic Technique." *International Journal of Psychoanalysis* 50: 237–48.

Kelly, A. F. 2001. "Toward an Etiology of Dissociative Identity Disorder: A Neurodevelopmental Approach." *Consciousness and Cognition* 10: 259–93.

Kernberg, O. 1975. *Borderline Conditions and Pathological Narcissism*. New York: Jason Aronson.

———. 1981. "Multiple Personality: Psychoanalytic Perspectives." Paper presented at the American Psychoanalytic Society Symposium, 1973, Honolulu, Hawaii. Reported by E. Berman in the *International Journal of Psychoanalysis* 62: 283–300.

Kinsler, P. J. 1992. "The Centrality of Relationship: What's *Not* Being Said." *Dissociation* 5: 165–68.

Kluft, R. 1982. "Varieties of Hypnotic Interventions in the Treatment of Multiple Personality Disorder." *American Journal of Clinical Hypnosis* 24: 230–40.

———. 1984. "Treatment of Multiple Personality Disorder: A Study of 33 Cases." *Psychiatric Clinics of North America* 7: 9–29.

———. 1985a. "The Natural History of Multiple Personality Disorder." In *Childhood Antecedents of Multiple Personality Disorder*, edited by Richard P. Kluft, 197–238. Washington, DC: American Psychiatric Press.

———. 1985b. "Using Hypnotic Inquiry Protocols to Monitor Treatment Progress and Stability in Multiple Personality Disorder." *American Journal of Clinical Hypnosis* 28: 63–75.

———. 1988. "The Post-Unification Treatment of MPD: First Findings." *American Journal of Psychotherapy* 43: 212–28.

———. 1997. "True Lies, False Truths, and Naturalistic Raw Data: Applying Clinical Findings to the False Memory Debate." In *Trauma and Memory*, edited by L. M. Williams. Newport, CA: Sage.

Kohlenberg, R. J. 1973. "Behavioristic Approach to the Treatment of Multiple Personality Disorder: A Case Study." *Behavior Therapy* 4: 137–40.

Kohut, H. 1971. *The Analysis of the Self*. New York: International Universities Press.
———. 1981. "On Empathy." In *The Search for the Self*, vol. 4, edited by Paul Ornstein. New York: International Universities Press.
———. 1984. *How Does Analysis Cure?* Hillsdale, NJ: The Analytic Press.
———. 1997. *The Restoration of the Self*. Madison, CT: International Universities Press.
Langs, R. 1978. *Technique in Transition*. Northvale, NJ: Jason Aronson.
Lalonde, J. K., J. I. Hudson, R. A. Gigante, and H. G. Pope Jr. 2001. "Canadian and American Psychiatrists' Attitudes toward Dissociative Disorders Diagnoses." *Canadian Journal of Psychiatry* 46 (2001): 407–12.
Lampl-De Groot, J. 1981. "Notes on 'Multiple Personality.'" *Psychoanalytic Quarterly* 50: 614–24.
Lenzinger-Bohleber, M., and R. Pfeifer. 2002. "Remembering a Depressive Primary Object." *International Journal of Psychoanalysis* 83: 3–34.
Lichtenberg, J. D. 1989. *Psychoanalysis and Motivation*. Hillsdale, NJ: Analytic Press.
Linehan, M. W. 1993. *Cognitive-Behavioral Treatment of Borderline Personality Disorder*. New York: Guilford Press.
Loftus, E. L. 1993. "The Reality of Repressed Memories." *American Psychologist* 48: 518–37.
Loftus, E. L., and H. Hoffman. 1989. "Misinformation and Memory: The Creation of New Memories." *Journal of Experimental Psychology* 118: 100–104.
Lowenstein, R. J. 1991. "Rational Psychopharmacology in the Treatment of Multiple Personality Disorder." *Psychiatric Clinics of North America* 14: 721–40.
Ludwig, A. M. 1966. "Altered States of Consciousness." *Archives of General Psychiatry* 15: 225–34.
Lyon, K. A. 1992. "Shattered Mirror: A Fragment of the Treatment of a Patient with Multiple Personality Disorder." *Psychoanalytic Inquiry* 12: 71–94.
Mannheim, K. 1936. *Ideology and Utopia*. New York: Harcourt, Brace, and World.
Marcus, S., P. Marquis, and C. Sakai. 1997. "Controlled Study of Treatment of PTSD using EMDR in an HMO Setting." *Psychotherapy* 35: 307–15.
Marmer, S. S. 1980. "Psychoanalysis of 'Multiple Personality Disorder.'" *International Journal of Psychoanalysis* 61: 439–59.
———. 1991. "Multiple Personality Disorder: A Psychoanalytic Perspective." *Psychiatric Clinics of North America* 14: 677–93.
Masson, J. M. 1984. *The Assault on Truth: Freud's Suppression of the Seduction Theory*. New York: Farrar, Strauss, and Giroux.
Matthew, R. J., R. A. Jack, and W. S. West. 1985. "Cerebral Blood Flow in a Patient with Multiple Personality Disorder." *American Journal of Psychiatry* 142: 504–5.
Merskey, H. 1992. "The Manufacture of Personalities: The Production of Multiple Personality Disorder." *British Journal of Psychiatry* 160: 327–40.
———. 1995a. "The Manufacture of Personalities: The Production of Multiple Personality Disorder." In *Dissociative Identity Disorder*, edited by L. M. Cohen, J. N. Berzoff, and M. R. Elin. Northvale, NJ: Jason Aronson.
———. 1995b. "Multiple Personality Disorder and False Memory Syndrome." *British Journal of Psychiatry* 166: 281–83.
———. 1998. "Prevention and Management of False Memory Syndrome." *Advances in Psychiatric Treatment* 4: 253–62, 369–71.
Middlebrook, D. 1991. *Anne Sexton*. Boston: Houghton Mifflin.
Mills, J. S. 1863. *Utilitarianism*, MetaLibri (PDF ebook), http://metalibri.incubadora.fapesp.br/portal (accessed November 5, 2010).
Mitchell, S. A. 1993. *Hope and Dread in Psychoanalysis*. New York: Basic Books.
Modell, A. 1968. *Object Love and Reality*. New York: International Press.
Moline, R., S. Singh, R. Morris, and H. Y. Meltzer. 1985. "Family Expressed Emotion and Relapse in Schizophrenia in an American Urban Population." *American Journal of Psychiatry* 142: 1078–81.
Mollon, P. 1996. *Multiple Selves, Multiple Voices—Working with Trauma, Violation and Dissociation*. Chichester, UK: John Wiley & Sons.

Murphy, D. 2006. *Psychiatry in the Scientific Image.* Cambridge: MIT Press.

Nielssen, O., and M. Large. 2008. "Post-Traumatic Stress Disorder's Future." *British Journal of Psychiatry* 192: 394–95.

Orange, D. M., G. E. Atwood, and R. D. Stolorow. 1997. *Working Intersubjectively—Contextualism in Psychoanalytic Practice.* Hillsdale, NJ: The Analytic Press.

Oxnam, R. 2005. *A Fractured Mind: My Life with Multiple Personality Disorder.* New York: Hyperion Press.

Parnell, L. 1997. *Transforming Trauma: EMDR.* New York: Norton & Co.

———. 1999. *EMDR in the Treatment of Adults Abused as Children.* New York: W. W. Norton & Co.

Piaget, J. 1954. *The Construction of Reality in the Child.* New York: Basic Books.

Piper, A. 1997. *Hoax and Reality: The Bizarre World of Multiple Personality Disorder.* Northvale, NJ: Jason Aronson.

Piper, A., and H. Merskey. 2004a. "The Persistence of Folly: A Critical Examination of Dissociative Identity Disorder, Part I." *Canadian Journal of Psychiatry* 49: 592–600.

———. 2004b. "The Persistence of Folly: A Critical Examination of Dissociative Identity Disorder, Part II." *Canadian Journal of Psychiatry* 49: 678–83.

Piper, A., H. G. Pope, and J. J. Borowiecki. 2000. "Custer's Last Stand: Brown, Scheflin, and Whitfield's Latest Attempt to Salvage 'Dissociative Amnesia.'" *Journal of Psychiatry and Law* 28: 149–213.

Pope, H. G, Jr., P. S. Olivia, J. I. Hudson, J. A. Bodkin, and A. J. Gruber. 1999. "American Psychiatrists' Attitude toward Dissociative Disorders Diagnoses." *American Journal of Psychiatry* 156: 321–23.

Putnam, F. W. 1989. *Diagnosis and Treatment of Multiple Personality Disorder.* New York: Guilford Press.

———. 1992. "Discussion: Are Alter Personalities Fragments or Figments?" *Psychoanalytic Inquiry* 12: 95–111.

———. 1995. "Resolved: MPD is an Individually and Socially Created Artifact." *Journal of the American Academy of Child and Adolescent Psychiatry* 34: 957–63.

———. 1997. *Dissociation in Children and Adolescents.* New York: Guilford Press.

Putnam, F. W., T. P. Zahn, and R. M. Post. 1990. "Neurobiological Changes in Multiple Personality Disorder." *Psychiatry Research* 31: 251–60.

Reinders, S., E. Nijenuis, A. Paans, J. Korf, A. Willemson, and J. den Boer. 2003. "One Brain, Two Selves." *Neuroimage* 20: 2119–25.

Reinders, S., E. Nijenius, J. Quak, J. Korf , J. Haaksma, A. Paans , M. J. Anne, A. Willemsen, and J. A. den Boer. 2006. "Changes in Regional Cerebral Blood Flow Patterns in Patients with Dissociative Identity Disorder." *Biological Psychiatry* 60: 730–40.

Renik, O. 1999. "Playing One's Cards Face Up in Analysis: An Approach to the Problem of Self-Disclosure." *Psychoanalytic Quarterly* 68: 521–39.

Rosenbaum, M. 1980. "The Role of the Term Schizophrenia in the Decline of Diagnoses of Multiple Personality." *Archives of General Psychiatry* 137: 1383–85.

Ross, C. A. 1989. *Multiple Personality Disorder: Diagnosis, Clinical Features, and Therapy.* New York: Wiley & Son.

Ross, C. A., S. Heber, G. Anderson, G. R. Norton, B. A. Anderson, M. del Campo, and N. Pillay. 1989. "Differentiating Multiple Personality Disorder and Complex Partial Seizures." *General Hospital Psychiatry* 11: 54–58.

Ross, D. R., and R. J. Lowenstein. 1992. "Multiple Personality Disorder: An Introduction." *Psychoanalytic Inquiry* 12: 1–12.

Sable, P. 2002. *Attachment and Adult Psychotherapy.* New York: Jason Aronson.

Saks, E. R. 1999. *Interpreting Interpretation: The Limits of Hermeneutic Psychoanalysis.* New Haven, CT: Yale University Press.

Sandler, J. 1987. *Projection, Identification, Projective Identification.* Madison, CT: International Universities Press.

Sandler, L. 1985. "Toward a Logic of Organization in Psycho-Biological Development." In *BiologicResponse Styles*, edited by H. Klar and L. Siever. Washington, DC: American Psychiatric Association.

Sar, V., S. N. Unal, and R. Ozturk. 2007. "Frontal and Occipital Perfusion Changes in Dissociative Identity Disorder." *Psychiatry Research* 156: 217–23.

Schafer, R. A. 1976. *A New Language for Psychoanalysis*. New Haven, CT: Yale University Press.

———. 1983. *The Analytic Attitude*. New York: Basic Books.

Schore, A. N. 2003a. *Affect Dysregulation and Disorders of the Self*. New York: W. W. Norton & Co.

———. 2003b. *Affect Regulation and the Repair of the Self*. New York: W. W. Norton & Co.

———. 2005. "Back to Basics: Attachment, Affect Regulation, and the Developing Right Brain Linking Developmental Neuroscience to Pediatrics." *Pediatric Review* 26: 204–17.

Schwartz, R. C. 1995. *Internal Family Systems Therapy*. New York: Guilford Press.

Searles, H. F. 1961. "Phases of Patient-Therapist Interaction in the Psychotherapy of Chronic Schizophrenia." *British Journal of Medical Psychology* 34: 169–93.

Segall, S. R. 1995. "Misalliances and Misadventures in the Treatment of Dissociative Disorders." In *Dissociative Identity Disorders*, edited by L. M. Cohen, J. N. Berzhoff, and M. R. Elin. Northvale, NJ: Jason Aronson.

Shapiro, F. 1995. *Eye Movement Desensitization and Reprocessing*. New York: Guilford Press.

———. 2001. *Eye Movement Desensitization and Reprocessing: Basic Principles, Protocols, and Procedures*. New York: Guilford Press.

Showalter, E. 1997. *Hystories*. New York: Columbia University Press.

Simpson, M. A. 1995. "Gulliver's Travels, or the Importance of Being Multiple." In *Dissociative Identity Disorder*, edited by L. M. Cohen, J. N. Berzoff, and M. R. Elin. Northvale, NJ: Jason Aronson.

Slavin, M. O., and D. Kriegman. 1992. *The Adaptive Design of the Human Psyche*. New York: Guilford Press.

Spence, D. P. 1982. *Narrative Truth and Historical Truth: Meaning and Truth in Psychoanalysis*. New York: Norton & Co.

Spiegel, D. 1993. "Dissociation, Trauma, and DSM IV." Paper presented at the 10th International Conference on Multiple Personality/Dissociative States, Chicago, IL.

Spillius, E. B., and M. Feldman. 1989. *Psychic Equilibrium and Psychic Change: Selected Papers of Betty Joseph*. London: Tavistock/Routledge.

Steele, B. 1986. "Child Abuse." In *The Reconstruction of Trauma*, edited by A. Rothstein. Madison, CT: International Universities Press.

Steiger, H., L. Gauvin, M. Israel, N. M. K. Koerner, N. Y. Kin, J. Paris, and S. N. Young. 2001. "Association of Serotonin and Cortisol Indices with Childhood Abuse in Bulimia Nervosa." *Archives of General Psychiatry* 58: 837–43.

Steinberg, M. 1991. "The Spectrum of Depersonalization: Assessment and Treatment." In *Psychiatric Update*, vol. 10, edited by A. Tasman, and S. M. Goldfinger (223–47). Washington, DC: American Psychiatric Press.

Steinberg, M., B. Rounsaville, and D. Cicchetti. 1990. "The Structured Clinical Interview of DSM-III-R Dissociative Disorders: Preliminary Report on a New Diagnostic Instrument." *American Journal of Psychiatry* 147: 76–82.

Steinberg, M, and M. Schnall. 2001. *The Stranger in the Mirror*. New York: Harper Collins Publishers.

Stolorow, R. D., and G. E. Atwood. 1992. *Contexts of Being*. Hillsdale, NJ: The Analytic Press.

Stolorow, R. D., B. Brandchaft, and G. E. Atwood. 1987. *Psychoanalytic Treatment—An Intersubjective Approach*. Hillsdale, NJ: The Analytic Press.

Sullivan, H. S. 1953. *The Interpersonal Theory of Psychiatry*. New York: W. W. Norton.

———. 1964. "The Illusion of Personal Individuality." In *The Fusion of Psychiatry and the Social Sciences*. New York: W. W. Norton.

Szasz, T. 1974. *The Myth of Mental Illness*. New York: Harper & Row.

Taylor, Charles. 2007. *A Secular Age*. Cambridge: Belknap Press of Harvard University Press.

Trevarthen, C. 1990. "Growth and Education of the Hemispheres." In *Brain Circuits and Functions of the Mind*. Cambridge: Cambridge University Press.

Turkle, S. 1992. *Psychoanalytic Politics: Jaques Lacan and Freud's French Revolution*. (Rev. ed.) New York: Guilford Press.

Vermetten, E., C. Schmahl, S. Lindner, R. J. Loewenstein, and J. D. Bremner. 2006. "Hippocampal and Amygdalar Volumes in Dissociative Identity Disorder." *American Journal of Psychiatry* 163: 630–36.

Viderman, S. 1979. "The Analytic Space: Meaning and Problems." *Psychoanalytic Quarterly* 48: 257–91.

Vincent, M., and R. Pickering. 1988. "Multiple Personality Disorder in Childhood." *Canadian Journal of Psychiatry* 33: 524–29.

Wilson, S. A., L. A. Becker, and R. H. Tinker. 1997. "Fifteen Month Follow-up of Eye Movement Desensitization and Reprocessing (EMDR) Treatment for PTSD and Psychological Trauma." *Journal of Consulting and Clinical Psychology* 65: 1047–56.

Winnicott, D. W. 1960. "Ego Distortion in Terms of True and False Self." In *The Maturational Process and the Facilitating Environment*. Madison, CT: International Universities Press.

———. 1992. *Through Pediatrics to Psychoanalysis: Collected Papers*. New York: Brunner-Routledge.

———. 1996. *Maturational Processes and the Facilitating Environment: Studies in the Theory of Emotional Development*. Boston: Maresfield Library.

Winograd, E., and U. Neisser. 1992. *Affects and Accuracy in Recall: Studies of Flashbulb Memories*. Cambridge: Cambridge University Press.

Wolpe, J. 1991. *The Practice of Behavior Therapy*. (4th ed.) New York: Pergamon.

Yalom, I. D. 1989. *Love's Executioner*. New York: Basic Books.

Yapko, M. D. 1994. *Suggestions of Abuse*. New York: Simon & Schuster.

Zuletea, R. 2004. "Post-Traumatic Stress Disorder and Dissociation." In *Attachment, Trauma, and Multiplicity*, edited by V. Sinason. Hove, UK: Brunner-Routledge.

Index

abuse, emotional and physical: in other cases, 63, 80; in Sandy, 45, 48, 55, 62

abuse, sexual: generalizations about, xn2, 3, 65, 95–96, 112, 124; in other cases, 62, 63, 81, 84; in Sandy, 27–28, 62, 127, 164; satanic, 63–65, 66–67, 74, 75n1, 111. *See also* rape

alcohol, 21, 32, 36, 39, 51

alien abduction, 111

alternative self-presentations: generalizations about, ix, 15–16, 73, 108, 120–121, 124; in other cases, 68, 69, 70, 73, 79, 80, 81, 82–83, 85, 86, 109, 153; numbers of, 70, 98, 103, 160n1. *See also* Sandy, alternative self-presentations

American Psychiatric Association, 65, 100n1

American Psychological Association, 100n1

amnesia, 15, 24, 27, 28, 41, 45, 58, 79, 107, 108, 117, 119, 132, 137

amygdala, 12

antilibidinal ego, 124

Arlow, J. A., ix

Atwood, G. E., 17, 142n2, 147, 155, 156, 173

auditory hallucinations. *See* "hearing voices"

Australia symposium on child abuse, 65

autohypnosis. *See* self-hypnosis

Baer, R., ix, 18, 61–74

Basch, M. F., 41n1, 171

Bergman, R. L., 36, 58

blending. *See* integration

Bliss, E. L., 1, 15, 18, 77, 104, 113n1, 135, 146

Bodkin, J. A., 91

borderline personality disorder, 36, 56, 119, 162

boundaries: in therapy, 11, 18, 19, 58, 59, 72, 74, 131, 142n1, 146, 151; in marriage, 51. *See also* telephone contacts

Bowlby, J., 177

Braun, B., 16, 123, 134

Brenner, I., ix, 12n3, 18, 137, 146

Breuer, J., 97

Bromberg, P., ix, 125, 149

Brown, Terrance, 93

bulimia, 98–99

Carpy, L., 176

"The Case of Anna O," 97. *See also* Breuer; Freud

Celani, D. P., 55, 57

"central ego," 128

Charcot, 112

chatting, 155–156

children. *See under* family

chronic fatigue syndrome, 111

Claire. *See under* alternative self-presentations

Cohen, L. M., ix, 131

Conrin, Sean, xi

core personality, 85. *See also* host personality

countertransference: in author, 4, 6, 19, 24, 25, 57, 139–140, 150; in other authors, 61, 70–71, 132, 146, 147; nature of, 176, 179n4

Craig, 1–2, 16, 19, 21, 23, 31, 39, 51–52, 52–53, 58, 59. *See also under* family

Crews, F., 163

Cruz, F. G., 153–154

Davies, J. M., ix, 7n5, 125, 147, 159

delusions, 94

dementia praecox, 97
dementias, 100n4
denial, 33, 41, 137
Dennett, D. C., 7n4, 115
dependency, 17, 21, 24, 36, 59, 119
depersonalization disorder, 106
depression: major depressive disorder,
    2, 78, 108; in other cases, 61, 62; in
    Sandy, 2, 175
desensitization, 37–38
*Diagnostic and Statistical Manual of
    Mental Disorders III*, 92, 93, 94
*Diagnostic and Statistical Manual of
    Mental Disorders IV*, 15, 91, 92, 93, 94,
    95, 103, 106
*Diagnostic and Statistical Manual of
    Mental Disorders V*, 103
DID. *See* dissociative identity disorder
disavowal, 41n1, 104, 108
dissociation: as a defense, ix, 106, 178;
    as a developmental failure, 124;
    descriptions of, 22, 23, 33, 45, 56, 59,
    86, 97, 118, 178; diagnosis of, 75n3;
    in infancy, 178; nature of, ix, 119,
    125, 135, 149, 177. *See also*
    dissociative identity disorder
dissociative amnesia, 106. *See also*
    amnesia
*Dissociation, The Official Journal of the
    International Society for the Study of
    Multiple Personality and Dissociation,*
    25n1
dissociative disorder, not otherwise
    specified, 106, 172
Dissociative Experience Scale, 106
dissociative fugue, 96, 106
dissociative identity disorder: biology
    of, 171, 172, 174; in childhood, 105;
    cultural niche, 98; demographic
    characteristics, 77, 167; as diagnostic
    entity, ix, 15, 79, 95, 101n8, 103, 110,
    115–116, 127–128, 171, 181;
    guidelines for treatment of, 131–132,
    145–146; as interchangeable with
    multiple personality disorder, xn1;
    legitimacy of, ix, 6, 15, 91, 95–96,
    104, 105, 118. *See also* dissociation
double-consciousness, 97

drawings, 23, 29–30, 31, 164. *See also*
    paintings
dreams, 3, 69
DSM III. *See Diagnostic and Statistical
    Manual of Mental Disorders III*
DSM IV. *See Diagnostic and Statistical
    Manual of Mental Disorders IV*
DSM V. *See Diagnostic and Statistical
    Manual of Mental Disorders V*
dysregulation, 149, 178, 179n4

EMDR. *See* eye movement desensitiza-
    tion and reprocessing
emotional abuse. *See* abuse, emotional
    and physical
empathy: difficulties in maintaining,
    11, 19, 24, 30, 57, 58, 141, 157–158;
    examples of, 30, 31, 40; failures of, 4,
    5, 17, 31, 129, 139, 147, 150, 175; role
    of in development, 174; role of in
    therapy, 132, 138, 140, 147, 151, 154,
    155, 158, 174, 175–176
enactments. *See* reenactments
Essen, L., 154
evolutionary biology, 126
expressed emotion, 169
eye movement desensitization and
    reprocessing, 37–39, 40, 41, 47, 136,
    138–139, 141–142

Fairbairn, W., 36, 56, 124
false memory syndrome, 15
false self, 68, 124, 127
false self-objects, 36, 58
family: children, 2, 31, 33, 43; father, 21,
    40, 43; grandfather, 3, 164; husband,
    2, 16, 19, 21, 23, 31, 39, 52–53, 58, 59;
    mother, 30–31, 40, 44, 127, 170;
    parents, 32, 28. *See also* Craig
family contacts: letters with children,
    53; letters with parents, 44–46,
    47–51; sessions with children, 1–2, 9,
    51–52; sessions with husband, 1–2,
    52; sessions with parents, 44
family minister, 45–46, 165
family systems, 31
father. *See under* family
fees. *See* money
feminism, 110–111

About the Author

Ronald A. Moline, MD, is an assistant professor of clinical psychiatry at the University of Illinois at Chicago and retired from the private practice of psychiatry, psychoanalysis, and couple therapy in 2008. He received his MD from the University of Chicago in 1962 and completed psychiatric training at that same institution in 1966. He served as an army psychiatrist in the U.S. Army Medical Corps from 1966 to 1968, stationed for much of that time in Ascom, Korea. He graduated from the training program of the Family Institute of Chicago in 1977 and from the Chicago Institute for Psychoanalysis in 1988.

Dr. Moline was awarded the Merton M. Gill Award for Excellence in Mentoring and Teaching in 2000, given by the psychiatric residents at the University of Illinois at Chicago Department of Psychiatry. He was designated a Life Fellow of the American Psychiatric Association in 2002.